Penny, Love,
We wear our
Crowns and let
The Shine ♡
Dr. Catherine
Miss Graham
Miss America

In Search of the Crown

Memoir of a black beauty queen during the Civil Rights Movement

She dared to challenge an unjust system.

Catherine Grace Pope, EdD

Copyright © 2018 Catherine Grace Pope, EdD.

All rights reserved. No part of this book may be reproduced, stored, or transmitted by any means—whether auditory, graphic, mechanical, or electronic—without written permission of the author, except in the case of brief excerpts used in critical articles and reviews. Unauthorized reproduction of any part of this work is illegal and is punishable by law.

This book is a work of non-fiction. Unless otherwise noted, the author and the publisher make no explicit guarantees as to the accuracy of the information contained in this book and in some cases, names of people and places have been altered to protect their privacy.

ISBN: 978-1-4834-9164-6 (sc)
ISBN: 978-1-4834-9163-9 (e)

Because of the dynamic nature of the Internet, any web addresses or links contained in this book may have changed since publication and may no longer be valid. The views expressed in this work are solely those of the author and do not necessarily reflect the views of the publisher, and the publisher hereby disclaims any responsibility for them.

Any people depicted in stock imagery provided by Getty Images are models, and such images are being used for illustrative purposes only.
Certain stock imagery © Getty Images.

Lulu Publishing Services rev. date: 10/10/2018

Dedication

This book is dedicated to my parents, John Quittman Pope and Juanita Hawkins Pope.

To my dad, for his tenacity and perseverance, and for providing me with a safe, secure, and stable home. He showed me the meaning of family by his presence during both the good times and the bad times.

To my mom, for showing me the kinder side of life through her gentleness, her thoughtfulness, and her intelligence. She opened the world to me through her love of books, her reading, writing, talent, and creativity. Through her life's journey, she taught me that each one of us has the ability to make this world a better place to live. She taught me to embrace the present by celebrating each day while instilling hope for the future.

To both of my parents, thank you for giving me unconditional love and for encouraging me to believe in myself and in my dreams.

In Search of the Crown

The mirrored image that I see
Reflects myriads of jewels at me
Unique precious jewels,
Embedded in my crown,
But soon the vision fades away.
It cannot last. It will not stay
This day in time.

What is this song—will it be sung
This fleeting race that makes me run
To catch balloons only to see them go?
I ponder where and why.
Alas, I find I do not really know,
But still I search.
Oh hurry—hurry! I reach to touch
For forging's my reality.

To levitate within my human need,
To soar as birds soar freely without guile
In search of crowns I go—
Collecting hope and justice to share along the way.
I bury pride, history, dignity
Deep within my genes.
I know, I know. I know.
This is my day in time!

—Joyce Goodwin

Contents

Acknowledgments xi
1 A Crowning Moment 1
2 His Eyes Are on His Sparrows 5
3 Test and Testimony 14
4 Rock-a-Bye Baby 39
5 The Radio Flyer 45
6 A Good Hair Day 53
7 The Black Book 57
8 Good Friends Are Forever 64
9 Elementary Years 80
10 Where Should We Play? 112
11 Our Sixties Facebook: Student Lockers 117
12 Peony Park 130
13 Technical High School 134
14 Yoshi 141
15 My Senior Year 145
16 The American Party Convention 152
17 Miss Omaha 1968 165
18 Can't Turn Around Now 179
19 The Semifinals 192
20 The Finals 198
21 The Journey 213
22 Miss Nebraska 1969 226
23 Beyond the Rainbow 254
24 Taking Back Control 263
25 Before the Demonstration 280
26 The Demonstration 295
27 A Breath of Fresh Air 344
28 Going Forward 351
29 I Did It My Way 360
   Epilogue 365
   Resources 369
   Contributors 373

Acknowledgments

I want to thank my sisters, Rose Mary Moore and Joyce Goodwin, for your strong sense of commitment to our family and friends. You spent hours and hours with me and provided me with so much information and insight into our family history for this project. Rose Mary, thank you for your support and guidance throughout my life. You have always been like a second mother to me. You rubbed my legs throughout the night to take away my pain when I was a small child. You helped me comb through my final manuscript before submission. Joyce, I want to thank you for loving, supporting, and caring for me. I will never forget how you made my beautiful gown for the Miss Omaha pageant, caringly and carefully placing each and every bead and sequin on it with love. But most of all I thank you for the beautiful poem that enhances my story.

William Carter, my husband, I would like to thank you for supporting and encouraging me through the long hours, sleepless nights, and fast-food dinners. You gave me a quiet place to work and study. Thank you for your enduring love and support. Also, thank you to the entire Carter family.

Ryan Ravelomanantsoa, my son, thank you for writing a thought-provoking passage for this book. You listened to passage after passage, encouraging me to acknowledge the truth wherever I found it. I would also like to thank my daughter, Reagan Jackson, for researching diseases such as tuberculosis, which struck African Americans and American Indians disproportionately during the late 1800s and early 1900s.

To William Moore, my brother-in-law, thank you for always being there for my family, welcoming us into your home and giving us unconditional love. You continuously sat up with me night after night in your home, offering me ideas and suggestions while I navigated through pages and pages of research. You fed me and cheered me on. To Alvin Goodwin, my brother-in-law, you also welcomed me into your home. I thank you for that and for driving me around the city of Omaha while I took pictures and spoke with Omaha citizens in preparation for the final pieces of my book. You also fed me and encouraged me through this process.

To my nieces, Melody Moore and Rosalind Moore, I really can't say enough. Melody and Rosalind, you are my personal cheerleaders. You gave me emotional support and were my organizers throughout this journey. You volunteered to take on any and every task in an effort to help me complete and publish this book. I can't adequately thank either of you. To the entire Moore and Goodwin families, thank you. Even with your demanding schedules, you made time to guide, support, and encourage me—I am eternally grateful.

To my grandchildren Ishmael, Mecca, Sumayah, Shaheim, and Yasin, thank you for allowing me to miss so many special occasions, events, and even birthdays. I'm hopeful that when you read this book you will discover that it was worth it.

I'm overcome with pride when I consider the struggles and all of the sacrifices my family, both living and deceased, made in support of my journey. As a special tribute to the many special angels in my life I speak their names: my grandparents, Rose Lee Hilliard Hawkins and Leonard Hawkins; my step-grandparents, Dr. and Mrs. D. W. Gooden; Aunt Cute, Aunt Janie, Uncle Tanner, Aunt Pinkie, Mary and Frank Pope, and Uncle Sam; Richard; Don Everett; my brothers John and Wallace; my nephews Wallace Pope Jr. and Geoffrey Goodwin; my niece Karen Goodwin; Aunt Audrea and Uncle Booker, Aunt Lucille and Uncle Leonard, Lenore, Helen, Leonard Jr., and Lynwood; Fannie Goodwin, Enid Moore, and Rosemary Fisher; and many other relatives, cousins, and friends.

To the entire Pope family and their descendants, I thank each and every one of you for living your lives courageously, intentionally, and with conviction on more than one occasion, stepping out into this world on faith. Your unconditional love for me and for each other gave me the support that I needed to follow through with my dreams. You encouraged me to push through the hard stuff and to embrace the present by celebrating each day, always with an open mind and with hope for the future.

Melissa Taylor, my first editor, thank you for taking a chance and going through the storm with me. When I discovered that we were both from Omaha, I knew this was no coincidence. You had to be the one who would help me as I struggled with getting to know myself and my history while writing my story. Your questions were thought-provoking and challenging. But together we stood the test of time.

Anne Geiberger, my copyeditor, thank you—you have gone the final leg of my journey with me. I know that it has not been easy, but with all of the changes, corrections, and sticky notes, we've survived. You have been patient and thorough; a writer couldn't ask for anything more.

Terese Danner, friend, thank you—you helped carry me back in time to the front stoop of our homes, to a time when we were children. You even searched through boxes and photo albums to locate pictures that would further enhance my story. Your friendship never wavered. Thank you for everything.

Samantha Miller, you humbled me when you chose me as your subject for UNO's Women's Archive Project; thank you.

Claudia Dunaway, your smile and kindness are infectious. I only had to ask once, and you agreed to be a reader for me. Again, I asked for your help, and you found me a copyeditor and a graphic artist. Above all you encouraged me to self-publish, and so I thank you for everything.

Melissa Hawkins, you opened several doors to my past through your research and tenacity. That baby girl in the Child Saving Institute thanks you, and so do I.

To the brave members of BLAC and those individuals throughout Nebraska who supported us, thank you.

To all of the businesses, newspapers, radio and television stations, magazines, school organizations, clubs, churches, individuals, and schools who supported me over the years and while writing my memoir, I say thank you.

I would be remiss if I did not thank the friends, mentors, colleagues, business associates, and advisors who have touched my life either personally or professionally or both. One individual who stands out is Dr. John R. Browne. You had the audacity to believe in me and told me that I was a writer, that I could write and publish my personal memoir. You mentored and encouraged me, and as my friend, you shared in all of my possibilities. Among the many others to thank are Jeri Elrod, Susie Buffett, Rodney Wead, Eve Christian, Sharon Rhodes, Cathy Hughes, Sandra Prior, Geri Brown, and Mildred Phillips.

I hope in my excitement to thank everyone I did not leave out anyone, but that would almost be impossible. So if you were excluded, I am terribly sorry and at this time, I thank you.

And for those of you who have ever had or will have a dream—this book is also dedicated to you!

1

A Crowning Moment

I opened the door, entered the assigned hotel room, and carefully looked around for a place to put down my crown and relax. The room was like most hotel rooms. It had large windows dressed in beautiful, cascading, oversized silk drapes. To one side of the room close to a window was a chaise longue, one of several pieces of furniture in the room. There was also a small dressing table lit by a beautiful Tiffany lamp. My immediate impulse was to settle down on the longue and massage my tired legs, but first I had to remove my crown so I could comfortably rest for a few moments. I knew that soon I would hear a stern knock on the door signaling it was time to return to the stage for my final walk, my final act as Miss Omaha. I sat down on the tufted velvet bench in front of the dressing table. I saw my reflection in the mirror as I slowly removed the crown. I wondered, *What happened to me? Who am I? Why was all of this so important to me?* I noticed that a quick look, a glance, can be far more revealing sometimes than spending years on a psychiatrist's couch, especially if that reflection leads to a much longer look, a look that reveals who you've become and who you are on the inside. I may never know the answers to my questions. But I will never stop searching for those answers.

I didn't want to wrinkle my evening gown, but I decided to lie down on the couch so I could massage my legs. They had been hurting since dress rehearsal. Time seemed to linger slowly, which was a nice respite for me.

I looked around for something to occupy my time. I noticed a book, a dictionary—the only book there—so I picked it up and began to thumb through it. My eyes drifted to the crown on the table across the room. It was my outstanding accomplishment. Others would consider the moment I had been crowned Miss Omaha to be the most memorable event in my life. Just one year ago, in the spring of 1969, I had become the first Negro girl to win the Miss Omaha Pageant. But even in that moment, I considered my commitment to bring about change through participation in the civil rights movement as just ahead of my participation in the Miss Omaha Pageant as the most memorable time in my life. I was a very young girl when I made these decisions. I had big ideas for myself and my future. But I also had responsibilities.

I dozed off with these thoughts. I couldn't decide if I was happy or sad about the bittersweet end of my reign. One door was closing, but just one door of the many that we walk through in our lives. Some doors bring hope, some fear, others opportunities, and some may bring joy, sadness, or other, deeply suppressed, emotions. I had always been interested in, intrigued by, and impressed with the journey of my race. Doors that were once closed were slowly opening all around us. As we walked through these new doors, we would encounter events pivotal to our lives: twists and turns that changed destiny and responsibilities.

So why did I open this door? Would there be a struggle on the other side of each door? Many individuals had done great things to break down the boundaries of oppression, racism, and hate, and they attempted to transcend the social ills in our society. Many heights had been reached by man, and many barriers had been broken by people who were determined, inspired, and had a burning desire to succeed.

It all seemed like a dream. I started as a young woman of little influence, status, or popularity. But I dared to challenge and change an unjust system riddled with bigotry and hatred, while at the same time confronting the social norms around what is or is not beautiful.

I have always wanted answers to my questions in life. I've often thought that they would help me become more intimate with my loved ones and even grow deeper in self-discovery. Over time, though, I've discovered that it's not the answers that matter the most to me; it's the questions, because those questions we ask help us understand ourselves and possibly others. I have held to the belief that if I continue to question I will find that I remain open to new thoughts throughout my entire life.

This is my story.

Ancestors.

Grandmother Rose (right), her brother, and a friend.

My father's grandfather Frank.

2

His Eyes Are on His Sparrows

My mother's parents lived in Oklahoma City and Chickasha, Oklahoma. My mother, Juanita, went to school there before her family moved out of the state. Her mother, Rose Lee Hilliard Hawkins, was a housewife and a domestic. Mom's dad, Leonard Hawkins, was a bricklayer. He also gambled and owned a bar. My mom had two younger siblings: a brother, Leonard, and a sister, Audrea Windola. When the Hawkins family left Chickasha, they moved to Council Bluffs, Iowa, some of the cousins went to nearby Omaha, while my mom's cousin Aunt Cute and her family moved to Chicago and some of the other extended family members moved to different parts of California. The Hawkins later relocated to Omaha, just across the Iowa-Nebraska border from Council Bluffs.

When my grandmother Rose became seriously ill with tuberculosis and could no longer take care of her children, she returned to her remaining family in Chickasha, thinking it best that she leave her children under the care of her husband Leonard. I have been told that on most days Grandma Rose was so exhausted and tired that she could hardly function. She became so sick that she could barely eat and was worn out by the devastating, hacking cough that caused her chest and limbs to ache, her eyes to bulge, and her skin to sag, exposing her small frail frame. In those days you didn't dare tell anyone that you might have tuberculosis: there wasn't yet a cure for this highly contagious disease, so most people didn't talk about it. They called it consumption, because you would gradually waste away. Many people were afraid to use the term *tuberculosis* because they thought that admitting they had the disease was a sure way to be sent away to die alone.

I remember seeing a picture of my grandmother, taken as she was leaving Omaha. In the picture, Grandmother is wearing a white ruffled blouse and a black skirt cinched at the waist. The neckline is made of a sheer lace. The lace is gathered around her neck and modestly covers her breasts. Her brother is wearing a black derby hat, a loosely fitted black suit, and a white shirt. The lady with them could be their sister or his wife. She is wearing a large white hat with lace and bows decorating the brim and crown. Rose and her brother, along with this very well dressed lady, are on the back of a train pulling out of the train station in Omaha, heading back to Chickasha.

Grandma Rose returned to Omaha one more time to look upon the faces of her children, whom she loved so very much. Consumption was still new to her body and had not yet made her so ill that she could not move among people from city to city. Some felt she was getting better; however, she soon went back to Oklahoma to continue to fight her awful disease. She stayed there trying to overcome the bitter cold and the evil disease that was bestowed upon her. Not too long after that she died.

What I noticed about the picture the most was that none of them were smiling. It wasn't really a sad look; it was a look of resolve, a look of acceptance. You could see smoke coming around the sides of the train as it slowly pulled away from the station.

In those days it was hard for blacks to get a ticket to ride a train. White people weren't concerned with their clothing or nice ways—what mattered most to them was where you were going or where you were coming from. Most black travelers, if they were allowed to ride the train, would experience a long, hot ride in close, cramped quarters. For most blacks it was a grueling as well as a frightening experience. Although my grandmother Rose was very ill she chose to make the journey by train twice. It was important for her to see her children, even if it was for the last time. She and her companions were confronted by segregated waiting rooms at each and every stop, along with segregated train coaches. The second time they made the journey the procedures were more familiar but the unfriendly attitudes of the conductors and the unpleasant looks of the passengers were no easier to endure. When the train stopped they were not allowed to get off and use the restroom in most places. Food and drink was rarely available to them, so they had to bring their food along with them on the journey. Where they got the money to ride the train, especially a second time, was unknown. During this time, fares were set high in order to deter migrants— especially black migrants—from traveling north. There are a lot of things that I don't know about our Grandmother's last trip to Oklahoma; but what I have learned is that she must have been brave and courageous with regard to her desire to recover and return to her children in good health.

I often wonder who they were waving goodbye to. Who took the picture? I would like to think that it was one of her children, my mom Juanita or her brother Leonard or sister Audrea.

I don't know exactly how long the children lived with their dad. I assume that they lived with him on and off for at least five or six years. My mom told my sisters that when she was eight or nine years old they would live from "pillar to post," or "place to place," and that she worked for several people when she left her dad, cooking and cleaning in their homes day in and day out. It was a hard life for her as well as the others. My grandfather spent a great deal of his time hustling and playing cards with friends and foe. He would win and he would lose. On one occasion he won a bar—or that's the way that he told it. My aunt Audrea was just a little girl when he took control of the bar and opened it in his own name.

When my grandfather had Aunt Audrea in his care he would take her to his bar. At times he would place her on the counter that stretched across the room and tell her to sing the blues. From what she told me, she could really sing her heart out. Most of the songs that she would sing were sad songs like *Tain't Nobody's Bizness If I Do.* (Although I don't think Aunt Audrea understood what she was singing at the early age of four or five.) Most of the time, they hardly ever saw their dad. He was what we would call "a rolling stone." But he was still responsible for them, and on most occasions he left them at home alone with one of his lady friends.

My mother also worked in Omaha for the priests within the local Catholic diocese while she was living with her family in Council Bluffs. Her friends have told me that she was as young as thirteen when she started working. There was even a story that a white man she worked for wanted to marry her. It would have been a common-law marriage, which was not uncommon in any community at that time. I also heard it rumored that he was many years her senior. What was even more shocking, we heard—and it was not from our mother—that he fell in love with her and in her words, "Didn't give a damn what anybody thought about it." My sisters always said that they had been stunned and surprised to hear this, because they just didn't see our mother as a woman who would be sought after by men—especially to the degree of not caring about what could have been violent repercussions from various communities. In any case, she had no intention of taking him up on his offer, although I'm sure the thought of having money and a roof over her head was tempting.

Following Grandma Rose's death, Grandpa Leonard married for the second time to a woman we respectfully called Grandma Helen. I don't know if this marriage was legal or a common-law marriage; in the twenties and thirties people were known to tie the knot without the added sanction of a justice of the peace. My brothers and sisters were all confused regarding the events surrounding not only that relationship, but our own relationship with Grandma Helen. It was called in those days "knowing your place." What they were sure of was that you were seen and not heard. Sitting quietly, not asking questions, and speaking when you were spoken to was the rule rather than the exception in most black families.

Only a few years passed before my grandfather Leonard also died of tuberculosis. There was some secrecy in the community surrounding his death, as well as Grandma Rose's. This awful disease took the lives of so many black people, it devastated black communities across America. My mother was twelve years old when her mother died, and not much older when her father passed away. That left three children without a mother. There are many tragic stories like theirs from that time, but this one is, of course, personal.

My mom, who was the oldest, never graduated from Abraham Lincoln High School. Before completing her last year she had to drop out. Leonard Jr. became a boxer and tried to make a living in cities and towns across the country. Audrea, the youngest, attended Long Elementary School in Omaha and later graduated from Thomas Jefferson High School in Council Bluff, Iowa. After high school, she began cooking and cleaning in Omaha for a local, well-to-do family, the Hurds. She later moved with this prominent family to Corpus Christi, Texas. She worked for them in their home and became a significant part of their family. From a young age Juanita, Audrea, and Leonard no longer lived as a family unit; but they would always be connected in their hearts.

Mom considered Grandma Helen a friend, just like her friends and close confidants Sister Lou and Ms. Watson, who were either distant relatives or dear friends of the family. There was also Cousin Doris and Cousin Anna. All of these people played an integral part in our lives and appeared throughout my own childhood and adult life. At different times they fed us, comforted us, and supported our mother emotionally as well as financially.

Each birthday I received a card, and with each milestone in my life I received a letter along with two or three dollars or a small present, encouraging me to continue to work hard, and telling me to search for my crown. For years, I never knew who was sending these lovely cards and messages. I later learned that my secret pal was another friend of Mom's, Ms. Shook.

John Pope, my dad, was always described by my siblings as a self-educated man. Dad was raised by his grandparents. His grandfather was a freed slave who came from Arkansas. When Dad's grandfather was freed he was given land to work, and later on to own. On this land he and his wife and family, including grandchildren and other relatives, farmed and raised horses. My dad said that one night white men on horseback came and terrorized the family, shooting guns, yelling, and setting the home on fire. They were forced off their land. They left everything and scattered to various parts of the South. My dad always said that this made it almost impossible for him to find any of his relatives outside of his uncles, brothers, and sister. He never gave up hope and always searched for them throughout his life. When the family broke up, my dad went with his grandfather, Frank Pope, to Chickasha, Oklahoma, where Pope served the community as a preacher. They had a large plot of land and a garden. They had pecan trees on their land and sold the pecans around town and beyond.

Dad had an unusual childhood. When he was a boy his family lived in Indian Territory. He would talk about how they cooked in a small pot in the yard. It was always said by his family that they were part Choctaw Indian. They lived in a small shack with wooden plank floors; you could see the ground below through the cracks. The walls were made of straw and tough Oklahoma mud. At meal time a peculiar thing would sometimes happen. The local Indians would come in, sit at the table, and silently eat the food right off their plates. None of the children went to school. My dad spent his day doing chores and playing with the local children, Negro, white, and Indian. They would entertain themselves swimming and fishing at the local water hole. He played an Indian stickball game with the Choctaw children. The game was played with a long, wooden stick fashioned at one end with the shape of a spoon. Dad claimed to have become very good at this game. He always felt that because the Indians were comfortable coming and going through their yard, entering their house without knocking, coming and going as they pleased without acknowledging or paying respects to the elders in his home, that they must have been living with them and even related to them. He said that in those days there were few if any formal marriages or unions among blacks, whites, and Indians.

He learned to ride horses without a saddle and to shoot a moving target with a shotgun, rifle, or handgun with a high level of accuracy. Even as a young boy he was responsible for contributing whatever he could to his family's survival. He used the hunting and fishing skills that he learned from the Native Americans to bring food to the table. It was obvious to me how much his family depended on him. All of the various groups seemed to depend on each other. There were even poor whites entwined in their small community.

My dad remembered more than one occasion when he was instructed by his family to hide several young white children in his bunk, covering them and instructing them not to move while strangers raided the house, stealing dry goods, vegetables, meat, wood, and coal. Most of these men were robbers, military men in uniform, renegades, or impoverished souls roaming across the country. My dad always said that for a little Negro boy it was a very hard and scary time.

He had a couple of brothers, and they were all fairly close. We don't talk about this, but people in their community always said, "Don't mess with those Pope niggers." And that's who Dad thought he was—someone not to mess with. His family, especially his brothers, didn't take any mess off of anyone. They protected each other because the law back in those days turned a blind eye when it came to the injustices that ravaged and terrorized black people in the rural communities of the South. I'm proud of the fact that the Popes defended themselves and their community.

Both of Dad's parents worked and sent money to the grandparents in Chickasha to help take care of their kids, but I'm sure it couldn't have been too much, because they didn't have that much. It was because of this that Dad started wanting to leave home when he was still too young to do so. I think he felt that they would have one less mouth to feed. By the time Dad and his brothers left home, their grandparents had died. My dad traveled around the country in boxcars and slept and ate with other kids and men hoboing around the country. He even ran across women traveling the rails. He noticed that some of the women dressed like men so they would have a better chance to survive. There were few jobs for white men and even fewer jobs for Negroes without skills in the small towns that he passed through. For most of his young life he rode the rails. He became skilled at playing cards and tricking the naïve out of their money in order to survive. Eventually he found himself on a train bound for a training camp in the United States Army. After a few weeks, he decided that the Army wasn't for him, and he disappeared from his camp.

He knew very little about city life when he ended up in Chicago, a place in the north that he was always hearing had jobs for men like him. Later he was somehow contacted by his sister, who was trying to unfetter herself from a male scoundrel who was just plain evil and abusive. Dad went to her aid, and a fight ensued. While saving her life, Dad seriously injured the man, who later died, and my dad was sent to prison for years. Thanks to his quick thinking without regard to his own safety, his sister lived a long and happy life. Dad never openly spoke of his incarceration, and neither did we.

My dad later moved to the Omaha–Council Bluffs area, where he worked odd jobs. Several years before he married our mother, he began to go blind. He moved about in his surroundings with uncertainty and confusion. Night became day and day night in his small world. He learned to successfully wash, shave, comb his hair, and dress himself in darkness. Months later his sight returned as strangely as it had gone away. Later he was told it was hysterical blindness. He never went to a doctor, so he never received a medical explanation for his condition. When he consulted doctors later about what had happened to him, they felt that his condition was more psychological than physiological. Following his illness he became a tailor for a time. He even was a showcard writer for a while. A showcard writer created handmade signs to display on the fronts of buildings and theaters, in store windows, and on street placards. These displays advertised goods, holiday sales, and special occasions. When an event came to town, Dad was hired to write an advertisement for it. He was an extremely good writer. He even went to a school for showcard writing.

He was a self-educated man, and like the other men in his family he enjoyed reading. He was always interested in what was happening out in the world. He would read the newspaper from front to back every day. He usually listened to the radio in the evening; he wanted quiet when he listened to the news. Because of that, we knew all of the local and world news. Daddy liked westerns; I remember him reading all of the western writers, especially Zane Gray. I appreciate that both of our parents were well read.

Dad was about twenty-seven and my mom about seventeen when they met. My brothers and sisters and I think that Mom married Dad because her parents had died; because of her dire circumstances stemming from this loss, she no longer had a real home.

My mother Juanita Pope (seventh from left) demonstrating with
the Citizens Coordinating Committee for Civil Liberties.
(photo courtesy of Omaha World-Herald)

My sister Rose Mary and others preparing to attend a hearing of
a proposed Nebraska fair housing practices bill.
(photo courtesy of Omaha Star)

3

Test and Testimony

I had always thought I knew who my mother was, her aspirations and dreams. I even thought I knew how she grew up and how she lived. But the truth is I should have just stuck with the questions.

I learned this as I embarked on an incredible journey to learn more about my parents, especially my mother. By questioning, I discovered that I never really knew the people that I called Mom and Dad, and I knew even less about the individual that others called Juanita, my mom, a daughter, a wife, a co-worker, a friend, a politician, and a community leader. I found I knew little and understood even less about the courage and strength that Juanita Hawkins Pope displayed throughout her life.

This particular journey of discovery began innocently one September, early in the school year. I was beginning my first year at Technical Junior High School, and although I was excited I was also afraid. I was afraid of the changes that I would have to make in a new school. I was also afraid of meeting new people, making new friends, and moving to a new neighborhood.

The first week of school I discovered that I wasn't the only one with the jitters in my seventh-grade classroom. There was a room full of kids who were sharing my experience. As a matter of fact they were just like me, I suppose my teacher had enough experience to know what we were all going through, since she had taught the seventh grade for years. In the second week of school she handed each of us a packet with large letters on the cover: *My Family Tree.* We had three days to complete the assignment. With this assignment I decided to embark on something different: to take a look at my parents when they were just starting out. Since I'd done several family tree projects before, I thought this was going to be an easy assignment. But then for me, nothing ever seems to go easy, just because I never let it. At the time I didn't know very much about my parents, and I thought this would be a chance to get to know each of them better.

We sat around the table that night and talked for hours: me with my tea, my mom with a glass of juice, and my dad with a tall glass of rum and Coke on ice. I don't know why, but as they began telling me their story tears slowly collected in the corners of my eyes and began to stream down my brown face. I had difficulty looking into my parents' eyes, and they seemed unable to look at each other. I don't know if Mom ever really forgave Dad for the events that turned out so badly that day. I know she must have tried, or they would not have been able to remain together over the years. Although I tried to analyze the situation and put myself in their place, I was only twelve years old, a junior-high student with very little life experience. Even at that early age, though, I did feel and have compassion for my parents while listening and writing.

I knew that I'd had two older brothers who had died long before I was born, but I knew little else. I asked my parents how my siblings had died, and my father told me a story about a day in 1939, when my mother was about twenty-eight years old. She decided to go to a public hearing with my dad. City officials were there discussing the benefits of and problems involved in the demolition of dilapidated housing in North Omaha, an area predominately occupied by Negroes, and where later we would live as a family when I was young. According to public records, the people living there would be displaced, forced to move out but lacking the funds to find new homes. Nevertheless, the city had decided that the $1.4-million expansion of the Logan Fontenelle Housing Project would improve the living conditions of families in the city. Most of the people at the hearing were not convinced that the city was doing the right thing. Many of the renters in the group were either out of work or on public assistance. They felt with this second phase of the project they would be put out of their homes with nowhere to go but the streets.

The proposed housing project would occupy the area between Charles and Clark Streets from Twenty-Second to Twenty-Third Street and between Seward and Clark from Twentieth to Twenty-Second Street, with one exception: land would be left vacant for commercial businesses.

Many people in attendance were not only in agreement with the city, but they were also excited at the prospect of more places available to rent. The people who owned homes in the proposed area thought they could sell them at a good price.

My mother, who was later described in the newspaper as a small-framed young Negro mother, stepped forward to address the panel. She waited patiently for the board to give her permission to speak. Then she began, speaking slowly.

"Hello," she said in her unassuming, quiet voice. "My name is Juanita Pope. I currently live at 2009 Clark Street, Second Ward." She paused. "If you have any questions please wait until I finish, then you can ask me questions. I'll try to answer if I can." She took a deep breath, then mustered up the strength to continue. She told the group that she felt that new housing would be good, but they must also consider the needs of poor people. She said that it was very important to make sure the city had plans for them. They needed somewhere to go that would be comparable, if not better, than where they were now living.

"Let me explain," she said. She then spoke of a few years earlier, in April 1936, when they were living at 2436 Charles Street. She was about twenty-four years old then, when her family had to relocate for the first phase of this same development project. She told the board how her very young family searched and searched in an effort to find new housing without financial assistance. They owned no home they could sell to the city, so they had no additional funding, as some others might have had.

They ended up moving into an upper-story room in a run-down apartment. The rent was twelve dollars a month. In those days, twelve dollars was a lot of money for a place that offered them so very little. She described the horrible conditions of the home and the cold, harsh winter they had to endure. She recalled how frightened she was that they could be forced out, with nowhere appropriate to go. That small, broken-down shack was really the best that they could do. She then went on to describe what happened that winter.

Several articles were later written about that meeting. The articles couldn't show the tears in her eyes as she continued to speak before the housing commission.

"That winter the heat had failed just before Christmas, and later two of my three children died of pneumonia."

Recounting this, my father said the room was deathly silent after my mother finished speaking. There were heavy sighs, and eyes were filled with tears. He was very proud of my mother for being so strong and smart. He said he never loved her more than he did at that moment. The chairman of the housing commission went on to the next speaker.

One by one, speakers stood up. One individual said that she was all for the project. Her husband was unemployed, but she wanted to find a better home outside of the city for her six sons and two daughters. Another man said that he had put a lot of improvements into his home and wouldn't move unless he got a good price. Another speaker said that he hadn't thought much about the change and that he had no idea where he would go.

Nonetheless, the housing authority declared that the demolition would start in the fall, and it did. My mother was so brave to stand up before people that she didn't know and tell her story in order to benefit others. But what could any of us do? We were powerless; we had to accept whatever they said. They went right ahead with the project. My father told me that years later they were allowed to move into the projects, which in the long run did benefit them. There were some at the meeting who felt any change would be better than where they were living. Maybe they had saved some money or maybe they had family willing to take them in, but it didn't benefit our family because we had nowhere to go, and with very little money our prospects were extremely dim. Nonetheless, they were forced to move to the cold, uncomfortable shack on Thirty-First and Corby Streets in North Omaha.

My father and mother had never spoken about that day in 1936 until I asked them what happened to my two oldest brothers.

I saw my father's sallow face and fixed eyes from behind his horn-rimmed glasses as he explained in great detail that horrible day. Mom had been home alone. Mom interrupted him then and told me that it all happened very fast. He began again, saying she was alone. I was sure he reiterated that point because he felt overwhelming guilt for not being there.

"There was a bad fire. . . ." he said.

Mom finished his thoughts. "The flames spread so fast. Much of the house was made of board and scraps of wood, and the smoke and fumes made me dizzy. Unable to think and determine my location in the room, I became confused. The flames consumed the small apartment quickly. All I could think was to call out to my oldest, John Junior, to get to the window. I snatched my two youngest sons—they were only one and two—from the crib where they were sleeping. I forced John Junior out on the ledge of the roof and awkwardly carried the other two out of the window." She turned to my dad. "Do you remember that apartment on the second floor of that old house?" She sighed audibly.

"The firemen finally arrived and safely helped the other tenants from the still-burning building. It was winter—and so cold. None of us had anything on except what was on our backs when the fire started. They put all of us into an ambulance. The doctors quickly discovered that one of my sons was not breathing on his own. At the time it was unclear who it was, but we knew it was one of our younger children. They didn't have the right equipment, but they performed a tracheotomy immediately. They cut a small opening into his throat and inserted a narrow tube into his airway so that he could breath."

She continued speaking, staring blankly and looking straight ahead. "As the winter months lingered on and seemed to last forever, our youngest, Richard, caught pneumonia. His brother, Don Everett, did not fare much better, and died later of complications from smoke inhalation. They were given the medical attention that we could afford, but even with the help of Dr. Gooden, our family doctor, we could not prevent their deaths. That's why we're here today."

My dad and mom held tight to each other's hands as my mom continued, "According to the paper, the fire started from a coal-oil explosion in a room below ours. The occupant, Mrs. Octavia Ward, was burned on her face and hands. As strange as it might seem, we were not mad at her. What good would that do? It certainly wouldn't bring back our children, Richard and Don Everett, both under five years of age, and both of whom died as a result of the fire. She was just as bad off as we were, and the fire wasn't her fault. All of us lived in that rooming house because we were displaced for the development of the first phase of the project. We had nowhere else to go."

Even though all of this was before my time, I strongly felt the loss of my two brothers as my parents related their story. Even so, I didn't want to lose myself as I often had a tendency to do and forget why I wanted to know these things about their life. As they continued telling their story, I tried hard not to think about the damage that it could have done to their relationship.

Tonight would prove to be one of the many nights that would change my outlook on family life and instill in me a heavy heart forever. Dad rarely spoke of this time. When he was asked about it you could see the anguish, sorrow, and grief in his eyes and the stress on his face. He could remember a time long before me and my brothers and sisters. He could remember his two sons who didn't make it through the times of poverty. He was determined to see to it that poverty did no more damage to his family.

I stopped writing at this point. My paper was complete for my project, but as time went on I continued learning as much as I could from whoever I could about my family.

My parents were still struggling financially when they moved the family to a two-story house on Thirty-First and Corby Streets in Omaha's Near North Side, but there was an unspoken commitment to hold the family together.

In the winter, the house was fairly cold. My parents had a potbelly stove in the middle of the dining room, and that's where they would feed the coal they brought up from the coal bin in the basement. I had not been born yet, but my brothers and sisters have told me that sometimes they would have to go down into the basement to fetch coal, and none of them ever wanted to. They would argue over who would go. The handrail attached to the crumbling, dirty wall was broken and sunken in several places. The stairs were of crumbling, sloping cement and were hard to walk down. It was always dark, muggy, and dirty down there. Every now and then they would see a rat (they never told me whether the rats were large or small). As soon as they noticed something shining in the dark or a wavy movement that they thought could be a tail they would hurry back up the stairs, sometimes moving backwards, and quickly shut the door. Of course, my parents would ask where the coal was, and they would merely bow and shake their heads. The boys would just laugh at the girls, saying that they'd probably imagined seeing something that scared them. But none of them would readily volunteer to brave the trip; even the dog would hide when it was coal-getting time. If it was one of the boys who lost the loud argument over who was to fetch the coal, he would suck it up and not let the others know that he was really afraid, and hurry into the basement and retrieve as much coal as a kid could possibly carry. Dad and the boys, John and Wallace, would have to tend the fire in the winter, keeping the stove glowing orange on the outside The kids were always cautioned to keep their distance from the stove, because if they fell on it they could get badly burned. So they knew not to play around it. My sister Rose Mary remembers a day when John actually volunteered to go down into the basement and bring up coal. He did a lot of chores on that particular day, because he had skipped school, and he knew it wouldn't be long before his parents would be getting a call telling them about it.

All of them took their baths in the same washtub, and the youngest one got to bathe first, on the assumption that the youngest was the least dirty. They had a bathroom upstairs, but it had only cold water; hot water needed to be boiled in the kitchen on the potbelly stove.

Men in the community used whatever they could to transport coal and wood back to their homes in order to stoke the fire in their stoves. Our dad used our brother John's red wagon. It wasn't easy to travel at night on foot pulling a loaded wagon behind you through the alleys and backstreets of North Omaha. Dad gathered coal that had been discarded or possibly dropped off of train cars heavily heaped with coal. He would make his way home with the wagon heaped with coal and other material collected along the way. Ward Four, where my parents lived, was a place in those days riddled with crime and scoundrels. Streetlights were few and far between in the overcrowded community.

For his entire life my brother John talked about that red wagon that his parents had given him. At first it was okay with John for Dad to use the wagon, especially since the coal that he collected kept all of them warm. But one night Dad came back home without the wagon, and that made brother John really mad and sad—so much so that he never took the time over the years to understand or forget about it. "I know I was just a small kid about three or four, but to me the wagon was like a man's first car today." He just wouldn't stop there, he would go on and on about how that really messed him up. Only he knew what that meant and, oh well, he did have problems committing to things and following through when he did commit. If you took the time to look at him when he told his story, you could almost see some sadness in his eyes. I don't know if he connected the loss of his brothers with losing his wagon or not. I do know that anyone who carries a childhood event like that into adulthood had to have taken that loss really, really hard.

Although they struggled with their circumstances, my siblings have all said that everybody seemed to be fairly content, even though they were very poor. They have even said that they didn't realize they were poor. There were apple trees and cherry trees in their neighborhood, and all the kids would steal the fruit. They did a lot of that kind of thing; it was a lot of fun.

All of these things went on with very few complaints. Our extended family sometimes had their issues, as most relatives do, but they lived together on and off throughout the Great Depression. I always heard from my parents that the Depression hit blacks in most urban and rural communities long before it hit the lives of more affluent people. In one sense, you could say most blacks were unaware of its impact; they lived their lives as if the Depression were a constant guest in their homes.

Oftentimes, Mom wouldn't go to church because she didn't have the right clothes to wear. She saw others with nice things, but just didn't have them. She wasn't vain, though—just proud. There were those around our mother that would make fun of her because of her old, used clothing, her housedresses, worn shoes, and unruly hair. She had a mole, a small growth on the corner of her right eyelid, that made her appear as if her eye were partially shut.

When people stared at her eye or made fun of how she was dressed, it make her sad. Most of the time they made fun of her behind her back, but on rare occasions strangers would whisper comments in her presence. She never publicly voiced her feelings of sadness or disappointment in others. She was self-conscious about the mole on her eyelid until she finally had it removed. She always said, "If given a lemon in life, try your very best to make lemonade." After the growth on her eye was removed she began to socialize more, laugh more, and even sing a lot. She began to smile more, and her smile was infectious. For some reason your attention was now drawn to her white, straight teeth. They were perfect. When she smiled, so would everyone around her. Makeup was something that she had rarely purchased before, but now she was not only buying it, she was wearing it to church and club meetings. Now when you noticed her eyes, you could see how they were actually—as our dad put it—sexy. She always had straight, beautiful legs, and now she was wearing modern dresses and skirts befitting the times, up-to-date clothes such as you might see in the newspaper ads. Most of her stylish clothes came from the closets of the women that she worked for, but she didn't complain about that. She was thankful that they thought of her instead of placing the clothes in the giveaway basket in their closets.

My relatives and friends said that some of the best lessons they learned in life were from my mother. My cousin Anita Jo said that my mom taught her how to dance and encouraged her to strive for better things. And in fact, all of my relatives had something to offer, and brought something to all of our lives for the better. My cousins have always given my mother most of the credit for the positive parts of their lives. In their youth, my cousins didn't understand that my mother was trying to teach them about having a strong desire and a thirst for education. She took time to help all of us with our homework or prepare for competitions that involved dancing, singing, and public speaking. My cousins later talked about how our family would sit down and have meals together, something that happened on rare occasions in their home. Their mother, my aunt Lucille, was younger and looked to our mother and father for guidance. While her husband Uncle Leonard, my mother's brother, was away in the hospital, the rest of his family lived with us for years. Our auntie relied on our mother. It was obvious over time that they were the best of friends: they respected each other and let it show to all of us.

Aunt Lucille and Uncle Leonard started their family when Lucille was young, before she'd had a chance to pursue any of her other goals. She was spirited and wanted to enjoy her life. Much of her young life was spent without her husband, because he was diagnosed with tuberculosis and had to spend years in a sanitarium, and she was forced to raise their children without his financial or emotional support. After he was released from the hospital the family lived in the projects. Later on they moved to a house on Hamilton Street, and things got a lot better for them. They were united; they were able to be a family again. With Uncle Leonard working, they were able to buy things for their home and their meals included more fresh fruits and vegetables as well as better cuts of meat.

People in the neighborhood envied Aunt Lucille's beauty. She didn't need makeup; she was just naturally attractive. She was shapely and would wear beautiful high-heeled shoes. She wore her hair short and colored it dishwater blonde. Negroes would speak of her hair as being a good grade of hair. Her eyes were hazel, and her skin was a honey brown. On important days, like Sundays, she wore a fox fur draped around her shoulders, with its small head and beady, piercing eyes still intact. Those eyes were made of glass, but that didn't diminish our fascination with it. That fox was Auntie's favorite thing to wear, although she had an extensive wardrobe, including other fur coats, beautifully fitted suits, and fine wool or cashmere sweaters. She had a look that would turn the head of any man, no matter what race or status he held. Contrary to what some thought about her, she was kind and giving. My sisters and I were lucky girls to have someone other than Mom we could talk to about personal things. It was her we asked about boys, and she never embarrassed us with the answers. She knew how to keep a secret, and would keep one unless she thought you would get into trouble or hurt, and on those occasions she would let us know that she was going to tell our parents.

At times, I envied her for the admiration she received from the other kids in the neighborhood. She could get practically anything from anybody, and I wondered what it would be like to have that kind of power. I was jealous of that power, wishing others viewed my mother with that same sense of awe. To my shame, I wanted my mother to be like that. I wanted my mom to turn heads and make men take a second look. She seldom wore makeup or fancy hairdos, even though she had dark bright eyes, flawless brown skin, and beautiful hair that she often wore in a pageboy. She was tall, and when she wore stockings the seam was usually slightly crooked on or both of her straight, shapely legs. She seldom wore fancy dresses that cinched at the waist like Aunt Lucille's. On her feet, she wore thick-heeled, black work shoes, with breathing holes in the top. She always spent her money on us for our school supplies, food, and clothing. I thought the whole thing about beauty, how people defined it and thought about it, just didn't seem fair, because our mother was a beautiful woman on the inside as well as the outside. She made heads turn with her wit, humor, and intellectual conversation. She could hold her own in a meeting on political issues with men as well as women. In the end men would find themselves attracted to her as they carried on discussions with her for hours. She was extremely intelligent, thoughtful, and kind. Some people just couldn't see that special kind of beauty that never fades. Life is funny. My cousins say that they envied us for having such a smart and talented mother.

While Uncle Leonard was recovering from tuberculosis in the sanitarium, Aunt Lucille and her children stayed with my parents. This strong, athletic man who sometimes boxed for a living was sent away from his home and family. For over five years, he was removed from everything familiar and safe. It was a special place, different from a regular hospital. He lived in a very small room, by himself most of the time, his only contact being with doctors or staff checking in on him.

According to various family stories, my uncle would slip out or my aunt would sneak in to him or meet him somewhere, and they would add to their family. He would return quietly to the sanitarium, and she would go back to our parents' house. I'm sure he would leave only briefly, but even so his family increased from two children to four, another boy and girl.

Many American Indians and Negroes from our community spent time in sanitariums. Negroes were not placed with whites in Omaha sanitariums. As in most large urban cities, they were restricted to certain areas on the hospital campus, and many of those areas were cold and secluded places. He had to cook for himself in thin, worn-out pots and pans on a small hot plate. He cooked greens and other vegetables, many of which he grew himself in the rough, dry ground on the premises. He made special brewed-pot liquor from the broth of wilted greens. He also ate a lot of oatmeal. He kept to his routine, prayed a lot, and imagined himself back at home with his family. I'm sure he was lonely. TB was a disease that held a death sentence for most. For black people, sanitariums were often equivalent to the worst of our prisons, because people could not gather together. They had to live alone for years, restricted from outside human contact. We never knew how Uncle Leonard managed to come and go without being noticed. Aunt Lucille said that because he was able to have some contact with his family, however brief, he was able to have hope and stay alive.

He was one of the very few to survive the ordeal that took both of his own parents. If you were unfortunate enough to be diagnosed with this disease you were sent away for having acquired it. You had no choice in the matter. Sometimes your family was even ignored and shunned because of it. It was a very hard time for many families.

In those days of the Depression there were often two, sometimes three, families living in our house at one time. Although my sisters were born later, they always said that they recalled hearing that our cousin Doris and her family stayed with us from time to time. Three families in one house, under one roof—and now even one family in a house can't seem to get along. There wasn't much space, and all of them ate together, slept together, cried together, and prayed together. They had very little food in the house. Our mother would go up and down the street asking her neighbors if she could pick the dandelions out of their yards. Some had no problem with her gathering the weeds from their yards. Others were planning to pick the weeds and cook them for their own families. The unpredictable weather in Omaha always introduced challenges when it came to living off of the earth. There were always extremes when it came to weather conditions: too much heat in the summer and too much cold in the winter. You could anticipate bad weather as surely as you could predict the sun rising each morning—tornados, floods, blizzards, and of course droughts, which were always the worst when it came to planting, growing, and harvesting a small crop. Omaha proudly accepted its designation as a part of the Great Plains, but sadly it was more well known as a part of Tornado Alley.

Resourceful as always, my mom asked the neighbors to gather at her home for a neighborhood meeting. Its purpose: to outsmart the weather. So many people showed up that she had to hold the meeting outside of the house. On that warm, sunny day most of the families agreed to put their resources together and create a neighborhood garden. They grew mostly potatoes, greens, onions, and carrots, and when they could get their hands on the seeds they grew squash. All of the neighbors shared in the work as well as the harvest. Both men and women canned the fruit from their trees and the vegetables from their community garden so that they would all have food, even during bad weather and tough times.

Of course in those days, the late thirties and early forties, everything was kind of rationed; you got your plate of food, but rarely did you get more. There was hardly ever any extra food in our home, and my mom made sure that the ones working the hardest got any second plates that were available. Everyone ate the same meal; not even my dad got preferential treatment. If there was meat, each person was served meat, even if it was only a small portion. Our parents were thoughtful and fair, and most of the things that they taught us they taught by example. As I look back on that, I'm kind of proud of the fact that everyone was treated basically the same in our family. I had friends whose parents always put themselves first, even when it came to food. For some reason that always bothered me.

My brothers and sisters always said that our mom was a good cook; she could make something out of nothing. In our house, she would find use for scraps and leftovers that other people would have thrown away. It was a well-known fact among our friends and family that she could cook just about anything. When the family all sat down at the table to eat, they would never put anything in their mouths without first giving thanks.

They were a close family. My mother loved reading and writing and literature, so the children were always encouraged to read. They didn't have many books in the house because they couldn't afford them, and they never had magazines. They only saw magazines on newsstands or in doctor's offices: they seemed like such a luxury. The kids did have library books that they brought home from school. Mom always helped them with their homework. The house was always neat and clean. It was furnished fairly well because the person our dad worked for gave him his old furniture when he bought new furnishings for his home. The furniture appeared to be new, so my family considered that they were doing fairly well.

Because of the potbelly stove the downstairs would stay fairly warm during the winter, but the upstairs bedrooms were always cold, so they would have to snuggle up in the bed with lots of blankets. In order to keep warm in the winter, they would sleep sideways so more people could comfortably fit on one bed, although most of the time the men preferred to sleep on the floor. Whenever either of my sisters would wake up in the middle of the night, she would check that the other sister was covered. In the summertime, most of the family liked to sleep on the porch. The cool breeze would come through the screens and pass over a bowl of ice carefully placed in the window to cool them off. They always said that it felt like camping.

My brothers and sisters were the second generation in our family to go to Long School. They always said that they had a lot of fun there. Some of them also went to Lothrop School or Howard Kennedy Elementary School. They all remembered coming straight home from school every day. Because my mom was still at work, John would be in charge of things at home. He was in the seventh or eighth grade at that time. They would get home from school and have whatever was left over from lunch—a sandwich or a piece of fruit. But if they had something special like cookies, John would lock the others in the basement, so he could keep the cookies to himself.

Despite such pranks, everybody loved one another. In those days my mom rarely went out anywhere. Sometimes she would visit with a neighbor, but she was always home with the kids when she wasn't working or volunteering. She liked to play jacks and other little ball games with the kids, or checkers and other board games. They all played outside a lot; sometimes they played in the dirt making mud pies, while other times they played stickball in the street, or a game called Captain May I?

They went to church. Wallace, Rose Mary, and Joyce would walk to Mount Moriah Baptist Church, or else down the hill to the Lutheran Church on Thirtieth Street and Corby. Sometimes even John would attend church. They also went to Bible school in the summer. The church folks were mostly white people, but they were very nice to them. As children, they never understood why these people were so nice or why they cared about them so much, but they did. The church put on plays, and they were the stars. They had programs on Saturday from early in the morning until late in the afternoon. My parents would attend their programs, in which my brothers and sisters would act and sing. They had fun, and it kept them off the streets and doing what they would call God's work.

In the summer they would go through the neighborhood and up a steep hill to attend the carnival when it came to town. They thought they were going a long way, but it couldn't have been even a mile up the hill. They liked to spend time there even after the carnival moved on.

My family always lived in rental houses. When their home was sold, they would have to move. Other times they moved to get into a better neighborhood or to get into a bigger house. But they always rented, and they always moved.

One of the things that my sisters remembered was how my parents felt about religion. "Mom and Dad didn't always go to church when we were growing up," they would say. Mother felt that we really didn't have the right kind of clothes. Other women would wear their fancy dresses, hats, and gloves, and Mom didn't have any of that. But she would always, always send her children to church, where they would participate in the musical programs, and most of the time she came to support them. She would show up to show her support even when she felt underdressed. During the winter months, she was especially conscious of her thin, worn-out wool coat.

As the children got older they began to get little jobs and with their extra money were able to buy her a coat, and she began to take more of an interest in church. Mom joined the usher board in the church, along with a few of the other church organizations. The usher board was responsible for assisting with the church service. They would greet people at the door to make them feel welcome. They would also assist them with finding seats, hand out fans, and even fan them if they needed fanning. They had their own group, and they were proud to be an essential part of the church and church service. My mother always said that she took this obligation seriously and that she looked forward to each and every Sunday that it was her turn to usher. What she didn't look forward to was someone becoming unhappy and falling out with the church. She considered her church meetings important, and I think that made her very happy. Dad wasn't really a churchgoer. He seldom attended church during our childhood. He was most dedicated to church in the decade before he died.

Mom always kept things nice and neat. When the embers would go out at night in the potbelly stove, it was time to go to bed. We would do our homework next to the stove at the dining-room table; Mom was always there to give us assistance. She would even sing songs: it made for a happy childhood. Sometimes our house even had a little lawn. I remember Mom going out and planting grass in the front yard. Because my mom and dad always believed in raising vegetables or some kind of fruit, we always had a garden in our yard. Mom and Dad would get together after harvesting the garden and do some canning. When my brothers and sisters were little my parents would put the food, fruits and vegetables, on the shelves in the basement, so all of them could eat from the garden long after the snow arrived.

My brothers and sisters often said that it was difficult for them to remember if Dad did anything special for them. Along with my sisters I do remember that he would let us sit on his lap, and he would blow smoke rings for us. I did that a lot—sat on his lap and bothered him to blow smoke rings.

One thing that my parents would speak about was our country's fear of communism. They said that the FBI had come to our home asking whether they were communist. The FBI claimed that some of my parents' friends, including their good friends the Watsons, had attended Communist Party meetings and were Communist sympathizers. And some of those very same friends were sometimes responsible for putting meals on our table, paying a bill so that our family would have fuel to heat the house, or seeing to it that the children had shoes on their feet. It was not uncommon for outside groups to offer help in our neighborhood, and communists were among those groups offering help to inner-city communities. My parents never understood why some of their very good friends, best friends at that time, were considered communist. I suppose Negroes helping each other without outside assistance must have seemed communistic to some skeptics unfamiliar with our community. I suppose that would frighten any white official, although it was something that anyone should have been able to understand. But as far as I know Mom and Dad were not communists or members of the Communist Party. I imagine the accusations came from the rumors that we were related to Malcolm Little, who was later known as Malcolm X. We could never own or disown that rumor. My parents were not aware of any basis for this rumor, and it has never been substantiated. Dad was a first cousin to members of another well-known Little family. Cleavon Little, the actor, was in that family. He was known for his starring rolls in *Blazing Saddles* and the Broadway production *Purlie*. He was in movies, on stage, and in television, and Dad was always proud of that.

My parents were determined to keep the family under one roof. They were afraid that social services would have to place their children in homes (now called foster care). They remained bound to the projects, the very place that had displaced them and set into motion the series of events that caused the greatest loss they would experience. It was hard, but it was home, where they ate, argued, slept, laughed. and prayed.

By 1950 I was one year of age, and things were better but not by much. There were five of us children at home. One evening my mother and another lady, Ms. Watson, went shopping for Christmas presents. My mother had $17.50 in her purse, more than she'd ever had to buy her family presents. She felt relatively flush, until she lost all but $2.50 of her holiday fund. A report in the paper related, "It was either stolen as she was walking through the store or she mistakenly dropped it unnoticed from her arm." But my mom said that she felt blessed just to be alive and well. This was reason enough to celebrate Christmas in 1950, reason enough.

By 1953, although my dad had a temporary job at Armour Packing Plant, he remained angry and disheartened at a system that he felt never seemed to give him and his family a break. A younger, angrier man approached him at work, knocked him down, and proceeded to fight him, even though he was unprovoked and Dad was almost twice his age. It was no wonder that my dad fought back. That twenty-five-year-old went to the hospital with severe knife wounds, although he later recovered. My older sister said she knew nothing about it until one day several kids from the neighborhood asked her why her dad did such a bad thing to that man. She ran all the way home to ask our mother if it was true. My sister was just devastated. She didn't have many friends who came to the house, and most of her social life revolved around the church. I'm sure that she wondered about the whispers and cruel remarks that she might have to endure the following day at school. She was embarrassed. What would everyone say and think about her family? Dad told the detectives who later came to investigate that he had acted in self-defense. He had his sheep-carving knife in his hands, and when confronted by the other worker he used it to protect himself. others at the plant substantiated his story. However, because he had been involved in a fight he lost his job at the plant. They couldn't allow violence to take place, no matter who was at fault. For a long time after that my mother and father didn't know how they would make it without his employment.

After my dad had been unemployed for several long months, my mother did a very brave thing. She took it upon herself to write the president of the Armour Packing Plant to try to get my dad his job back. Not long after that, my dad received a certified letter in the mail notifying him of his reinstatement. Mom must have written a hell of a letter.

Most of the people in the projects were very impressed when they heard that my mother got my dad his job back. Suddenly they all wanted my mom to hear their troubles and give them advice. She began giving advice and writing letters for a lot of families.

My mother had no qualms about aspiring to be a lawyer. She was intelligent. She was also a little different: she was not a run-of-the-mill person. She would talk the talk as well as walk the walk when it came to publically standing up and addressing social ills with vocal and written solutions. She wasn't afraid to be a soldier for justice. She would get depressed sometimes and keep to herself. She would seldom get mad. Most people who knew her couldn't remember ever seeing her get angry. She was a humble, kind, and thoughtful person. She was very interested in children and in their education. She took an interest in student activities and the school system, and that involvement sparked an interest in politics. She would give kids in the neighborhood money for showing her their grades. Most students would work very hard so that they could show her good grades on their report cards. Depending on their grades she would give them a nickel or a dime, or whatever she could afford to give them. Her opinion went a long way with the kids in the projects.

Later in her life, she started showing her anger and asserting herself. Dad didn't want her to be so public about her involvement in social and political causes. When we were little, she put a lot of her energy into us. But as her older children grew up and moved away, she participated in political and social groups more and more. Dad felt that by keeping her at home, he could protect her from the cruelty of racist people. He knew only too well what that was like. He had been turned away at stores. A young man he had been told that he could not attend schools for penmanship, tailoring, and suit making. He was not allowed to apply for jobs that he felt he was qualified for. The thing that stood out the most for him was not being allowed to attend a grammar school so he could learn to read and write. Many doors had been slammed in his face. He would never disclose to my mother the fact that in his early life he was locked away for protecting his sister and was never given a fair trial among his peers. His was a Jim Crow trial with little hope that he would see justice.

Because she wrote letters for so many people, Mom became even more active in the community, especially in civil rights. In 1962, when I was thirteen years old, she wrote to the Public Pulse, the open editorial column of the *Omaha World-Herald*. She wrote many letters to the Public Pulse, but on this occasion her letter was about six Negroes who molested and beat up two airmen in the air force. Her article was entitled, "Not Right to Judge All."

"It's too bad that all Omaha Negroes must be judged by the actions of a few hoodlums who molested two airmen. It was bad, I admit, but if we are going to judge the morals of a whole race by a few, I'm afraid the white citizens wouldn't look too good, either. I can remember myself as a child in Omaha being rocked and run down by white youths who were three times my age. May God have mercy on all of us."

My mother not only wrote, she demonstrated. On Monday, September 9, 1963, she was on the front page of the *Omaha World-Herald* along with eight others as part of a civil-rights group called the Citizens Coordinating Committee for Civil Liberties (4CL). Their membership was picketing. They were protesting against the policies of the *World-Herald*, which seemed biased and unfair when it came to reporting news and other information regarding African Americans. The group, including my mom, demonstrated for over an hour in front of the newspaper offices. They were led by the leaders of the 4CL, Reverend Jones, Reverend Rudolph McNair, and Reverend R. F. Jenkins. Unless policies were changed, they said, they would be returning again and again, and I had no doubt that they meant what they said. Senator Edward Danner, the only Negro member of the Nebraska legislature, and Reverend John Markoe, SJ, a retired associate professor of mathematics at Creighton University, also participated in the demonstration. It was noted by the paper that they were "peaceful and quiet" and that there were "no arrests." By the end of the demonstration there were over forty people involved; my mother was the seventh to join.

By November of 1967, the year before I ran for Miss Omaha, my mother was running for political office. Dozens turned out in support of her. Her opponent received 22 votes to my mother's 121 in Near North Side Precinct Five. She was elected to the Greater Omaha Council Association board. She would serve a one-year term beginning in February 1968. The board controlled about $5 million of federal funding for antipoverty programs in Douglas County.

In addition to Head Start, a program that my mother and I strongly supported was the Sunshine Cultural Center. It was the only local school and youth cultural center dedicated to the performing arts. University students serving in Volunteers in Service to America (VISTA), along with local artists and teachers, gave their time and talents in support of the program, which established a school and provided dance, art, music, and acting lessons to children who otherwise could never afford such programs. Children of preschool age attended the school. Students in grades kindergarten through twelfth grade received tutoring, and many of the children participated in other components of the program, such as performing arts, being offered at the school. Many of the programs encouraged the academic achievements of the students. Many people on the Near North Side, including my mother and me, several of her friends, and other community members volunteered daily in the school. Others volunteered in special projects three days a week. They were there to assist, working with the children, reading to them and helping them with art projects and their homework.

I was not surprised to see Omaha Public Schools step in and give their opinion about the school and its director. As far as a majority of the community was concerned, the school had a wonderful program. Omaha Public Schools, however, considered that since all of the instructors and volunteers at the school were not credentialed, they could not possibly provide good instruction. I believe that it was primarily a matter of economics that motivated them to admonish the performing arts school. The funds being offered to the school were city and federal, making some of those unavailable to the school district. The school did a very good job of providing students with skilled teachers and volunteers. The *Omaha World-Herald* reported that the Tri-University Project in Elementary Education at the University of Nebraska had become a participant in the school's program, as a volunteer at the school. The newspaper also stated that the school was not like Head Start, nor was it like the Montessori schools., even though it embodied "a similar kind of discipline" to that of the Montessori program. According to the paper, district representatives claimed to be "alarmed."

I volunteered there and saw to the day-to-day operations. I was extremely skilled in all forms of dance as a result of my studies at Kellom Recreation Center, my high school, and the University of Nebraska Omaha (UNO). I had studied music and had become especially accomplished in classical singing in the Dory Passolt music program. I had studied piano at the Valentine School of Music, and I could play enough to accompany myself during practices for vocal performances. I was also an actress, and

I had performed in school plays and musicals, as well as at the Omaha Community Playhouse and in Los Angeles community theaters. Artists came from all over the city to volunteer, and the school even had artists-in-residence, something that most programs in the city had probably heard very little about or had little access to.

Black children, who were usually relegated to stereotypical or minor roles—or given no roles at al—in productions, for the first time had an opportunity to have roles in plays and musicals about themselves. They were allowed to write, to direct, and to make their voices heard. More importantly, they were given every opportunity to tell their stories. They were also instructed by people who looked like them, something refreshing and to which they were unaccustomed. And all the while they were being told that they were smart, talented, and beautiful. In addition to my education in the arts, I learned the importance of volunteering and of giving back to my community, which, in turn, could only make my city a better place to be.

As for the parents and community members of the Near North Side, I am sure they gained a sense of pride and purpose, even respect, from their children. The volunteers were humbled by the experience. They learned so many positive things about the children, the parents, and the community. They learned of their struggles and about their family lives. They saw the spirit and the beauty in black children. It was evident that the school was not there to take the place of the services offered by the city, but it was there to provide a rich cultural experience through the lens of the black community. I guess the truth about the Sunshine School could be found in the always-long waiting list of those wishing to attend. It could be found in the number of volunteers working without salaries. It could be found in the young and old men volunteering to repair and remove old plaster, paint the building inside and out, and remove old and add new wiring and fixtures so the children would have a safe place to go. It could be found in the multitude of mothers making and delivering lunches so those children who stayed late did not go hungry. Finally, the truth could be found in the music, singing, teaching, learning, and laughter coming from inside those walls located in the heart of the ghetto. In the aftermath of so many of the events of 1968 and 1969, my experience at the Sunshine Cultural Center made me feel worthwhile. I felt like I had something to contribute to the children in my community, and I knew that they had given so much to me, including an opportunity to work side-by-side with my mother.

The Sunshine Cultural Center was insignificant to most outside of my community, but it gave me the opportunity to teach many things. As a young woman whose parents were once told that I might never stand or walk on my own, the center gave me the opportunity to teach dance in my community.

The school gave me more than I could ever have imagined it would. I remember that before I began a new class, whether with young children or adults, I would often tell the students the story of a baby who had numerous physical problems, one of them being the inability to walk. I would then walk to the center of the room. Standing on the hardwood floors, surrounded by wall-to-ceiling mirrors with ballet bars on both sides, the music would start. Then I would dance around the room in my small, hard-toe ballet shoes to beautiful piano music. I would pause and say that I had been talking that whole time about myself.

I remember how silence fell across the room and on one such occasion one small girl in the second or third grade sitting quietly on the outer edge of the floor asked me how I could dance so well when I couldn't even walk when I was a little kid. I leaned over and smiled at her, and I said, "Divine intervention. And it was also my vision for my life."

As I look back, I wish I would have said those things in another, simpler way for her and the children seated around her. I guess that I could have also said that my family and friends never gave up on me. They would spend hours taking turns massaging my legs and helping me exercise and walk awkwardly in my leg braces; I could have said that I was walking today because of their help and also because I never gave up on myself. When I was alone, even at that very young age, I would close my eyes and visualize myself moving around, spinning and dancing. It was divine intervention. It was in God's plan for me all along, and I was never allowed to forget it.

For years my mother fought to improve the conditions of those in her community. She fought tirelessly for the human and civil rights of others. She often went to the school board and demanded justice for those she felt were not being treated fairly and justly. My mother always said, "It is your responsibility to speak out if you are able to give voice to the voiceless." She was a fighter, even though it was difficult for most to grasp the idea that through it all she was sometimes very ill. In fact she was ill most of her young-adult and adult life: she had a bad heart, and throughout her life she struggled with depression. It was hard for those who knew her to believe that she suffered with debilitating illnesses when she was always giving so much of herself to others.

She was always at city-council and school-board meetings. The school board even changed their format because she refused to quit talking about the injustices in inner-city schools. In 1971, at an Omaha school board meeting held at Joslyn Castle Carriage House, in response to my mother's outbursts and her refusal to adhere to the four-minute speaking limit, members voted to add a penalty to speakers who exceeded their speaking time. According to the board, they were attempting to improve public relations and public participation. At the next meeting, my mom was told that visitors who talked longer than five minutes would not be allowed to speak again for three months. My mother began speaking and waving an American flag. I always drove her to the meetings, and I was shocked because I didn't know that she even had a flag with her. She spoke in favor of Ernest Chambers, a civil-rights activist, and against what she considered "a dual system of education" for Negroes and whites. She exceeded the allowed time by three minutes, despite being warned to stop talking. Needless to say, my mother was banned from future meetings. According to the *Omaha World-Herald,* one Omaha citizen wished the school board a "complaint-free New Year."

My mother attended many more meetings, even though the board made it clear that she was not welcome there. She also attended many public events that year, despite being very ill, including my graduation from UNO, where I received a bachelor of science degree in speech pathology and audiology, minoring in speech and drama.

Relatives said that some of the best lessons they learned were from my mother. My cousin Anita Jo said Mom taught her how to dance and encouraged her to strive for the better.

Over the years, my mother tolerated a lot. She had to help raise her younger brother and sister. She lost two children to poverty. She overcame her episodes of clinical depression and later used her energy to fight for justice for blacks in the workplace and in the schools.

Despite all of that, she would joke quite often. Even when others weren't laughing, she was not at all shy about laughing at herself. Her jokes often made us stop a beat and think before we would erupt into laughter.

On Saturday, October 7, 1972, on a damp and dreary day, my mom was preparing to go with me to an all-city event at Elm Wood Park in Omaha, where I was scheduled to open the event with a couple of songs. The first song was *Let There Be Peace on Earth*, a song written by Jill Jackson Miller and Sy Miller in 1955. It is a song of the life-saving joy of God's peace and unconditional love. The other song was *Give Me a World*, the lyrics for which were written by my mom, Juanita Pope, and the music composed by her niece, Betty Jo Ford, a well-known Los Angeles musician. This song was written to encourage world peace and love for one's fellow man. The song was later recorded. Later that day, at 2:12 p.m., my mother died in a local hospital of an apparent heart attack.

I can't remember much about my mother's funeral, but I do remember that it was raining like sheets of water washing roughly down a rocky waterfall. The long row of cars randomly pulled up behind the large limousine carrying the casket and the three limos following closely behind with immediate relatives and other family members. The mortuary placed flags on the lead cars with stickers on the back of the windows. From 1513 North Thirty-First Street the long train of automobiles moved slowly, winding through the bumpy, uneven streets of North Omaha. People from all over Omaha joined the caravan. The children and teenagers who had received instruction at Sunshine School, the adults who as children attended Head Start, students who had received a better education in the Omaha Public Schools as a result of her relentless activism and steadfast desire to correct wrongs within the school system were all in attendance. Community activists came from across the country. City officials were in attendance. Even members of the government respectfully graced the pews of her beloved church, Mount Moriah. Following the graveside service a young man who had been our paperboy for many years came by our house with a card and flowers. We asked him in, and he told us that our mother had pushed the school board to help him obtain a scholarship to attend Omaha University. He attended and graduated with a degree in engineering. He told our family that our mother always encouraged him, helped him, and gave him a monetary gift each and every Christmas.

The obituary in the *Omaha World-Herald* read:

> *Survived by her husband, John; daughters Mrs. Rose Mary Moore, Mrs. Joyce Goodwin, Miss Catherine Pope; sons John F. Pope and Wallace L. Pope, all of Omaha; sister Mrs. Audrea Burnett, San Diego, California; brother, Leonard Hawkins of Omaha; and ten grandchildren.*

But there was so much that it didn't say, that it didn't know.

She was survived by so many others. Throughout her life, she touched and changed the lives of so many children, adults, and community members for the better.

I now felt like Alice, peering through the looking glass, unaware of what I could and would encounter in my life, but knowing I was on a journey that would always be guided by the love and compassion of a woman who inspired so many, my mom.

Mom.

Uncle Leonard.

Aunt Lucille.

4

Rock-a-Bye Baby

❧

For years I wanted to know something about the children who lay in the beds beside me when I was a baby. Why were we put there? Why did society need orphanages? There weren't many options for babies and older children in crisis. In some societies, children have always been overlooked, with people placing little value on their well-being. In the United States, social organizations began providing help for children as early as the 1800s. Later, as more and more people began working, even woman were working outside of the home, creating a greater need for caring for children by others outside of their immediate family.

As time went on the majority of children in unstable homes were placed in state homes, shelters, and orphanages by the courts, some due to child abuse and neglect. Others were placed in institutions when parents were unwilling or unable to take care of them. My circumstances would fall under the latter.

I was not born under any unorthodox circumstances. My life began in a hospital ward. My mother shared a room with other mothers. I later became friends with several of their children. For me that softens the beginning of this story.

My mother and I weren't in the same hospital room for long, because my mother was transferred to a psychiatric unit in the hospital, where she eventually received shock treatments. She didn't volunteer for these treatments. But hospital staff felt she was incapable of making decisions for herself and for me. Women in general, and especially Negro women, so I have heard, were the medical guinea pigs of the forties and fifties, used to explore ways to "fix" women and men who appeared sad or severely depressed. Of course it is public record that people were often misdiagnosed. One example of an individual being misdiagnosed was the famous author Mary Jane Ward, author of the book that later became a movie, *The Snake Pit*. Most doctors didn't know then to look at possible or obvious underlying causes for depression such as poverty, poor housing, lack of healthcare, poor nutrition, or spousal abuse. The system only wanted quick fixes, the kind that shock treatments apparently delivered. There was very little regard for meeting the emotional needs of women, especially Negro women. The treatments would cause women to forget what brought them to the brink of despair, so they could quickly return home, resuming their roles in the household.

Because my mother was in a psychiatric unit at a hospital, I had to be placed in the care of an institution. I was admitted to the Child Saving Institute on May 25, 1949.

My father wrote in the file that my mother was a thirty-seven-year-old housewife and he was a forty-seven-year-old sheep butcher who made good money but worked sporadically. I was described as having three siblings who remained at home with my father; they were thirteen, eleven, and eight at the time. My father stated that he was unable to provide for my three older siblings and me, which led to my placement at the Child Saving Institute. My aunt Audrea came all the way from Texas to visit me while I was there and told the nurses that my mother was worried about me.

I can only imagine what life was like for my mom in that hospital. Nothing around her was familiar; she had none of her own things there. She was probably supplied with everything—comb, brush, toiletries, even the thin, starched gown with loose ties that immodestly concealed her curves. She was probably allowed to bathe several times a week in communal showers. I wonder if white women bathed with black women?—just a thought. Was the food, probably served on heavy, worn out trays, still warm by the time the aide or nurse reached her room with it? Oatmeal or Cream of Wheat was probably served most mornings. She would like that. Lunch was likely to be a small sandwich and soup or something like that, and dinner usually a stew containing small vegetables and some type of meat.

My mom, I understand, wasn't eating much. She didn't have an appetite. So they checked her weight more than once a week. No one really had time to visit, and she had very little money or credit on the books to buy snacks or personal items from the hospital store.

The rooms in a state hospital had to be somewhat dark, with creepy shadows dancing across the wall. They were small rooms with red and white or gray and white linoleum floors, the kind you see on hospital floors. The plaster walls were gray and drab-colored—no bright, cheerful colors that might lift people's spirits. They knew very little about the therapeutic benefits of colors then. Two beds sat on opposite sides of each room with the feet of the beds clumsily facing each other. The larger wards were crowded with beds, charts attached loosely to the foot of each so as not to mistake one patient for another. The beds were made of iron painted in various colors with lead-based paint. The head and foot of each bed was sectioned with evenly spaced iron bars. Windows were difficult to see out of. Patients, anxiously trying to look beyond the dismal walls, were confronted with rusted bars obscuring the hopeless view. The same covers adorned each bed: plaid wool, one no different from the other. There was a small side table with a single drawer for each patient, and inside it a small brush and comb that would obviously snap if used on some black women's unkempt heads. In this hospital ward there were probably no mirrors.

I've avoided thinking about what the doctors finally prescribed for her treatment. I was informed years later that she received shock treatment. That was so personal, something most families never talked about when their loved ones returned home. According to documents from the institute my mother came to see me on July 6, and was described as quiet but crying. She was happy to see me, and she could see that I was doing well. She was looking forward to bringing me home. She talked about her four other children, including a son who had joined the Navy and was now gone. She told the doctor that she had not wanted him to join the Navy, but he was "Navy struck." The reports describe my mother as a nice-looking woman who was neatly dressed and clean in appearance.

I don't really know if my mother was aware of anything that was going on with me. I think that she had very little knowledge of what was actually happening or going to happen in the months to follow. I could imagine my mother spending weeks and weeks confined to a room that she had to share with strangers. Just because she had been there before I can't imagine that it was any easier on her. She must have been frightened as well as lonely; she had to be.

There were now two dresses hanging in my mother's closet: the one that she had worn into the hospital so many months before, and now the dress, coat, and hat that my aunt Audrea brought for her to wear home. And finally after a long stay she did.

My mother was discharged from the hospital on June 30, 1949, but her doctor explained that she could not yet care for me. She needed at least three weeks of follow-up care before taking me home. There was talk that I might not go home at all.

Although my mother was sent to the hospital out of concern for her physical and mental health because she had a baby—me—out of necessity my needs had to be addressed, so I became a major concern.

While I was at the Child Saving Institute, I was provided boiled skim milk every three hours. I was described as having bloody stools, so I was given a prescription of sulfadiazine four times daily. Upon admission I weighed seven pounds, four and a half ounces. When I was discharged back to the care of my father on August 1, 1949, I had gained two pounds and four ounces. If a personal story ever took a turn for the better, it was mine. All of my family took an active part in my journey back to health. My mother was still not able to fully care for me because of my health problems. I had been born with a nonfunctioning pancreas. I began to lose the weight that I had so miraculously gained. After some worry and an interesting treatment, my pancreas slowly began to function.

A discarded drunk, living in the streets of Omaha, suggested to my father that he should take the pancreas of a sheep, boil it and drain the juices, and slowly feed it to me. Because of Dad's job at the packing house, a sheep's pancreas was actually available.

I had become smaller than when I was born. I could fit into the palm of my dad's hand.

My dad thought about the drunken doc's advice for several days, considering the naysayers' comments. We couldn't afford what the doctor was prescribing, and Dr. Gooden didn't have access to what I needed. I'm sure Dad looked to God and then at me and saw another child slowly slipping away from him. My tiny body was becoming smaller and weaker. My eyes began to bulge, and the wrinkled skin around my limbs was sagging off my frail bones. It must have been a nightmare for him.

So my dad took the advice of his alcoholic friend. He filled one of my mother's jelly jars with the boiled juice from a sheep's pancreas and fed it to me with a small spoon. I still have the baby spoon he used.

Day after day my family attended to me. My aunt Audrea had come from Texas to take care of my siblings while my mom remained in the hospital. Aunt Audrea had visited me at the institute and knew how worried my mother was about me. She looked like a younger version of my mom; she was a beautiful angel. They were very close sisters. She didn't stay long because she had to return to her own family, but she was close enough and dedicated enough to leave her home with little notice to come take care of us.

Medical and financial concerns among the black community in Omaha did not begin or end with me. There were many more African Americans in our city and across our country who experienced devastating illnesses as a result of poor health conditions, poverty, and racism.

It was always whispered by people who liked to gossip, very softly—or in some cases very loudly—that I would have been put up for adoption or given away if my mother'd had her way. But I never believed any of it. As a child when I went to sleep I would have dreams, bad dreams about what I would sometimes hear adults say about me, especially when they would say that I wasn't wanted by my folks. Even my relatives would speak in the kitchen about it when they thought that I wasn't in hearing range. When I was very young, about four or five, I would sometimes cry softly in the dark in my bed at night. Over the years my ears, human ears, could not, would not hear that I was once a baby placed like so many across our country in a home under very precarious circumstances. Didn't anyone ever tell them that I could have been listening and that their words would hurt me—hurt me badly? Didn't anyone tell them?

A visit with my father's Aunt Janie.

5

The Radio Flyer

Cha-Ching!

Here are a few things that I can remember! As far as I know there were very few pictures taken of me as a child. However I do remember two pictures in particular.

One picture of me was taken in a photography studio. I wore a blue-green satin dress with a large bow pinned into my natural hair on the side of my head. My hair was not straightened. It was dark brown, thick, kinky, and soft like cotton. I had three braids, one on top and one on each side of my head. That however wasn't as important as the thick bangs that framed my small face from ear to ear. Even though my bangs were thick, my mother made sure that they didn't cover or cast a shadow over my dark brown eyes. On that day she made sure that my hair was perfect—at least, as perfect as it could be for a little colored girl, or so the photographer said. Years later I remember my mother referring to that comment while talking to her friend, Mrs. McIntosh. She said that the man in the store had no business talking rudely about her child, and Mrs. McIntosh agreed. I was glad my mother had her for a friend. They always supported each other in so many ways. As with most children in those days I was positioned for the photo on a thick rug that resembled a short string mop. I remember my shoes were Mary Janes, made of a shiny black patent-leather material and secured by silver buckles tightly fastened on each side. My socks were white with wispy, short, white lace cuffs that were trimmed in blue. They were neatly turned down one time on each ankle. My mother made sure that my knees and elbows were greased with Vaseline. She did this to make sure that the eye of the camera was not distracted from my smile by ashy legs. It was customary for Negro mothers to make sure that their little girls were oiled down from head to toe. It was not possible to do a retake unless you had extra money, and my mother made it clear that everything had to be just perfect, or at least meeting her expectations. I was positioned on the rug with one leg slightly crossed over the other, and my small hands were gently crossed as well. My dress casually cascaded over my legs. The dress was supported by a petticoat made of white crinoline, an inexpensive material made of open-woven stiff netting that would itch if you moved too often or unexpectedly. Most mothers expected the crinolines on their little girls to slightly show in the picture. Boy, was that pose uncomfortable. As I was posing, my legs began to hurt a lot but I didn't let on because I was sure that my mother had spent a lot of money to make sure that I was memorialized. Besides that, she just looked forward to her children doing the same things that other children were able to do. I smiled and waited patiently while the photographer adjusted the lens several times. He then moved behind the large camera and finally took the posed picture. When the picture came back from the studio I remember looking curiously at it. My mother hadn't put makeup on me that day, but when we picked up the pictures that my mom had selected and I looked at them, my lips and cheeks were colored a rosy red and my eyes were outlined in black, emphasizing my long black eyelashes. While growing up I was accustomed to my legs hurting; they would hurt a lot and they would hurt often, but the main thing that I remember about that day is how much my legs hurt; I wasn't accustomed to sitting in that position, especially for such a long time.

The only other picture that I remember was one of me next to a large, scraggly Christmas tree that was placed in the corner of our living room; at least the tree seemed large to me. It also appeared to be dry and somewhat brittle. In the picture I was seated happily on a small red tricycle. I remember that Christmas in particular because it was a very cold winter that year, and the concrete floors made it even colder. I was so proud of my tricycle. It was red with a red-and-white seat. I remember touching each and every part of the tricycle; I also remember that I was afraid to ride it for fear that it really wasn't my trike—silly, huh? My parents looked at my face. For some reason they could always tell what I was thinking.

"Yes it's yours," my mom said. "Well, isn't a trike what you wanted?"

"This isn't just any trike, it's a Radio Flyer, and one of the fastest," my dad said with pride.

By this time everyone was watching. They were all looking at my face and laughing at the same time. How did I get it? Where did it come from? The questions just kept coming.

"Why, Santa, silly," my sister Joyce said in her matter-of-fact sort of way. And that was that. I didn't ask any more questions. I just kept admiring it. It had silver paint on the metal handlebars and large, black wheels with silver spokes. The wheels were covered with metal fenders. It had long, red-and-white plastic tassels hanging from the red handgrips. The seat could be lowered and raised. It also had a seat on the back for passengers and a foot stand on the back so you could give a friend a lift anywhere they wanted to go. I was so excited that I wanted my parents to go for a ride. I believed that my trike was the fastest one in town.

But I think I left out the most important thing: my legs didn't hurt; I rode my trike all night long, ringing the large round metal bell that you could ring by pulling the lever on the side of the handlebars snapping it back by quickly letting go. The bell had a tinny, brassy sound. *Cha, Ching, Cha, Ching* sounded the bell, and I rode and laughed and rang and rang the bell over and over again. It almost sounded like a cash register when the drawers open and close. My family couldn't wait for me to stop and get off. But to me it sounded like music, sweet and strong like a xylophone. Not really a xylophone, but when you think back, it was a sound that would make anyone smile.

On that cold winter Christmas the weather was very chilling. The sound of my trike on the concrete and red-and-gray linoleum was very irritating. Most of the time when I rode on my trike, I was vigorously pushed around the room by my brothers. I would drag my feet across the cold floor. Other times, I would pump and pump the red pedals, roll for a while, and then stretch out both legs and use the heels of my shoes to stop. Most kids would stop that way, but our parents didn't like it because it would wear out the heels of our shoes.

My inability to lift my frail, thin legs, whether I was pedaling my trike and or walking with a steady gait, was seldom talked about. In our family, as I later discovered, there were many things that were not talked about.

There were so many secrets. For some reason I didn't like secrets, and we seemed to have a lot of them in our family. But in this case, well, I guess I didn't mind. When I saw my trike I can only remember that I was so surprised. I think that Christmas was the best one ever. I just knew that there weren't going to be any presents that year—and boy, was I wrong. Many young men were now coming back from war, and at the time no one had much of anything. My father lost his job that year, and just to have a tree and a Christmas dinner was enough for all of us. I think my oldest brother John bought that bike because he knew that it would make me happy.

John had just returned from the Korean War. It was fought from 1950 to 1953. My brother told me that the war was in support of the Republic of Korea (South Korea), and that we took part in it, backed by the United Nations, because we believed in it. Although I was only four or five he never spoke to me like I was a small, unaware child with few experiences. He spoke to me as if I were a part of the whole world with a significant investment in its success or failure. All of us enjoyed my brother John's stories. He spoke about so many places—places far away, many of which we would probably never go to. I don't remember the year that my brother came home and bought me that trike, and that's not the important thing; what's important is the fact that my red tricycle with the long, dangling tassels was a very big unexpected surprise that came just in time to make a little girl happy. What made me even happier was the fact that this was the first time that I met my brother John whom I had heard so much about. And I wasn't disappointed in the least. As I recall he was tall, dark, handsome, and the smartest brother in the whole wide world. Seeing him for the first time made me realize how much an individual could miss someone they had never met. When he walked into the living room I noticed his tan. He was a beautiful bronze color. His hair was medium length, cut close to the sides of his head and longer on the top. I noticed his piercing eyes. His dark and strong voice would charm anyone, even me.

Dad, however, appeared to have a different impression of John. Dad's expression was one of dissatisfaction with my brother. He was not at all impressed by his charm, and he was far from overjoyed by his return. He would sometimes call him his prodigal son, because he had lied about his age to join the service. That being said, as a little kid it didn't matter to me. I liked him a lot: he was my big brother. Now that I think back on things, even I could feel the tension in the house, along with my brothers and sisters. As a child I wasn't capable of understanding what was actually going on in our house most of the time. All I knew was that both of my brothers—John as well as Wallace—were finally home and all of us were glad, including my dad, even if he didn't know it at the time. When I grew up I learned that on several occasions my brother John made my mother sad, and in turn that angered my dad.

There are other things that I remember about several other Christmases. There was one in particular that came along several years later. I remember an evening in our home several days before Christmas. Many things were missing—food, a tree, and presents. My father had temporarily lost his job at the Armor Meat Packing Plant due to an "in-house group altercation" (or so I was told). Anyway, food and Christmas were bypassing our 2220 Seward Street address on Christmas Eve. I went to bed early because there was little for me to stay up for. At about seven o'clock I awoke to the sound of a knock at the door. It was the Salvation Army. They told my mom and dad that they were out for the entire night. They were not workers, but volunteers. I heard my dad offer them something to drink. It was cold and windy, with large amounts of snow falling swiftly to the roof and ground. Three men and a lady came in. They were dressed like Eskimos and outdoor workers against the severe weather. I remember hearing laughter. As I looked through the stair banister I could see an occasional smile on my mother's face as she walked through the room. I heard my father ask them how much they earned for coming out on such an awful night. One of them did not hesitate to respond, "Nothing—we do it just because it brings happiness to others. We help others and in return, believe it or not, we help ourselves in ways most people can't even imagine."

The next day I woke up to the smell of food cooking. I came downstairs to a small Christmas tree with a few decorations and several presents under it. You may not be able to understand, but for me that was one of the best Christmases ever. That scraggly tree was beautiful. As I look back I now know the satisfaction that those volunteers from the Salvation Army must have felt. And if they could have seen the expression on my face—all I can say is those volunteers were priceless.

Many of the memories that I had were those created for me by my beloved family through their stories. Most members of my family were quiet and didn't talk much, especially about their childhood or life growing up in the inner city of Omaha, Council Bluffs, Chicago, the rural areas of Oklahoma, or even Arkansas. My family would speak even less about our parents and grandparents, either because it was too sad and painful or just because they had very little information about them or other members of our family both past and present. I suppose that's because time just slips away from us—or, as some would say, time and stuff just happens. I was told the present is always occupied with the past and the future but very little time is spent in the moment. I assume the moment for most people is involved with trying to live in it, making it from day to day and not asking why or philosophizing about the what-ifs. Asking those types of questions wouldn't do much good and could cause a great deal of damage to your future investment, yourself.

As for me, I always liked stories, especially when they were about my life, whether I was actually present in the story or not. You're not always *in* the past, but you can rest assured that you are always *of* the past. That's how I always thought about things, anyway. I saw my family history as the foundation that I am a part of, whether I was strong enough to acknowledge that fact or not.

A young Mrs. Gooden.

My father at about age thirty. 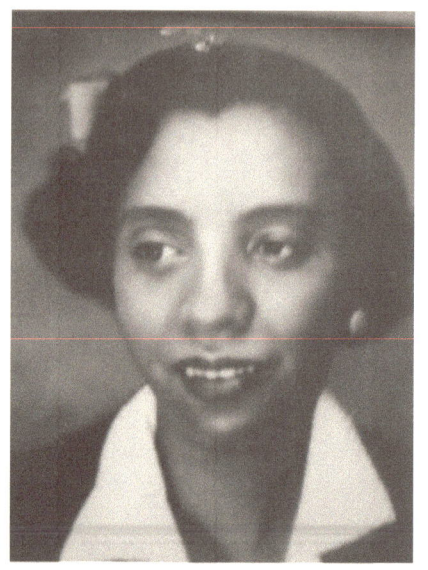　　　　My very special mom.

Mom's friend Iola (left), Aunt Audrea (middle), and Uncle Booker (right).

6

A Good Hair Day

In the 1940s, because of the war, there was less of everything. Most people participated in the sacrifice. Those sacrifices included material for clothing because there wasn't enough material to go around. Hem lines were shorter; most skirts and dresses went to the knees, and styles were somewhat masculine. Most women, my mother included, wore thin dresses, with large, overextended shoulder pads. Unlike the twenties and thirties, little skin could be seen. Modesty was the word of the day. I think that was because men and women were now required to work side by side. Even though the war had been over for a few years, in 1949 and the early fifties poor women like my mom happily wore the styles of the past.

My mother was a domestic so she wore what could be described as Kitty Foyle dresses. In my community they were simply called housedresses. I remember how my mother looked as if it were yesterday. A couple of times I can even remember seeing her in trousers. Women who worked in military factories wore them to work during WWII. Most people said that they were safe clothes since they were worn mostly by riveters, who had to work around large machines that built airplanes and aircraft carriers.

Most of my mom's clothes were made of denim, cotton, or wool blends. From what I remember my mother only had one coat. The winters must have been even harsher for her because of that. I could tell that the coat wasn't purchased as a new coat off the racks because the first time I saw it the cuffs were frayed around the wrists and the lining hung slightly below the back of the coat. My sister Joyce, who could sew, immediately repaired it when my sister Rose Mary called it to her attention.

In the late forties and early fifties fur trims were still popular, and my mother had one. She must have found it at a thrift store, or perhaps it was given to her by Dr. Gooden's wife. She cleaned it up and on special occasions wore it proudly. During the day she usually wore brown oxfords or saddle shoes. Her saddle shoes were her favorite for working and walking. She always wore her hair in a peekaboo style, fashioned after the movie star Veronica Lake—parted on the side with a wave of hair slightly covering one eye. Several times I saw my mother's hair in a bun, and on many occasions she covered the back of her head with a large, heavy, black snood.

My dad normally wore overalls to work. Under them he usually wore white shirts with the sleeves rolled up to his midforearm. Rarely did I see him in a suit, although I know that he owned one. Most people during this time had few items of clothing. My dad had heavy work shoes and large rubber boots that he wore on the job. He had a hat that was sometimes called a fedora; most men wore that style. When he did want to dress up he wore his white shirt and an old suit that was slightly smaller than it should have been. He would also wear suspenders and cufflinks for dressy occasions. On rare occasions he wore a tie and at times even sported a tie clip. My mother found him a pair of wingtip shoes in a Sears and Roebuck catalogue, and Dr. Gooden gave him an old pair of spectator shoes. Neither of my parents wore fancy clothes. Their clothes were usually drab colors: browns, faded greens, and grays. For most people clothes were a necessity, and my parents were no exception.

My mother usually wore her hair the same way, but on one occasion when she came to my school her hair was very different. I was in grammar school. We were having an afternoon performance program, and my mother entered the classroom looking beautiful. Her hair was covered by a scarf. She never went anywhere without her scarves, even on a clear nice day. Sometimes she would even wear a turban, but on this particular day she wore a scarf. When she took the scarf off, I could see her hair was softly rolled into a French roll. The top was waved and positioned into an updo with large curls loosely cascading to the side of her face. She wore large, glass clip-on earrings that looked like sparkling pink diamonds, with a simple necklace to match, hung close around her slim neck. She was wearing makeup on her beautifully tanned face, and her thin lips were adorned with a bright, iridescent, red lipstick. Even as a child, in that moment I thought that she looked so contemporary and smart for the times.

I recall that day so clearly, not because I was performing, but because all of the other kids whispered and chattered respectfully about how beautiful and pretty my mom looked. That would be one of the few times I would hear others—even the teachers—comment in a very good way about my mother's appearance. My good friends told me that some of them even looked at her with envy. I didn't care what any of them said or thought, because on that day I knew my mother was special and beautiful.

At dinner that night my father took a long, hard look at her. He never said a word, but I could tell that he was very pleased with the way his wife looked. That night during dinner, she wasn't just our mother, she was his wife. It was as if they were meeting for the first time. I didn't say a word at the table, and neither did anyone else. We just enjoyed the evening.

I know that my dad felt special, as if my mom had gone to all that trouble for him. I didn't mind a bit, because in the back of my mind as I lay in bed I knew that my mom really did love me, and she loved me a great deal to go to so much trouble for me that day. I would never doubt the love that she felt for me again, no matter what.

I learned later that my mother did everything possible to prepare for that day. At home, with the help of her very best friend Iola McIntosh, she took a great deal of time with herself. I even discovered some of the hair secrets that she used the night before to prepare for the following day. That night I watched her unroll the hair that was positioned into a smooth side roll on the back of her head. First Mrs. McIntosh straightened my mom's hair with a large, heavy, iron tool that had thin teeth and a smooth wooden handle. It was called a straightening comb. They heated the comb on the small gas stove in the kitchen; I was mesmerized by the blue-and-yellow flame as it separated when the comb rested on the iron grid. You could tell that my mom was pleased as she watched her hair being straightened and then curled with the curling iron. I continued to watch as they stuffed an old stocking with pieces of dark cloth to create a simple tube-shaped hair piece. They positioned it with bobby pins and wrapped her hair meticulously around the hairpiece so it couldn't be seen. I think that even my mom liked the way she looked, because that night she gently tied a head rag around her head and had it on when she said good night to me.

The day following the school performance I came down to breakfast, sat in my usual place, and saw that Mom had returned to her usual attire: a long, loosely fitted housedress and her old everyday dark-brown shoes. She may have worn those same things the day before, but I didn't notice anything below her neckline. It just wasn't something that I remembered. Maybe I was too young to understand what was happening to me in that moment, but somehow I realized that what she wore or how she looked wasn't what was really important. She was beautiful because she was my mom, and that would never change.

7

The Black Book

The Project Workers

Day in and day out you could hear the kids playing outside—hide-and-seek, stickball, jump rope, and jacks. It really didn't matter. You could hear the arguments and fights, the yelling, the sadness and the pain. Sometimes you could also hear the laughter and joy. Family and friends celebrated and anticipated the good times—births, graduations, weddings, homecomings, deaths—and each milestone would be marked with pictures and letters to family far away unable to attend.

The Logan Fontenelle Housing Project, was owned and operated by the federal government, which employed inspectors to oversee things. These project workers could come and go whenever they wanted to without making an appointment. Their job was to police the housing projects. According to Housing Commission guidelines they were responsible for conducting visits to each and every home in the projects to make sure that the tenants were living within their financial requirements. You could not purchase anything, including food and small appliances, that was not financially accounted for on their books, because your rent was based on your income, which had to qualify you as low income. If you purchased anything outside of those guidelines that meant that you and your family were getting money or help from other sources and you had not declared those funds and reported them to the government. My mother was always stressed out before our appointments, and most visits were unscheduled, so my mother was stressed out and nervous most of the time. The inspectors had been instructed by the main office to go through your things, to make sure you weren't spending money that you hadn't accounted for on their prior visit. My mother always said that we had to be careful with everything that we had. If our grandparents gave us anything we had to hide it. My mother was always nervous whenever the workers came around, and that made me nervous. Whenever they came around she looked sad, and I always wondered if I just ate a little less or my parents didn't spend so much money on medicine for me maybe things would be different; maybe she could rest a minute or they could just have a break for once. Inspectors were also required to count the number of people living in the home. If adults were home, they would ask them intrusive questions regarding their personal lives. I thought they treated my parents like they were their parents. They were just plain nosy.

If I was home alone, although at five or six I hardly ever was, they would still barge in and ask me questions. Most people said I was precocious, and my family knew that I could hold my own. The things that I had faced and seen over the years shored me up to face a lot of things. I wasn't a timid child, but like any kid at times I was afraid of something. Take the dark for instance—I had my concerns with the lights out! Anyway, I thought it should be against the law to ask a child questions. Did I lie? Yes I did, about any and everything, from where we got the shiny new breadbox to the beautiful dress that my sister Joyce was making that was draped across a living-room chair. It was a good thing the sewing machine that Mrs. Gooden had given us was stored in the coat closet, or I would have had to lie about where that came from. I knew that we were already getting very little money. I could see that from the way my mom would always serve us at the table. We would get "just enough," as she would put it. "It's not going to run off," she would say. "Chew your food. There'll be some for seconds, so just take your time." Usually there weren't any seconds, and sometimes the first lacked any meat, especially when my dad didn't get called in to the packing house to work. Even a little girl like me knew that I had to do my part and protect the family, even if it meant telling a lie every now and then.

After they left, I would go upstairs, climb up on the toilet, and look in the bathroom mirror attached to the medicine cabinet. I wanted to see if my nose had grown. I had been told that would happen if I told too many lies.

Many times, I would lie about taking my money and spending it on candy, although the worst lies were about going outside when the others weren't home—that was not allowed. But breaking the rules was "a part of my DNA," as my oldest sister would say, and she knew because I was her responsibility most of the time. My dad always said that we weren't on welfare, and I knew that he was proud of that. However, by the way we were treated, we might as well have been. I heard it was because we lived in the projects.

My sisters told me that our neighbors would yell up and down the street, "Project workers are coming! Hey, they're here! They're here! They're pulling into the parking lot." The neighbors would yell up and down the block, "Miss Furry is coming! Miss Furry is coming!" In this way, they were put on notice to pick up everything that they could and put their things away so the worker couldn't report them out of compliance to the government, whatever that meant.

Residents would peep outside through their thin, frilly curtains. If they were outside hanging their clothes out on the lines, they would rush to remove the clothespins, take down their clothes, shove them into their baskets, and cover them up so the workers wouldn't be able to see if they had purchased anything new. Some people would hide in the basement entrances at the end of the buildings so the projects police wouldn't know they were at home. But there were also people who would open their doors as the workers approached their stoop, stand behind their screen doors, and ask what they wanted. I always admired those people; my dad was one of them. He wasn't intimidated for a second.

One worker was usually assigned to all the families within a square block. Our worker was Miss Furry, who would use her keys to our homes to let herself in and inspect the premises. Miss Furry and another government worker came to our door one day, opened it, and without knocking just walked in. On this particular day, Miss Furry was wearing a brimmed hat, I suppose to keep the blazing sun off of her fair skin. She was also wearing her ever-present white gloves. Her dress was green taffeta, falling slightly below her knee. She reminded me of most of the white women who worked downtown in the tall office buildings.

Behind her came a strange man, someone I had never seen before. I don't know why the man was with her. It was my thought that he was watching out to make sure no one got in her way or tried to stop her from doing her job.

I peeked around a corner and watched as they went through our drawers in the living room, moved into the kitchen, and then went into the pantry and the laundry room. I watched the man take his handkerchief out of his suit pocket and wipe the sweat from his brow. They returned to the kitchen, opened the icebox as if they knew what they were looking for, and helped themselves to popsicles. I was dumbfounded! Those were ours, and we loved them. I couldn't contain myself. I leaped from my hiding place and told both of them to get out of my house. I was only six, but the popsicles were the last straw. I said that they had no right to go through our things.

Miss Furry stopped and stared at me, hard. "Why you disrespectful little snot," she said. "You had better watch who you're talking to." She pursed her lips and told me that my parents would be hearing about my disrespectful behavior. She was writing in her giant notebook as she spoke.

"You little nigger, where are your parents? Are you here alone?" She quickly looked around the room, keeping her eyes on the windows and doors. Her co-worker moved to the door and began to tap his shoes and turn the knob to signify that it was time for them to go.

I was alone. My mom was next door, but I wouldn't tell them that. I didn't want Mom to get into trouble, even though I was scared. "My mom is upstairs." I knew they wouldn't go upstairs. There was something about doing that that wasn't authorized, or they were just plain afraid. I knew that I would get into trouble later, but I didn't care. Nobody had the right to intrude on our privacy and treat us as less than citizens.

She stared at me for a bit longer. Then the man opened the squeaky door, pushed the screen open for her, and she walked out. She stopped.

"Hey, this is a school day. What are you doing home in the middle of the day?"

Next door, my mom heard them talking to me. She quietly went around back and began hanging clothes in her basket on the clothes line to dry. Then she came in through the back door. Coming into the room, she told the project worker I was sick—my legs. "The liniment didn't quite help last night, and the pain kept her up for most of it. So her father and I thought it best that she stay home."

You could tell that Miss Furry really wasn't buying any of it.

"What else do you want to know?" my mom asked. There was an

awkward pause while my mom tried to figure out what she should say. "I had to stay home with Cathy until one of her sisters comes home."

I couldn't understand then why my mom felt the need to go into so much detail, why she had to explain so much to her, but as I think back on it, she was young and my mom was much older.

I bravely jumped in. "Lady, my legs hurt bad—that's why I'm home today." I was at odds with this adult, and I didn't understand why. What I did know was that an explanation was important, otherwise my mother wouldn't seem so insecure. The worker just stared at my mom and quickly accepted her reason for not being with me. I suppose she suspected that my mom had been outside of our house and was probably next door, but she just wanted to move on. I didn't know what the worker would do if she knew the truth, so I lied. In our neighborhood under these circumstances it really wasn't uncommon.

I did get into trouble. My parents felt that my actions had jeopardized the well-being of the entire family. My dad explained that they had tried hard to get into the projects and that many people who tried were not accepted because they didn't have any prospects of getting a job or they didn't have a decent referral from someone. So we had an obligation to follow the rules and to do our very best to keep the place clean and not make any trouble.

Later, I heard my parents talking. "I'm glad Miss Furry didn't get so mad that she wanted us thrown out of here," said my father.

"Yes, John, so am I. We wouldn't have anywhere to go. We could become homeless," my mother responded with worry in her voice. I think they slept fitfully that night, but not without much pause and prayer.

As I lay in my bed thinking about that day and about Miss Furry, even through my anger, I thought it would be nice to look like her and my white teachers—to someday have the money to buy the makeup, the shoes, the clothes and accessories. I also thought it would be nice to have the straight hair with curls that glistened in the sunlight. I was jealous, even through my hurt, fear, and anger. I knew I never wanted to be like her on the inside, that lady who came to our house to snoop around. I wouldn't want a job like that. But I did want for myself some of the things that she had.

As I grew older, I still had to welcome people like Miss Furry into our home, only now I did it without talking too much. I wondered what it was like to have so much power over people that were essentially strangers to you. With a pen and a large black notebook, you could decide the fate of others. You could mend or break up families. You could provide homes for the homeless, or with the stroke of a pen put them back in the streets. I wonder what she thought about the families in the projects' red brick buildings. They were put on notice to pick up everything that they could and put their things away so she couldn't report them to the government as "out of compliance." Did she think about them at all?

When I really thought about it, she really wasn't pretty, and I didn't want to look like her in any way! However I always wondered how so many of my people got here and why we had to live in this place called "The Projects."

Later I learned that the projects were a legacy of a horrible summer in Omaha in 1919. The Omaha race riot led to the creation in 1930 of housing projects that later became home to hundreds of African Americans in the 1940s. The practice of redlining by the banks and racially restrictive housing covenants had resulted in decades of racism in housing in Omaha. According to news articles and records, blacks were not separated from whites, but when you actually lived there as we did, the separation, the difference, was obvious. Buildings in different locations were occupied either by whites or by blacks. Most of the time black children and white children played in different locations. The first buildings were built during the Depression, with another addition added in 1941, to improve conditions for working-class whites. This housing was closed to Negroes in general up to the 1950s. My family, along with my cousins and a few others, were allowed to move in during the late 1940s, when we relocated to the Logan Fontenelle Housing Projects.

During the Civil Rights Movement of the 1960s, policies that kept blacks out of public housing began to change. Until then, the real-estate market remained segregated, and housing in most white areas was difficult for the majority of African Americans to purchase.

The Logan Fontenelle Projects was a place for most of us to call home. And we did. It wasn't great, but it was all we had.

My best friend Terese's fifth birthday party.

Goodwin's Barbershop on Twenty-Fourth Street.

8

Good Friends Are Forever

"Terese, Terese, are you home? Can you hear me?" I yelled, vigorously knocking on her screen door. "Can you come out and play? What are you going to do today?"

When it came to friends there was none better than my friend Terese Hudgins. I lived at 2220 Seward Street and she lived on the other side of the plaza, at 2229 Franklin Street. She lived with her mother Inez, her little sister Renata and her other siblings. We met when we were three or four years old. She was of medium height, slightly shorter than me, and had thick, long, wavy, dark-brown hair. She always wore ribbons or barrettes, usually with one large braid or twist on top and two other braids hanging on opposite sides of her head. She had deep dimples and always wore beautiful clothes and shoes. She would come down the street with a peppy skip and a large smile on her adventurous-looking, caramel-colored face. You could see all of the ideas swimming around in her head by looking into her sparkling, dark-brown eyes. She would usually have paper in one hand and a box of crayons or a large pencil and eraser in the other.

As she reached my stoop she would say with assurance, just a few steps away from me, "Hi, Cathy! I've got an idea! Do you want to hear it?"

Of course, being her best friend, I would usually respond, "I'm all ears!" Then Terese and I would laugh so loud we could wake the dead.

We'd walk down the street not too far and breathe in the tantalizing smells of my Aunt Lucille's wonderful donuts, fried pies, or cakes, cooling on her windowsill. Terese would want to immediately go in so we could gorge ourselves.

"No hurry," I'd say with confidence. My aunt always made sure that I got two donuts, so I knew we didn't have to rush. It was always more fun for me to share with Terese.

Terese was always sure of herself, yet she could be shy. Her walk was strong, and her legs were straight. At times I was shamefully jealous of her solid gait. She was special to me because she never criticized or made me feel unsure or inept in any way.

"Cathy, do you know you're my best friend?"

"Yes, and you are my best friend," I would always say back to her. We made this pledge almost every day, joining our pinky fingers together in solidarity. "Now that's that. We're friends for life."

On afternoons we sat on the concrete step in front of Terese's house and colored in our coloring books while eating donuts. "Cathy, don't forget to thank your auntie," my cousin Christine, who liked to hang around us, would say. She was next to the youngest in her family. Christine was beautiful and always treated me like her little sister. We sat in the sun, coloring, trying to figure out what else to do that day. We could spend half of the day trying to decide what we would do with the rest of it.

I remember one time when several friends on skates glided toward us and stopped with a quick twist of their feet, showing off. "Do you want to race?" one of them called out.

"On skates?" I asked.

"Of course on skates!"

"Can't you see we're busy? We don't want to skate right now," Terese called, looking down at my legs. She knew I was tired from walking through the neighborhood.

"Thanks," I said when our friends left. She just smiled.

Later, as adults, whenever we would talk, Terese would describe the Fontenelle projects as a close-knit community. "Everybody knew everybody," she would say. "Every family had something to do with every other family." I always nodded my head in silence, knowing too well what she meant by it. She meant that if we did something that could get us into trouble, like the time we took a shortcut through the alley, our parents knew about it before we got home. The people in the projects took care of each other, and we both really missed that. Kids played outside all the time. We played everywhere in the projects. There were so many kids. Even children who didn't have brothers or sisters always had playmates. All of the little kids played together. We were predominantly black. Just a block away, across Twenty-Second Street, the kids were white. We called it "Patty Land," because it was where the white folks lived.

"What do you think we should do today?" Terese asked.

"I think we should look through Miss Anderson's window. She's the closest one to us with a TV set," I answered.

"We can't hear it, and the last time we did that, well . . . you know what happened," she fired back.

How could I forget? Someone saw us looking in Miss Anderson's window watching her TV and told our older sisters, and they in turn told our parents. That's the way it always worked in our community. Whatever you did would get to your parents faster than you did.

The games we played depended on our mood and the season. Everybody played Monopoly, bingo, Chinese checkers and regular checkers. When we were in the mood for something creepy, we would tell ghost stories or fortunes using an Ouija board or a magic eight ball that looked into our futures. The kids who went to the summer programs at Kellom Recreation Center learned to play chess, and they taught the rest of us so they would have more kids to challenge in local tournaments. We always played cards: old maid, match, and on rainy days when we were alone, solitaire. We also played commercial games: Candy Land and Chutes and Ladders. Some of our mothers, grandmothers, and even teachers taught us how to sew, knit, embroider, and crochet.

I wanted to show my friends how to weave on a loom. One summer in Chickasha, my great-aunt Janie, my dad's aunt, taught me a kind of loom weaving, a lost art form her Choctaw relatives, or so I was told, had taught her. When I went back to Omaha, I couldn't practice anything that I had learned about loom weaving because we didn't have the necessary tools, so each summer when I went back I had to learn all over again. Aunt Janie and her two daughters, cousins Gro and Viola, never said a word about it. They would just teach me all over again as if I were a brand-new student. I liked being taught by them, receiving all the attention. Gro also knew how to make liquor out of the plums and pears that grew on the trees in their backyard. But I guess I was too young to be very interested in that.

Terese and I usually entertained ourselves by playing school, drawing, writing, dancing, and singing inside and outside, no matter what the season. But when the winter months passed and the snow melted, kids would come together from all sides of the neighborhood and fill the streets. The boys in the neighborhood would sometimes take our skates and attach them to a board and make scooters. Then they would pick sides according to the street they lived on and play stickball or line up for relay races. Among the girls, Anita and Nancy were always chosen first: Nancy for baseball and Anita for relay races.

My favorite game was always Captain May I? You would have to ask before you moved. I begged my friends to play it daily. I always liked Captain May I because it was a slow-moving game and I was successful at playing it. I had an opportunity to use my brain as well as my athletic abilities.

When we played hide-and-seek (we called it hide-and-*go*-seek), whoever was "it" would lean up against a tree, post, or wall, cover their eyes with an arm and count backwards from a hundred. Only the smart kids didn't have a problem with that, so we let the others count up from one. Usually, though, you didn't have to wait very long before everyone was hidden out of sight.

"All-y-all-y-ante!" we would yell out. "Here I come!" All of us who were hidden would freeze and hold our breath until someone was found. Then the game would start all over again. No one ever got tired. When the streetlights came on we knew that it was time to go inside; we were usually having so much fun that we could have played outside all night.

"Christine, Catherine Grace, Terese, Cathy, Betty!" our parents would call. "Better get in here! Lynwood, Ronnie, it's getting dark. Get in here!" Across the plaza and park you would faintly hear the names of the others.

"I heard the office men are coming tomorrow." Terese sometimes wanted to talk about the "office men" and when they were coming around to our street. They were the people who came around the projects and cared for the government properties. They made sure that the bulbs in the streetlights turned on at night. They saw to it that the grass was cut. There wasn't any trash anywhere because they would empty the communal trash cans and keep the place clean. They took their jobs seriously and would walk around the neighborhood with an air of authority and importance.

I also remember that there were a lot of people who came to deliver a variety of personal and household items to us. It wasn't because we were rich, but because most of us didn't have cars; so the businesses would come to us. The cleaners would pick up clothes from those who could afford dry cleaning. The bread man sold sweet rolls and cakes as well as bread. The milkman would pick up the empty bottles from the milk crates we left outside on the porch. He usually left a large bottle of milk, a bottle of half-and-half, cream, eggs, and butter, and—if you had the money and left him a note in one of the empty bottles—chocolate milk and ice cream. The iceman brought large chunks of ice to some people. There was a fish man and a vegetable man. The junk man traveled up and down our concrete streets. Food vendors even had scales on the back of their moving stores.

There was also the insurance man, who would show up at the door carrying a large, black briefcase. We would clear off the table, and he would place the briefcase on the floor. When he opened it, there was a large ledger inside with rolls and rolls of names and addresses. Both of my parents would sit down with him, and he would go over their life-insurance policies.

"Hum," he would say. "Mmm, that will be five cents for each of the children and a dime for each of you."

If you were any kind of parent at all, according to some in the black community, you would pay the insurance man without asking any questions regarding his accounts. He would then write in his book and your book so you had your own records. Then he would open a small ink box, check the stamp to make sure it was turned to the right date, roll it back and forth in the ink, and stamp both books. Mr. Jenkins, our insurance man, came every month for years. When we moved, he came to our new home to collect the insurance money. That was about the only time that I was able to see my parents conduct any kind of official business other than when I went downtown with my mother to the bank.

At least once every other month, a man would bring a large truck loaded down with furniture into the neighborhood. My dad always said that he wouldn't buy any of that furniture no matter how bad my mom wanted it, because "once you start buying the stuff on credit you'll be paying for it until you die, and then you kids will have to pay for it even though the furniture will be long gone to the junk man."

Some of our regular neighborhood vendors made distinctive sounds. We didn't even have to look from under the shades to know who was traveling down our block. Some rang bells, others announced their coming by way of megaphones, and a few sang songs. Some just shouted things like

"The fish man's here! We got carp, catfish, and some fresh local crawfish. Better come and get it before it's gone."

The Spiegel man drove down our street in something like a milk truck. When he opened up the back you would see pots and pans and brooms and mops, swaying on their hooks. I always liked this man who sold pots, pans, and utensils because I could hear the metal making sounds like beautiful chimes as he traveled up and down the streets searching for buyers. He also had several Spiegel catalogs that we could look through so he could bring back or mail something he didn't have with him. We didn't buy any brooms from the Spiegel man. There was an old, blind Negro man who made brooms and sold them door to door. Once he sold us a broom, he would share news from the streets like who got married or who just got out of jail.

I felt safe in the projects. It was the ghetto, but in those days I felt safe. People would leave their doors open and their screens unlocked. We didn't have air conditioning, and in the summertime our mothers would put a cot outside on the front lawn and take their naps. Terese's mother enjoyed doing that. No one bothered the nappers.

Years later, Terese and I would talk about a lot of the people in the projects. The first people that popped into her mind were usually the Hawkins. My aunt Lucille Hawkins was the president of the Kellom PTA. Terese remembered her kids, my first cousins Lenore, Christine, Lynwood, Anita, Helen, and Leonard. When Terese grew up the oldest sister, Lenore, moved next door to her. But I remember Lenore as the cousin who spent so much time helping to sooth and massage my legs when I was a baby and little girl. She took so much care with me.

Both of us remembered the Woods family. Mr. Woods was an insurance man, and Mrs. Woods was a homemaker. They had three children; Cathy and Donald were the ones that we knew the best. Our playmate Cathy grew up to become Cathy Hughes, the owner of radio stations and later TV1, an outstanding television station. We always played together when we were youngsters and grew up to respect each other and care about our community.

There was also Betty Green. She lived across the parking lot from us on Seward Plaza. She was tall with long, dark hair that she usually wore in two or three braids. Betty also had long, pretty eyelashes. She always seemed to be older than she was, like she knew things that we didn't know. Terese and I always thought of Betty as the peacemaker in the group. When kids would disagree or a new kid in the group would try to bully his or her way in or out of something it was Betty who would rise to the occasion and bring calm to the situation. The next thing we knew we'd all be playing like nothing had ever happened.

We didn't have all of the conveniences that people who lived in houses had, but still Terese and I remembered that our lives were good. If we really needed a personal item or medicine, it was there. We had about three drugstores within walking distance of where we lived. All we had to do when we needed a cold drink or ice cream was to go right up the street to Reeds Sundries. It was originally a drugstore before Mrs. Smith bought it and took it over. We also remembered the Rexall drugstore. Terese said that if you needed to buy sanitary napkins there, you asked for them and the druggist would quietly wrap them up for you in a plain, brown, paper bag. It was odd, but you knew that he didn't want you to be embarrassed. The people who lived in the projects were respectful of one another.

There were clothing stores. A lot of us shopped at the Salvation Army farther down the street. No one would have a clue where our apparel came from. One clothing store was the Rialto, where sometimes the clothes were so old, like stockings that would rip before you finished putting them on. Farther down the street was a black-owned dress shop. They had the most beautiful clothes, and the ladies who worked there looked like they had just stepped out of a fashion magazine; their nails, hair, and clothes were just fabulous.

Farther down the street was a restaurant. They had a little puppet and band playing on top of a jukebox. It was really something special when we had the money to make the band play music. In our neighborhood there was a huge ice house that took up almost a half a block. At night from our houses you could hear the water circulating through a large revolving mill as the ice was made. That was a huge business back then. When you walked through the projects, on one side was a parking lot and on the other side was the ice house.

On the corner of Twenty-Fourth Street was Jones Body Shop. They were a premier body shop, doing work for people all over the city. Before Jones Body Shop was built, there was a poultry house. I remember most of the people in the community going there to buy chickens. Feathers would be everywhere—on the walls and the ground. If you inhaled quickly, feathers would find their way into your nose or mouth. You could also hear the squawks of the chickens as the men wrung and snapped their necks before chopping off their heads. Some people who lived in houses and had their own yards and chicken coops would buy live poultry. At Easter time I remember a few friends in the projects who had baby chicks as pets.

I remember going across Fontenelle Plaza, the large open park that separated the whites from the blacks, to the free health clinic. We would go there as kids and get all of our shots. I can still smell it, like a strong, minty alcohol. I can still see the doctors and nurses standing in the doorway waiting patiently for us. The nurses would wrap our arms to stop the bleeding from the shots they gave us. There was a large trash can by the door where they would discard used needles, gauze, and bandages. You could hear kids crying, and parents yelling at them to stop, long before you reached the door to the small, red-brick building. My mother had them give me my polio vaccine on my back so no one could see a scar.

My parents read in the newspaper that it was important to keep children out of standing water. As children we would play on Franklin Plaza on the swings. The pavement sloped down toward the middle of the swing set and rainwater would collect there, so most kids weren't allowed to swing until the water dried up. They had us so scared we didn't want to anyway! We were told to stay out of standing water and even out of the high, uncut grass that grew quickly after it rained, because mosquitos bred there.

The news media often carried stories about polio, showing kids in wheelchairs and on crutches. The worst thing would be seeing kids confined in iron lungs—that was extremely frightening. As time went on, the doctors started giving us oral vaccines. I can still taste the syrupy, sweet-tart medicine, but it was better than a shot. Slowly it would go down my throat as I thought of avoiding the devastating disease that left so many children crippled, unable to walk and spending their lives with little hope for a cure.

Our friends the McIntoshes lived on Seward Street. Grover, Mrs. McIntosh's son, was a big guy with a broad smile. He always made us feel like we were his friends. He could make a ship in a bottle, using tweezers to carefully put the small parts inside the narrow, glass bottle. He also made flowers from colored paper and would have most of us walk up and down the street selling them on the Saturdays before Mother's Day and Easter Sunday. He would always give us something for our efforts, but I never thought that it was quite enough. Nevertheless, we all worked for him year after year, and we even looked forward to it. It was fun to make all of the ladies in the neighborhood feel special and happy. Grover was very creative. He seldom had a job, but he knew how to make a buck.

Terese and I started kindergarten at Kellom Elementary School. The school was only a year old when we started there. Edythe K. Hall was the principal throughout most of our years there. She had white, curly hair. She was a very kind lady, but as principal she didn't play around. She meant business. Her philosophy was that we were there to learn, and that was all there was to it. I started kindergarten off by getting into a bit of trouble, but by first grade things were getting better.

In first grade in Mrs. Chase's room we made Easter bonnets out of paper plates. We decorated them until we decided they were beautiful. The day before we got out of school for Easter break we had a parade. We walked around the school from room to room showing off the hats we made for Easter. Our parents were allowed to come, and they sat on the sidelines and watched as we paraded down the middle of the cafeteria. Afterward, we had a tea in the cafeteria.

At the end of the program our parents were asked to join the parent-teacher association. Along with our parents we helped the parent-teacher association by collecting money when people signed up as members. We would go around the school singing, "Join the PTA, we joined the PTA, we joined the PTA, hi-ho the dairy oh, we joined the PTA." That was so cool. I think we received a medal pin and wore it proudly when someone in our family joined.

There was a boy in our second-grade class named Billy. He was from one of the poorest families that we knew. Billy's family were good people. They lived in our neighborhood next to an unpaved parking lot. We would have clothing and money drives at school to help less-fortunate families like Billy's. We also had Red Feather drives, for which we would put money in an envelope in exchange for a red feather. That program later became United Way.

In the Logan Fontenelle Housing Project buildings were red brick with forest-green doors. The front doors faced the streets that ran around the central plaza, and everybody had a large concrete step and a patch of green grass with some bricks and iron railing around it painted green. The poles in the front and back were also painted green. Later on, the city put an overhang over each step to protect visitors from the elements while they waited at the front door. The grass turned brown and died when the weather turned cold, and our mothers usually replaced the dead grass with flowers in the springtime.

The clotheslines were all lined up in the backyards. We mainly used the back doors because they were the most convenient. The parking was at the back and faced the back door. From our unit, we had to go down a shallow hill on a walkway to get to the parking lot. There was an alley that led to our school, and across from that was Logan Field. On our way to school through the alley, we had to step over the drunks; they were usually people we knew. Sometimes they were the parents of our friends. We never said anything disrespectful to them or made fun of them. Some of the bad kids would chunk small rocks at them or call them names like wino, but we never did.

The plaza was made of concrete. We could play hopscotch and jump rope on it. People would throw their kids' birthday parties in the plaza. Adults would bring out their kitchen tables if they didn't have card tables and play cards all night long in the plaza. It was the neighborhood's entertainment center. Informal singing groups were formed by teenagers, who would harmonize to the latest songs and music. Some would play instruments, and others would dance, rehearsing for shows around town. Whatever the occasion, there was something for everyone to enjoy. During the summer months one of our favorite things to do and look forward to was to make up a routine, practice with our parents and friends, and enter the parks and recreation Show Wagon talent show. The Show Wagon was a fully equipped portable stage that traveled from park to park during the summer. We were never turned down from participating, and we would perform our acts in front of family and friends. Harry Eurie and others we grew up with appeared on the Show Wagon at Logan Field.

Terese's mother held Terese's fifth birthday party in the plaza. She carefully loaded a tub with dry ice and filled it with ice cream. She hung balloons all over the place. She hung apples on a string and people had to bite them. The invitations told the guests to wear play togs, which were casual clothes. She didn't want them to wear the fancy party dresses that most girls wore to parties in the fifties. She was concerned about the girls that didn't have fancy clothes to wear, which would make them feel uncomfortable or even keep them from attending the party. For some reason I didn't attend that party, but my friends Cathy Woods, Terese's sister Renata, and our friend Ronnie was there along with other kids in the neighborhood. I can't think of any reason why I wasn't there, except maybe I was sick. In those days I was always sick at home or in and out of the hospital, but whenever I missed any of Terese's parties she would always come by and ask about me and bring me a piece of cake or a balloon. That's the kind of friends we were. Terese's mother and my mother always thought about the other kids in the neighborhood and were concerned about their feelings, and they taught us to think the same way.

We used to sit down outside in front of our homes and plan an arts center. Kellom had elementary-school crafts but not a true arts center. Our plan was to solve that problem. We would sit on the project steps and plan our center. It would be a visual and performing arts center. We wanted to have someone who would make costumes and an art teacher and dance instructors. Kids would learn a lot about music. We would have classes so students could learn all of these things, and an arts gallery to show off the visual arts.

Our parents were invested in our education and social development. Terese's mother sent her to charm classes downtown at the Goldstein Chapman Department Store, and also arranged for her to take art lessons at Joslyn Art Museum. She made sure that she knew how to travel back and forth to the museum on the city bus and that she had the paint supplies she needed. Mrs. Hudgins also saw to it that Terese's brothers and sisters were well taken care of. Although our mothers had very little money, they both had a whole lot of vision.

In junior high, Terese and I slowly began to drift apart. Both of us were taking a deeper interest in our own activities. She was interested in art and I was very interested in singing and the theater. We did, though, go to each other's churches as visitors.

When we got to high school, Terese went to Central, and I went to Tech. We were in a community-organized dance troupe in high school, and we both participated in a production called *Africa Speaks,* produced and directed by Sherry Alston. That was a special time for us, one of the few that we would share as we continued down the road of life.

When we graduated from high school we went on to attend UNO. There we pursued different careers but joined the same African American organization, Black Liberators for Action on Campus, a political and social student organization. Terese was considered one of the original members. In the sixties black organizations were springing up on college campuses across the country, and Omaha was no different. The years did not diminish our desire to work together for social justice and equality.

Most people thought that both Terese and I were a little odd. That might be why we became such close friends. From the time that we were very little girls, people both young and old made comments about us being different. According to Terese, some people thought that we felt we were better than them. We could see things that hadn't happened yet. We always had a vision about life's possibilities for us. We could mentally transport ourselves far away from the stoops in the Fontenelle Projects while physically remaining seated on the hard, cold concrete steps. Our environment never hindered our dreams, and even if others would not dream with us, we knew that wouldn't stop or prevent us from traveling on our joint and individual journeys.

My cousin Lynwood Hawkins.

My cousin Leonard Hawkins.

Joyce's class photo.

My brother John.

Rose Mary and Joyce, my sisters and friends.

My brother Wallace.

Three peas in a pod: Rose Mary, Cathy, and Joyce.

9

Elementary Years

A lot of things in life came hard for me. Some things I brought on myself, while other things were bought on by society or just because of the times. In any event, along with my family and neighbors we would try to survive through it all.

Hopscotch could be challenging and jumping rope was off the table because of what my family called "my condition." They never meant any harm; they were just afraid for me and didn't want me to get hurt any more than necessary. Of course to most minor bumps and scrapes would just be considered kid stuff. To my family every fall I took could mean a trip back to the doctor to reevaluate my gait or possibly for more therapy.

Most of the time they wouldn't come out and just tell me things—you know, lay it on the line. Now that I look back on things, like most people of my parents' generation they would use what I call code words. However, no matter what my parents said or how they said it I was always determined to try and do any and all of the things that the other kids did. My elbows were always scarred up and my knees were usually red and scabbed over.

For I while I even sported a knot on the left side of my head that I got while trying to hurry past a moving swing as my sister Joyce, who was taking care of me, yelled at me to come back to her so we could go home. Of course, I wouldn't listen to her. I saw an empty swing, and I was determined to get there before anyone else. She couldn't stop me. I fell to the ground and lay there, not moving. Joyce told me to get up several times, but I just kept lying there.

Joyce quickly picked me up off the ground and began running with me across the open field past the other play equipment and past the first block of buildings to our house. My mother saw us, flew out of the screen door, took me from Joyce's arms, and placed me securely on the living-room couch. I learned later on that my mom lit into my sister with one uncontrollable wallop after the other. My mom was very angry with Joyce. As for me, when I woke up I saw a lot of adults standing over me, shaking their heads. I could hear my sister in the background saying, "Mama it wasn't my fault." Of course she couldn't keep her mouth shut. She had to tell on me, and it wouldn't be the last time!

All of my mishaps and personal disasters were for the most part because I was just plain hardheaded and stubborn. The other things that happened—well, they just happened. As with each and every one of us, I was susceptible to the times, and the times that I was susceptible to were from 1949 on. I was born in 1949, during the Cold War. People were fearful and began to build shelters on private and public property. At first I thought they were storm shelters or basements, which was where we kept trunks, lots of junk, and the washer and dryer. But later I found out they were concrete buildings with enough canned rations, dried milk, and bottled water in glass jars to last for several years. Camping stores started selling clothing and gas masks. One of the men that my dad worked for gave him a mask. I remember it looking like an elephant head, with the long hose in the middle and gargoyle-like eyes. That's frightening for any kid, and to say the least, I thought it was very scary.

Kellom Elementary School, located in North Omaha, opened in 1952 as a community school incorporating a community center with a swimming pool. It was Omaha's first new school in twenty-seven years. My kindergarten teacher was Miss Holtz. The school still stands at 1311 North Twenty-Fourth Street. Kellom was always considered a black school, especially in the pre–civil rights era, but I only saw it as a beautiful, blonde-brick building with large windows wrapped all the way around it. You could see the gardens from most of the classrooms. We began the school year off learning how to protect ourselves in case of an emergency.

I asked my dad questions about bomb shelters. "What will we do if there is a war?" He'd just tell me that it wasn't for kids to worry about.

Being the precocious kid that I was, I just couldn't accept his response. I knew it was very serious.

"We have no place to go," I would say to Dad despondently.

"Well, in a way we do," he said, trying to be encouraging. "We can go underground. There's a place in the projects where no one would want to go unless it was absolutely necessary. It's at the end of our building. Wide concrete stairs lead to a large, cold, damp, musty space overgrown with cobwebs and chunks of hard, brown only God knows what. I'm sure that you get the picture. Anyway, we can all go there in case of an attack," he responded, with a little uncertainty in his voice. Dad always told it like it was, even if it was hard to swallow, and it usually was. His caution and description of our "shelter" left me with a lump in my throat.

Everything wasn't gloom and doom. Day-to-day life still went on. I somehow managed to stay a dreamer, always with the big ideas. My parents always had something for me to do, something for me to dream about to keep my mind off of serious adult matters. I went with my mom to church and to visit sick neighbors and take them food. She knew the families that did without but never embarrassed them. We would just drop in and drop off a chicken or one of her delicious pies. I would sit quietly on the front steps while she went in to talk women's talk. Mom wouldn't stay long. She would say her goodbyes, and we'd be on our way.

My mom would play games with me, jacks and word games. She even wrote plays with me—little one-page and sometimes five-page plays. My dad was the perfect audience. The plays, which were like fairy tales, always kept me focused on what I could be: fearless, a champion for those who had little and did much. Despite everything else going on, those big ideas made me dream big. My dad told me that when I grew up I could do anything, be anything: a doctor, a teacher, a judge. He even told me about the Supreme Court. I could visualize myself in a long, black robe, seated among powerful people, making a difference.

"Stand up straight, Cathy. Hold your head up, don't look down," they would say to me from time to time. "The world needs you, and you need to be ready for the world." Because of my parents I always knew that there would be a better world because I was a part of it.

On my first day of school, Miss Holtz walked us down to the auditorium to participate in our first assembly with the entire school. "You're walking too slow," she said to me. "You're holding up the line." She sounded slightly irritated. I looked down at my feet, and noticed the other kids doing the same thing—looking down at my feet. Miss Holtz's words seemed to echo through the halls. She could have been using the megaphone tucked under her arm, as loud as it seemed to me. All summer long, while the other kids in the neighborhood were wishing for new clothes to start off the school year, I had prayed to be rid of the large, heavy shoes that my mom purchased for me through my doctor's office. As I surveyed the feet on both sides of the long, narrow hallway I saw that no one, not even the older teachers, wore ugly, chunky, heavy, orthopedic shoes. Now Miss Holtz saw them, too.

"Oh dear, I didn't realize. I couldn't tell that you're handicapped. So next time I'll send you down earlier, with another student of course."

"I don't need any help, and I don't need anyone to walk with me because I don't need to go first!" I blurted out in front of the other kids without thinking.

"But honey, that's school policy," she said in a caring voice.

In the beginning of the year Miss Holtz purchased a large aquarium and placed it in one end of the classroom. Gradually she filled the tank with water and funny-looking, wiggly green stuff. She added several rocks of various sizes, colorful rocks that shined, smaller ones that looked like small diamonds, and other colorful stones. On the side of the tank was a large tube that blew bubbles into the water. All of us sat on our squares on the floor and watched with our mouths open. We watched the bubbles in the otherwise empty tank for several days before she added fish. One by one, they were slowly and carefully placed into their new home. As I sat on the alphabet rug on my spot I watched them intensely. They were something to see. Some of them just seemed to stay in one place all the time, while others busily explored their new home, a large, rectangular, glass cage. They had sand, toys, food, houses, and even castles, but for some reason as they blew wonderful, beautiful bubbles they just didn't seem very happy.

I asked my best friend Terese if she knew how fish felt swimming around and around not getting anywhere, finding themselves right back where they started. I think she thought the question was sort of silly, even though she couldn't help but think about it.

"Fish always swim in tanks," she said, very sure of herself. But I went fishing all the time with my dad and his close friend Mr. Redman, so I knew there were fish living out of tanks, in lakes and rivers.

What I was really concerned about was the fact that the fish were swimming in this glass cage with all the kids staring at them. I began to think about how I was going to free them from their sad existence. And one day when everyone went out to recess, Terese and I hid between the coats in a coatrack near the classroom, waiting for the teacher to leave the room and close the door. When she left neglecting to lock the door, I motioned to Terese that it was okay to quietly enter the classroom. We tiptoed through the sweaters and coats and over the lunch pails, becoming more scared as we got closer to the door. Both of our hearts were beating loudly. Terese stood on her tiptoes, quietly turned the knob, and slowly opened the door to the classroom. I moved a little slower than she did so that my shoes with their heavy, steel-toe plates hit the wooden floors quietly. We left the lights off. We knew we had to move quickly before someone discovered that we were missing.

"Cathy," Terese said, "are you sure you want to do this?"

"Uh huh," I responded, nodding. "I don't see how we can do anything else. We have to let them go. They don't belong in a cage. Look at them. They look so sad!"

Terese turned to me. "How can you tell?"

"I can just tell—why, look at their eyes."

I walked right up to the aquarium and pulled it over toward us. The tank stayed on the edge of the table without hitting the floor. The water spilled out onto the floor along with at least ten fish of all sizes. We hadn't even had time to name them. Just as I yelled, "Run, fish, run!" the door to the room flew open and the entire class came rushing in, led by Miss Holtz. For a moment I thought that the whole world had stopped. There was total silence. Then I broke it. "It's my entire fault. I did it." The kids' shoes made a squishing sound as they shuffled around in the water. Jake, who always went overboard no matter what happened, jumped up and down in the water, making his own war cry as he moved fearlessly across the floor. "Oh, teacher, I did it. It was my idea. It was all my idea," I said.

"But why, Cathy? Why would you do such a thing?"

"Well," I began, hoping that she would understand. I was distracted by the other kids happily slipping and sliding on the water, jumping in it as if it were rain. "Teacher, I was really sad about the fish living in the cage. I had to free them, I just had to." By now I could see the fish slowly dying on the floor in front of my very eyes. They were flopping all over the place. It was truly an utter disaster with great consequences—I was sure of that if I wasn't sure of much else. I didn't know then what the lesson was in all of this, but years down the road I would discover that there was a price to pay if you wanted freedom. Right now for the fish, it was death for most of them.

Miss Holtz didn't say another word. The water oozed from her shoes as she paraded us down to the principal's office unannounced.

First the principal spoke with Terese, and then she spoke with me. Our mothers were called. Her mother picked her up first. My mother arrived a few minutes later, although it seemed like hours. She went into the principal's office calmly but came out with a puzzled look on her face.

"Let's go home." That's all she said. The walk was interminable. When we finally arrived home my mother was very quiet. She immediately went upstairs and stayed there for a very long time. Finally she came back down.

"Have a seat," she barked at me. I was already seated so I knew this was going to be bad. "Catherine Grace," she began, "you surely are different, and that's okay. You have unusual ideas about this world, and I can tell you stand by your convictions—and sometimes that surely is okay. But there is something wrong with not respecting the ideas and property of others. You might not agree with people, and you really don't have to, but you do have to respect the ideas and property of others. When you don't you have to be willing to accept the consequences. Do you understand me?"

It was a lot for me to take in, but I did understand her. I was going to be punished, and so was Terese. We were going to be punished by the school, and our parents wouldn't allow us to see each other for several weeks. That seemed to be the worst of all. I knew further punishment would be on its way when my dad heard the news. Either I was going to get a whupping and have to do all of the kitchen chores or I was going to get a whupping and have to stay indoors for a week; but in any case I could almost bet and win on knowing that I was going to at least get a whupping.

Terese was allowed to return to class the very next day, but as for me, the principal held another conference with my parents to determine if I was even ready for kindergarten. Some of the administration at the school felt that I needed to mature another year.

The following day I wasn't allowed to attend school with the other students. Both of my parents went with me to school to meet with the principal. My dad was not happy. My parents didn't know where to sit so they squeezed themselves into the small chairs outside of the principal's office, the ones that I sat in whenever I went to the library.

The secretary appeared with the formality that usually made parents uncomfortable. "The principal will see you now."

When we walked in, I immediately blurted out an apology and promised to never do anything like that again. Then my parents said that they intended to replace each and every fish in the tank and pay for all damages to the tank as well as the classroom. I don't know why they said that. They didn't have the money. They would have a hard time just affording the fish. They were trying so hard to save face, and my dad kept glaring over at me. I saw his eyes fill with tears—a rare sight. I don't know if it was because he was disappointed in me or if he was fearful of what would happen if he couldn't find the money to pay for the damages.

Fortunately we were told that the damage was minimal and that the only one to pay was me. Mrs. Holtz understood; she knew that my dad would have difficulty paying the damages. I sat on a small chair looking up and glancing at both of my parents to see if I could catch a hint from either one of them, sighing, smiling, or frowning at the thought of their baby paying. Even my piggy-bank money couldn't possibly cover everything. But I didn't see any compassion for me in their eyes. What I did see was two parents who stood up, shook the principal's hand, and assured her that they would deal with me to her satisfaction at home and that whatever the punishment was at school, it was all right with them.

Each morning I picked up the trash in front and back of my block and at school. I had to clean my room before I went to bed and make my bed in the morning. I even had to pick up behind my sisters, who shared the room with me. That was hard because one of them had drawn a line down the center of the room during a shouting match about my things vs. your things—woo.

I knew I would have to apologize to my teacher and the entire class. I wasn't looking forward to that, but I knew that it had to happen if I was ever going to be accepted back into the school—and I loved Kellom, even after these few short weeks. I didn't want to go down in history as the youngest kid expelled from an elementary school, especially during the first two weeks. I was sorry for all the trouble that I had caused, but was I sorry for letting the fish die?

I was allowed to return to school the following Monday morning. I asked if we could go to school early that morning so I could apologize to the school custodian, Mr. Johnson. When we arrived, my mother took me right through the cafeteria and toward his small office. We snaked our way through a narrow passage full of mops, smelly rags, pails, and brooms. We carefully stepped over several plastic containers holding bleach-smelling liquids. My mother politely knocked on the closed door. He answered and kindly asked us in. His office didn't look anything like the principal's office. At first I was afraid to look at him, but when he looked at me through his round, wire-framed glasses, I was able to find the right words.

"Mr. Johnson, I'm so sorry. I know what—" but before I could get the rest of the sentence out, Terese and her mother entered the room. It was now pretty crowded, but it was comforting.

"We—" Terese said, speaking up in a strong voice.

"We," we said together, "are terribly sorry for the mess we made and all of the damage that we caused."

Mr. Johnson spoke calmly through his wiry gray mustache. "I hope you kids learned your lesson. Your teacher took her own money to buy that tank and the fish that went in it. I know you're both sorry for what you did. Now hurry on before you're both late to class, and thanks for coming by."

Because of the incident, my parents were told that I was probably too immature for kindergarten. But my parents knew better. I was already reading, and I could correctly spell and write the names of everyone in our family. I was singing in the children's choir and had memorized each and every line in the Easter pageant. I was ready. As frustrated with me as my parents were, they still demanded that the school let me back in. After a stern speech and me agreeing to follow the rules, the principal allowed me to return to school. Miss Holtz welcomed me back into the classroom with a smile. I don't think she held it against me, although it seemed like I had to clean the paintbrushes and bang the erasers more often than the rest of the kids, usually during recess!

Our classroom no longer had a fish tank. I finally got up enough nerve to ask Larry, a short, stocky kid who said little but knew a lot, if he knew what happened to the fish and the tank. He did. The fish tank and the remaining fish were now in the principal's office. Everything, no matter how noble, has a cost. I couldn't change anything that happened that day with the fish and the fish tank. The only thing I could do was learn from it, and accept and live with the consequences. I had no intention of ever being sent back to the principal's office for troublemaking. I would prove, however, to be a regular there.

I resigned myself to the fact that we're sometimes creatures of habit, like fish swimming around in tanks, afraid to try new things. We can get used to almost anything, especially if we don't experience life or take risks.

I was a kid of the fifties, and most black kids in the fifties could have sworn that Elvis was black. My sisters stopped everything to listen to him on the radio. They owned records by Jackie Wilson, Chuck Berry, Sam Cooke, Fats Domino, Little Richard, and James Brown. I remember "Red Sails in the Sunset," a thick, red record made of something that looked like plastic that my sisters played on their record player, which I was never allowed to touch. They would slowly remove the records from their jackets, place them on the table, move the arm to its place, and turn the player on. I always liked watching the record fall onto the velvet turntable. My sisters would quickly wipe off the record on the sides of their clothing and place the needle on the outer edge of the record. Boy, did Nat King Cole sound great on a record player! I always hated it when the records wore out or became scratched. By the late fifties, my sisters were listening to the Frankie Lymon and the Teenagers, Little Anthony and the Imperials, the Platters, the Dells, the Silhouettes, the Coasters, and the Drifters.

After my brothers John and Wallace completed their service in Korea, they came home to the music they loved, jazz and the blues. Later, along with their friends Bill and Al, they would listen to the sounds of Charlie Parker, Miles Davis, John Coltrane, and Thelonious Monk. John loved the ladies and their music: Ella Fitzgerald, Sarah Vaughn, and the love of his life, the beautiful Dinah Washington. Of course all of my family loved Ray Charles, whose genius would set them on fire at the community dances whenever he came to Omaha.

There weren't a lot of black actors and actresses for us to enjoy. But whenever my brothers, sisters, or parents got an opportunity to go to a show they would swoon over Dorothy Dandridge, Sidney Poitier, Lena Horne, Harry Belafonte, Diahann Carroll, and Eartha Kitt. Mom always imitated Kitt's purring sounds, and she just loved Sidney Poitier and would save up her money to take in all of his movies.

My dad wasn't much for the movies, but he loved baseball and would drive to Kansas City whenever the Royals played against his favorite players: Jackie Robinson of the Brooklyn Dodgers, Willie Mays of the New York Giants, Ernie Banks of the Chicago Cubs, and Hank Aaron of the Milwaukee Brewers and the Atlanta Braves. Later on, my dad would take me along to visit my cousins in Kansas City and we would take in a baseball game to watch a local boy, Bob Gibson, play for the St. Louis Cardinals.

By the second grade I had a brand-new classroom with a brand-new teacher, Mrs. Palmer. Mrs. Palmer's hair was reddish brown and styled in tight, short curls. She was very young, thin, and stylish and kind of pale.

Her face was narrow, with freckles that prominently stood out across her pixie nose. I always had to hold myself back from wanting to touch them. All of the kids thought she was beautiful as well as smart.

I had settled down somewhat. I was walking better with my knobby knees and looking a little better, though I was still skinny enough to look undernourished. Regardless, I was smiling a lot more. I even won the smile contest sponsored by the local dentists for having beautiful, straight, white teeth.

Terese and I were really into playing school. Of course both of us wanted to be the teacher, because we were both the student all week long. When we couldn't agree on who was going to be the teacher we would drop the chalk and pointer stick, fold and put the lined black chalkboard into the closet, and pull out our red-and-white jump ropes and quickly go outside.

With keen eyes we'd search out other friends and start a jump-rope line. We'd gather the kids together and form two lines, and I would always ask to twirl the rope. I was much better at twirling than jumping. When it came to double Dutch, I was better at twirling two ropes than anyone on our street. My hips had a rhythm that was second to none.

When Terese wasn't around I would meet up with my older cousin Lynwood and we'd shoot marbles. I had several beautiful aggies and cat's-eyes. Lynwood always insisted on winning them so he could secretly give them back. He was my second-best friend. Aggies were supposed to be good luck, so I made sure that if he or his friends won them from me I would have a fair chance to win them back. I usually did.

The last time I beat the boys in the neighborhood we were all bent down on one knee in a small, awkward circle. Charles, who always carried a stick because he was afraid of running into dogs when walking home, carefully made a circle in the dried mud with his stick. Then he made a smaller one in the center. Kevin, a friend of ours from the white side of the projects, had asked us to participate in a marble match on the white side of town, so that's where we were. My marble bag was almost empty, and Lynwood looked discouraged. When it was his turn to shoot, he pulled out his favorite peewee, bent down close to the edge of the dry, dirt circle, rubbed the marble back and forth in the palm of his small, chubby hands, spit on the marble, and shot with his thumb, eyes partially shut. No one moved.

Lynwood had challenged some of the rougher kids from South Omaha to play a game of marbles or shut up about how weak and what kind of babies we were in North Omaha. Most of those kids I hadn't seen before, but he knew most of them since his dad, Uncle Leonard, coached a lot of juvenile boxers on the other side of town. Most of these kids had watched their older brothers and cousins participate in matches, including the Golden Gloves.

They were arriving, mostly boys our age, except for their older brothers who had brought their girlfriends to watch. I was there to look after my skates and for no other reason. Lynwood told everybody the rules. If they weren't playing or were playing for "keepers"—keeps, that is—they had to stand or sit behind jump ropes that were tied to several trees in order to rope off the playing area. Kids continued to arrive on bikes, scooters, and foot. Dirt was flying everywhere, and frankly I have to say it was one of the most exciting afternoons ever. I was in about the second grade, and Lynwood was one year older. Lynwood asked for quiet while he called the game as Ringer and gave the rules. "Five to eight players," he shouted. "What will it be?" He sounded just like a huckster on one of those carts that traveled down our streets peddling their wares each week. About seven boys stepped forward. They were serious, and they appeared anxious and determined. The boys playing asked why I was there. One of the boys from North Omaha told them that I enjoyed the game of marbles. "She's here to help and to keep the score," Lynwood said. I quickly got on my knees with a large, gnarly stick in my hand and drew a small circle with 100 points written in the center of it. Then I drew an outside one worth 75 points, another worth 50 points, and finally the largest one around all the rest, worth 25 points. It stretched eight feet across. By the size of the circle it was obvious that this game would be hard to win.

Everyone pulled out the individual pouches or sacks containing their marbles. As they poured them into their small hands it was apparent that they loved each and every marble and didn't want to lose even one. Each player sat outside of the circle and knuckled down. The first player placed his shooter in the crook of his index finger with his knuckle on the ground. Everyone held their breath as the marble was shot straight out with the shooter thumb. Marbles were shot one after the other as North Omaha and South Omaha played and racked up points. Finally, it was the end of the game. Marbles were being picked up by both sides. It appeared to be a tie. "We need to play another game!" someone yelled. "Lynwood, you play Steve."

"Yeah," kids shouted. "Play for the win!"

Lynwood looked at me. I don't know why, but he asked me to shoot for him. "Cathy, if you win this round for us—"

"Hold up, cuz, if I win this round you have to promise not to make fun of the way I walk and, well—not to take my skates anymore for your box-car scooters."

"It's a deal," he said.

One of the older boys was pushed out by his girlfriend, but he balked. "Wait a minute—not so fast. We don't have anyone willing to play against this girl. We don't care if she is your cousin."

"I'll play her," spoke up a boy named Jake from South Omaha. "But I'll play her bullseye marbles, one-on-one."

The circles were drawn, and a line was drawn several feet behind the circles. We were each given three marbles to shoot. The one accumulating the most points would be declared the winner. I went first. I was so nervous that I scratched,

"Oh, give the girl another turn. Can't you see that she doesn't know what she's doing?"

No favors for me.

Jake went next and scored 50 pts.

"Zero to 50!" someone shouted.

We went again. This time I made 75 points, and Joe made 100.

It was the final shot. I shot 100 to Joe's 25. The score was now 175 to 175.

"Tiebreaker, tie breaker!" the kids shouted.

I stood up, my knees hurting, and then I moved back behind the freshly made line. Jake was right beside me. For some strange reason I felt like he was rooting for me, but I knew better. I shot a 75, and Jake shot a 50. North Omaha had won.

"We won!" I shouted. Although most of the marbles belonged to me, after that game, I gave them to Lynwood and considered him my hero.

Over time I gave all of my marbles to Lynwood. I thought he could use them more than I could. My mother told me that giving the marbles to my cousin was a nice thing for me to do, but I think she was actually just happy about not having to continue patching the knees of my pants or tripping over the stray marbles that would somehow get loose from my small suede bag. In exchange for the marbles, I made him promise to leave my skates alone. He would take a skate from me and attach it to an old crate, an open box of slats made of wood used to carry items for shopping, to make a scooter. All the boys were doing it, but making this deal ensured that I had both skates instead of having to scoot down the block with just one.

World War II was long over, and even though we were involved in the Cold War, we felt safer than ever before. My brothers were coming home from the United States Navy, and my sisters had boyfriends coming and going. I thought most of their boyfriends looked much better going. I always seemed to get myself into trouble when they were around, although I always had extra money for candy because the boyfriends gave me money to keep my mouth shut. Usually this hush money came at a high cost. I couldn't divulge to my parents any information surrounding my sister's activities. On one occasion one of my sisters invited a boyfriend over to the house. I can't remember if he came in or not, but I do remember her spending a lot of time talking with him through the screen door while she debated over whether or not to ask him in, as she had been told not to have company in the house when she was babysitting. I kept interrupting, asking my sister to fix me something to eat. They ignored me, laughing and talking about a dance the week before. She went outside, and they both moved further away from the front door. I could see them outside leaning against a car, talking. I was becoming very agitated, so I decided to cook my own dinner. I went to the icebox, got out a wiener, put it into a pan with water, turned on the stove, and patiently waited for my dinner. I decided to watch a show while I waited. I never got to watch television that late, because I was usually sent upstairs to bed by then. I turned the television on, sat in my dad's favorite chair, crossed my feet like he did, and dozed off to sleep....

The smell of the wiener woke me up. I hurriedly pushed myself out of the chair, rushed to the stove, and reached for the pot. It was so hot that I couldn't hold onto the handle. I had two options: drop it or fry my fingers— but where to drop it? It landed on a plastic kitchen chair. The wiener was as charred black as the inside and bottom of the pot. It was bone-dry. I began blowing on the pot, hoping it would cool off before my sister or anyone else came back to the house.

I waited about ten minutes before touching the handle to make sure it was cool and clumsily tried to lift the pot off the chair. It didn't budge. It was stuck. It took both hands and all my strength to pry the pan from the chair. It was hard for me to believe what I saw when I freed it. The plastic seat of the chair had come up with the pan, along with the padding. Straw was spewed out all over the floor. All that was left of the chair was the wood that supported the bottom.

I had to think fast. I quietly carried the pan to the back of the pantry, wiener and all, fanning the smoke all the way. Next, I slowly dragged the chair across the floor, opened the hall closet and pushed it all the way to the back. Finally I picked up the loose straw that covered the floor and put it in the garbage can. I was so focused I barely heard the screech of the screen door opening. When my sister came in, she asked me if I was hungry, all the while looking around with a puzzled expression on her face.

"No, Sis, I'm not hungry, I'm really tired," and I meant it!

"Cathy, what's that smell? It smells like something's burning."

"I think the neighbor's outside getting her hair pressed again on their back porch," I said nervously.

Still looking puzzled, she continued asking questions. "At this time of night? Okay, then, you'd better go to bed, and don't be slow about it."

I knew that our mom would be home soon from her occasional night job at the Ritz Theater. It was Saturday, and on weekends she stayed later than usual to clean up. Dad also stayed out late at the Bomber, a club he often frequented, taking every opportunity to gamble and win money from men who had gotten paid the night before.

Sunday was the day of the week that all of us went to church, except Dad. "Get up and come down to breakfast so you won't be late to Sunday school!" he hollered the next morning. Going to church was not something my dad did on a regular basis. He usually went whenever we were in a play or musical. Quite frankly, he didn't have much confidence in preachers. He would say that most of them held us back with their ideas. They wanted us to turn the other cheek even when we knew that we were right, and that didn't sit well with him. But even though he didn't think much of organized religion, he liked for us to attend church even thought he tended to think that it was just another way for the white man to control us.

I was a slowpoke, so by the time I arrived at the kitchen table everyone was seated. "Well, sit down," my father said in an anxious voice. He seemed to be in a hurry to get us all out of the house. But I just stood there.

"Catherine!" That was the name I was called when I was in trouble. "Don't you hear your father speaking to you?" My mother was chiming in, and if we upset her in front of him, all hell would usually break loose. When my mother got upset she would hum religious hymns or sweep the floor, even if it wasn't dirty. It was a way for her to soothe herself, a way to make herself feel better since she had no way to deal with her anger inside. Neither activity made my dad happy. Sometimes I think that it was also a way for my mom to annoy my dad, maybe even get back at him for being so unkind and at times even thoughtless. They were insisting that I find the chair and sit in it. I responded that I preferred to stand, pray, and eat on my feet, but they weren't buying that.

"Does anyone know where the chair is?" Mom asked. "Joyce, Rose Mary, you were here babysitting. What happened to the chair? Speak up! Don't just sit there like you're deaf and dumb." The air was thick and sticky.

"I see it! It's right here!" One of my sisters pulled it out of the closet and dragged it across the room, straw, soot, and all.

My guilt took over. My voice was low and shaky. My words made very little sense but were sincere. "I'm sorry, Mom. I'm sorry, Dad." They were used to hearing those words from me, but I could tell by the looks on their faces that they weren't impressed. They weren't impressed at all, and we didn't have time to argue about it. It was time for me to go to Sunday school.

After Sunday school, my sisters planned to stay at church for the 11:00 service, but my mom and I went home. After we got home I went to my room and quickly changed from my church clothes to my everyday dress so that I could help with dinner. "Cathy, when you come downstairs, go to the pantry and carefully get on the step stool, get down several jars of okra, and bring them to me. I already have green beans, cabbage, squash, and ground beef."

"What are we making?" I asked as I took the okra off the shelf.

"Goulash" was her answer. I knew that was what we made when the money jar was almost empty, something that happened a lot. But it was delicious. Mom was a great cook, and this was one of her specialties. As I heard her voice so soft, so peaceful, I turned to put the step stool back into the corner and saw the burnt pan with the hard, shriveled-up wiener stuck to the bottom. I walked out holding the jar in one arm tightly against my chest and the arm of the pan in my other hand.

"Oh, thanks," Mom said as I placed everything on the table. "You're such a big help. I couldn't do this without you." Then she saw the pan. "What's that?"

"That's the pan I used to cook the wiener."

My mom looked inside. She paused, and there was silence. She never yelled at me, not once. "What a mess, we'd better scrape and soak this pan. I only have a few."

She never said anything more about it all the while I helped her in the kitchen. "Take that apron down off the hook in back of you and put it on so you won't get your dress soiled." After dinner she never said a word. That night while lying in bed between my two sisters I couldn't figure out why I didn't get a whupping.

I remember another occasion when one of my sisters' boyfriends came over to our house and fell asleep in my dad's favorite chair. My sister had to spend a lot of time taking care of me, so I guess he got tired of waiting. She was making a lot of noise upstairs, moving around quickly. I could hear drawers squeaking and closet doors opening and closing. I thought they were going out on a date, and Rose Mary would eventually come down and entertain him while she waited for someone else to come to take care of me.

Rose Mary's boyfriend wiped his forehead and opened the collar of his shirt. He began sweating, so he removed his nice shirt and hung it on the back of a chair. I looked the guy over thoroughly. He looked annoyed and asked me why I kept looking at him. Then he just fell asleep. I didn't think that it was common or even possible for a young man to snore and drool at the same time, so it became a science experiment for me. Watching the spectacle, I had my doubts that they were going anywhere. There was a mass of wiry hair growing wildly on his chest. I had never seen so much hair in any place other than on someone's head or on a bear at the zoo. I slowly moved around the chair, looking at him long and hard. I got the razor from my dad's shaving cup in our only bathroom, located upstairs, and tried to shave his chest. While working my way down his chest, I nicked him and he woke up.

"Shit, what in the hell is going on around here? Rose Mary, where are you? What's wrong with your little sister? Get me something. I think she cut me. Why, I really believe she did."

I did understand why he was upset. He didn't look right. From time to time I stood on the toilet seat and watched my dad shave. He had told me that a razor was dangerous and not to ever use one until I was ready. I guess I thought I was ready. This guy needed some help with his looks. If only he would have given me a chance to finish the job, I really think he would have liked it. Besides, my sister didn't seem like the type to like hairy men. To be honest though, I was mad at him for intruding on my time with my sister. Now that she was older, when it came to guys I usually took a back seat. Anyway, he left the house running without even saying goodbye.

My sister hurried down the stairs after hearing the door slam. "Where's Joe?"

"Was that Joe?" I shrugged. "I think something came up. He just left."

"Did he say when he's coming back?"

I paused, not answering.

Then I politely took her hand and said, "Let's eat now."

My parents had their hands full, feeding, clothing, and keeping a roof over our heads. I didn't help any with my antics, but I didn't necessarily know that then.

I kept thinking, am I going to go to jail? What would my punishment be? Would the judge have me locked up for good? Maybe, I didn't know. What I did know was this guy was mad, and so was my sister. He probably wouldn't come back to our house again, let alone take my sister on a date. But I wasn't worried; my sister had plenty of boyfriends. My sister threw the razor away. She never said anything because she wasn't supposed to have him in the house at such a late hour, especially when my parents weren't at home.

Secretly I liked his new look. It was probably easier for him to button up his shirts, seeing that all that chest hair wasn't in the way and showing if the first two buttons were left open. Besides, now my sister had more time to read to me and play games with me, something she was doing less and less as she got older. Other people and other activities were now occupying more of her time. She was my older sister, and she always took care of me like a mother when my mother couldn't.

My sisters loved and protected me. They made me feel safe, and the thought of being alone was something that started to keep me awake and scared at night, especially if they were out and I had to go to bed alone. Whenever I would cry out in the night for my mom and she didn't come, my sisters would hold me and rock me. "Momma loves you very much," they would say, and I would slowly fall asleep.

When I was a baby I slept in the same room with them, and as I got a little older in the same bed. In the bed my sisters would laugh and talk together about any and everything, and I would lie there as still and as quiet as possible for a little girl. I knew that it would change someday. It was inevitable. I just wasn't ready for it to change now.

My sisters were spending more time away from home, and my mother finally convinced my dad that if we had a TV like our neighbors maybe my sisters would spend more time at home. It seemed like forever, but the day finally came when my father saw a need to have something in the house besides a radio—an old, used television set that failed to work more often than it worked.

I don't remember going shopping, but I do remember coming home one day to a large console TV positioned right against the wall in our living room. The rabbit ears weren't hooked up yet, but when that was done all we had to do was plug it in, turn it on, and wait for the picture and sound. The first few weeks there were no rules around watching the TV set. Then my dad decided that it was on too much and we were studying too little, so he set down rules. During the day hardly anyone watched the TV except on the weekends when we had more free time. On the weekends I preferred watching cartoons in the morning and playing outside the rest of the day. School occupied my weekdays, but I was the first to arrive home after school so I could see some of my favorite shows before my dad got home.

The console part of the TV was not as pretty as some of the other ones in the neighborhood, but the black-and-white picture was clear and all three channels came in with no problem. The antenna on top had a dial to adjust the picture and rabbit ears that kept the picture operating in a storm.

Mom was very proud of her new television, and one afternoon she invited several of her friends over to watch their favorite soap operas. *The Guiding Light* and *Search for Tomorrow* were their favorites. She always managed to find something to serve them to eat, even if it was a watery soup and a few soda crackers. Her friends loved her fried chicken, string beans, and sweet bread, even if she didn't make it very often—or maybe because she didn't make it very often. She also made a wonderful-tasting cake without icing on top.

The day before her soap-opera party, Mom sent me to Jake's Grocery Store, our neighborhood market, to purchase bread, lettuce, tomatoes, sweet tea, and other odds and ends for our meal. She was determined to serve the leftovers the following day. She told me, as usual, not to buy any candy. It was bad for my teeth. On several occasions I had been inspected for worms, which my parents said came from eating too many sweets. I just couldn't believe that. How could you get worms from eating sweets? I later learned that parents told that to a lot of children to keep us away from the treats we loved. Parents were always telling us scary things to make us act the way they wanted, although it never worked well with me.

I went to Jake's, and as I was leaving the store with Mom's groceries, I reached in my pocket, found some pennies and nickels from my hush fund, turned around, and asked for some penny candy, licorice and my favorite dot candy—small sugar pieces on long rolls of white paper. When I got home, I dropped the sack of candy on the side of the stoop to get later.

I usually went to my room whenever I had a sack of candy in my grips; however this time I didn't have time. Later that evening, I went out and brought my sack into the living room to enjoy a few pieces. Just as I pulled the first piece out of the bag, the doorknob turned and my father walked inside and said, "I'm home." He was standing right in front of me but was looking elsewhere. I knew I would get a whupping for having the candy. I was near the TV when he came in, and I reached behind it to the heavy board that covered the picture tubes. In a panic, trying to hide my candy before my dad caught me, I dumped it into the back of the TV.

The next morning I heard my dad swearing, which was rare. "Get down here, Catherine! Right now!"

I sighed. Catherine, not Cathy. I must really be in trouble.

"Little girl," he said. "Look what you've done. You ruined our brand-new TV." My mom was between us, protecting me, even though she was probably mad, too. "Juanita, move. She is going to get it. The next time she lays eyes on a television set it will be in color." He was pointing to my mess. Oozing out of the back of the TV was a gooey, runny mess. It had melted onto the wires connecting the tubes. The TV no longer worked, and we couldn't afford a repair man.

After that, I had to go to the McIntoshes to watch TV. Cheryl McIntosh was my mother's best friend's daughter, and she was the only person in the neighborhood at times who seemed to be on my side through my punishment.

When I first became aware of the McIntoshes, I was about three years old. They lived right next door to us, in an identical house. Iola McIntosh always worked for prestigious people in Omaha. As my father put it, "Those people run this city, and I get tired of reading about them all the time in the paper. Doesn't the *World-Herald* have more important things to write about?"

Mrs. McIntosh always brought home the finest clothes and shoes, so many that she gave the ones that fit Joyce and Rose Mary to them—if, of course Cheryl didn't want them. The girls would sometimes spend Saturdays cleaning and trading them. Cheryl came to expect these fancy clothes and wouldn't tolerate the ones we usually wore that came from Goodwill. She was a very pretty girl with beautiful, dark curls that usually hung in a sophisticated Shirley Temple style. She had a perfect figure and strong, curvy legs. Her skin was honey brown and her large, deep dimples were prominent on both sides of her smile. My sisters called her pretty, but the boys referred to Cheryl as sexy.

Dad sometimes made mean comments about the McIntoshes. He always described the family as moochers without regard for our situation. Dad was always complaining about people my mom called friends, people who liked and supported my mom and whom she liked and supported in kind. He didn't seem to know that whenever the McIntoshes had anything, they always shared with open hands and hearts. Mom and Mrs. McIntosh were like sisters, and they spent a lot of their free time together. I just think Dad was a little jealous of their relationship. But there was something that the two women didn't share in, and that was working continuously and tirelessly for the rights of Negroes. That was my mother's passion, and from time to time it separated her from her friends and even her own family. The views and suggestions of others never swayed her from doing what she believed was right.

On one particular day in the late fifties or early sixties, I remember coming home from school and seeing my dad at home. My mom had left the house the same time I did that morning. She had on an extra-nice dress—one of her church dresses—along with a small scarf on her head. She was carrying her purse in her hand. Usually my mom was home when I got there, but instead my dad unlocked the door to let me in. I immediately went upstairs and changed out of my school clothes, came down, and got a snack. I sat on my favorite rug in front of the TV. We had a new TV now, and I felt lucky to be allowed to watch it. I even changed the station. While I was eating my sandwich, my show went off and the news came on. I got up and took my saucer into the kitchen. I began looking in the icebox for something to drink when I heard my dad. "Cathy, get in here."

He was moving his glasses around on his face from front to back and back again. "Is that your mom in that group of people? They're putting them into police cars and into the back of paddy wagons because they refused to get up off of a stool at a Woolworth's store, and your mother is definitely among them."

"Is mom in trouble" I questioned.

"Sssh—let me hear this."

On the news they said that the protesters were removed from the stools at Woolworth's because they refused to leave the area on their own. "As you know, people across the South, even young college students, are traveling from the North. They are called Freedom Riders; white as well as black students are attempting to integrate segregated public facilities, even public drinking fountains. These black and white students, some of them in elementary school, are saying that even in Omaha, Nebraska, they will be allowed to utilize and be served in public facilities because they are citizens of the United States and they will no longer accept second class status."

Thinking back, I remember that during the week darkness would come fast, and Terese and I had very little time to play together. On Saturdays it always seemed to rain. Since I was still in trouble for the candy/television debacle, I had a lot of time on my hands. I stayed out of the way as much as possible, and was usually on cleaning duty. I also used the time to enter the Douglas County American Red Cross Writing Contest. We were allowed to participate throughout elementary school, and I entered several years in a row. I would often watch my mother write in her beautiful penmanship. She was passionate about so many things, but whenever she wrote stories, she did it with such enthusiasm other things took a back seat. Nothing else measured up to the pleasure that writing gave her. At night I would peek into her bedroom and find her sitting on the edge of her bed or at her night table writing, thinking, and writing some more.

My poetry was accepted for the *Junior Red Cross Highlights,* a magazine that published student work around the county. I took a first-place ribbon in the second grade, and my friend Terese also won a prize for her artwork. One day not long after, we put together a plan for writing, publishing, and distributing a small newspaper about our neighborhood.

There were so many stories to tell, and we were sure that if we told them they would be the talk of the town. Terese and I asked our mothers what they thought about a neighborhood newspaper. They said that it was a good idea as long as we stuck to the facts. It was going to be quite an undertaking, but we were sure that we were up to the task. We went around the neighborhood asking for stories to put into *The Nosey News.*

One of the first stories that we wrote was about a young boy on our street whom we learned had come down with polio. George attended our school and was well liked. One Friday afternoon in school our teacher asked us to write get-well cards to him expressing our concern and how much we missed him. It was easy, because we all shared these sentiments.

Polio had been a growing concern in our community long before I was born. Everyone was afraid, and the fear grew boundlessly with news like George's because no one really understood how you caught the disease or how it spread. Rose Mary was terrified of being placed in an iron lung. After seeing a picture in the newspaper of a kid living in one, she was so frightened she couldn't eat or sleep for days. She was not alone. So we were careful in the summer to not leave the lids off of the trash cans, because most people believed any exposed garbage would attract flies, fleas, and maggots and make for an environment where germs would expose kids to polio. We also didn't swim in public pools.

So for our first edition of *The Nosey News,* published with the help of our moms, the cover story was on polio. We wanted people to know that we were concerned about our neighbors. It was late spring, and all of our believed conditions for polio were present. We found an old newspaper and began using segments of the paper to give us ideas and help us write our articles.

I remember coming home from school one day. I was six or seven and my parents were doing something very unusual—at least, unusual for them. They were reading the front page of the newspaper together. Even though I wasn't paying a great deal of attention, I do remember that they were smiling at each other. Just then my brother Wallace came through the door, and my dad announced that a man named Dr. Jonas Salk had found a cure for polio. "He comes from Pittsburgh, and he says that he has a vaccine."

"How long is it going to take before they give it to us?" my sister Joyce asked. No one had noticed her entering the room.

"The paper says that the government licensed the vaccine for distribution this afternoon."

"I have no idea who will get vaccinated first in Omaha," interjected my mom, "but whenever it's our turn we will definitely show up."

I didn't understand what it all meant, but I was excited because everyone else seemed to be. It wasn't unusual for kids like me to be interested in and even scared of polio. We saw our neighbors, friends, and family members broken and saddened by the cruel realities of this disease that would paralyze and even kill children and adults. Every week there would be a student or friend missing from his or her seat in my school. My church would take up money for either their care or their burial. Frightened faces could be seen in the stores and on the streets. Stories and rumors—sometimes false ones—spread across all racial and economic communities. It was frightening, and it didn't skip the young minds of children.

Most of the articles that Terese and I wrote for our newspaper came from our parents' suggestions—things like cookie recipes, neighborhood sports, and local weather reports. The other stuff we got from the school newspaper, the *Weekly Reader,* and a local black paper, *The Omaha Star.* We wrote about kids who didn't have clothes and food. There was even a food-and-clothing drive because of our paper. Of course, every now and then we still slipped in a little gossip, but most of the time when people had time to help us they offered recipes and poems written by their kids. This wasn't what we had envisioned. We were becoming discouraged and frustrated. How could we write a newspaper without any real news?

One gloomy day our paper was rescued by fate. We were sitting on the back porch when we overheard two ladies gossiping while they were hanging out their clothes to dry.

"Did you hear about the police going to Linda's house down the street?"

"No, what happened?" A clothespin fell out of her hand and for a moment, we could see her arms, bending down to swoop it back into her apron.

"Well, I heard from Janice that two police cars pulled up in the back of this building. The officers got out and walked around to the front door and knocked, and when the door opened they said a few words and then Linda let them in. Janice of course doesn't know what happened inside, but when they went back outside Linda was loudly telling them to find out who stole her money off the clothesline. She expected them to get to the bottom of it: arrest the person and get her money back."

The lady mimicked one of the officers. " 'Let me get this straight. Someone stole your money off of your clothesline?' "

Now she used what we could only assume was Linda's voice. " 'Not only that, I expect you to arrest them and put them in jail.' "

The officer's voice sounded again—they were giggling at her acting, really having a good time with their impromptu play. " 'What was your money doing on the clothesline in the first place?' "

" 'I washed the money. Money is dirty, and I won't carry around anything with so many germs. I won't handle it. I just won't, and you shouldn't either.' " The ladies cackled at the thought. The storyteller continued, finished with her fake voices.

"I saw the officer taking down the information; what else was he going to do? Then he just shook his head, nodded to the other officers who stood there looking at the clothesline, and they got into their cars and left. Do you believe that?"

Now *this* was a story that people would read! We began collecting stories by listening to the men talk over their card games or dominos, or listening to women talking about any and everybody in the neighborhood while they hung out their laundry or gossiped in their kitchens over coffee as they sat in front of open windows. We heard about the neighbor down the street who was seen with another woman in the back row of the Ritz Theater. It was all just gossip, but boy was it interesting. Before school began that next year the paper was shut down, and rightly so. We were obviously headed for big trouble!

Third grade was filled with my studies, and during the summer I was able to take dancing lessons at the Kellom Community Center with my friends.

I was now ending the third grade. We were now living in a house at 2023 Ohio Street. This meant changing to a new school—Lake School—in the fall, which I resisted. During this time my mother was taking me with her to political meetings in the community. She was inspired by Martin Luther King Jr.'s visit to Salem Baptist Church in Omaha. She was concerned with what she called the poor education that black children were receiving in Omaha public schools. She didn't think that it would do any harm to sit in a chair quietly and listen to the speakers.

By the fourth grade I was comfortable in my new home. It was the first time that I had lived in a single-family home, and that meant that we didn't have people living on each side of us any longer. I missed listening to my neighbors through the walls, arguing, laughing, and fighting. And upstairs—well, upstairs at night on one side of us I would hear other sounds that I couldn't recognize. Sometimes they were faint and then they became louder. Anyway, when you're living in a house, especially if you're renting, things seem very different to you. The old house was beautiful with its wide, wooden porch. It had a large entry, and the stairs had a long banister made of wood that curved gracefully from top to bottom. It made a smooth ride when no one was looking. It was a shotgun-style house, and when the pocket doors at either end were open you could see from front to back, from the living room to the kitchen and from there straight out the back door to the yard.

Our fenced-in yard wasn't large. There were several large oak trees and plenty of tall bushes growing in along the fence. Next to the back gate was a large, white, two-car garage. Nothing was ever in it but trash and old tools along with a spray of leaves, and in the winter mounds of snow whenever the door was left ajar. Across the fence was the alley that the garbage man traveled up and down once a week. A large lamp stood on the other side of the alley in the back of Myers Funeral Home. On Saturdays several streets along with the alley would be temporally blocked off so funeral services could take place without disruption.

It didn't take long for me to make friends in the neighborhood. I was doing just about everything—playing stickball in the streets, cutting hair ribbons to use during tag races, playing jacks, and practicing on and off whenever time allowed for the Show Wagon. Since my sisters had married and moved, I now had a room to myself. Kids from my old neighborhood would visit whenever they could, but for the most part I wouldn't see them because of little or no transportation.

As it got closer to the start of the new school year my parents were still trying to convince me to attend Lake instead of Kellom. I began to understand why they wanted me to make the change: it would save them money, time, and worry if I went to Lake School. At the last minute I changed my mind, and they enrolled me in Lake. During the first week of school a lot of things happened: enrollment cards had to be signed; there was meet-the-teacher night; and on the first day, walk-to-school-with-a-parent morning. All of these things were familiar to me, even the first semiannual duck-and-cover drill, followed by a fire drill—but there was one thing different about this drill. Before we left the classroom our teacher reviewed what would happen during the fire drill. Well, before I knew what was happening the bell rang. We all lined up at the door, row by row, and then entered the halls along with the rest of the classes. Walking down the hall, I thought that this school was much older and the halls much darker than at Kellom. The windows were higher and narrower than Kellom's, and for most of us it was hard to see out of them. We had just come out from under our desks, lowering our arms from over our bent, safely guarded heads. Now two bells sounded, ending the duck-and-cover drill, and the fire drill began.

Our class moved swiftly, following the class in front of us as we went upstairs and then turned down a long, narrow hallway. We were instructed and shown what we would be doing in each and every classroom the day before. At the beginning of the week several students had talked about how anxious and excited they were to participate in the fire drill. I heard the firemen talking to the principal in the hallway. After we had reached the end of the hallway, each of us was instructed to step forward, put our hands straight up over our heads, sit down on our bottoms, and scoot forward. It was almost my turn, and I started sweating. My new friend Emily was in front of me now, and then without saying a word she was no longer there. It was as if she had simply disappeared—and, oh well, she did. Now it was my turn. I sat down with my arms up over my head while the teacher caringly demonstrated what to do. I closed my eyes and down I went. It should have been fun, but it wasn't. I was scared to death. I had just sent my body down an old escape chute used to evacuate students and staff during a fire. Only I don't recall any teachers or staff going down the chute with us. I felt my body knock against the sides of the large, dark tube. We were provided a pillow for our heads and a padded blanket under the rest of our body. The large tube was made of galvanized steel, and it extended from the upper floor to the ground outside of the building. It was set at an angle so people could slide through it with little difficulty. It was called a pipe fire escape and was used to speed the emptying of large buildings. It could be converted to reach any floor so people could be whisked to safety. The experience left me utterly speechless—and that was rare.

Over the weekend I pleaded with my parents to return to my old school, where we just walked outside in a single file at the sound of the fire alarm. It wasn't exciting, but I sure preferred it to the drill at Lake School. I should have tried to enjoy myself, because it certainly was the last time that I would ever go down anything like it. The slide on the playground was the only experience that even came close.

All of my friends were glad to see me back at Kellom, and I was certainly glad to be back. There was one thing though; I wish I could have traded the mean fourth-grade teacher that I had at Kellom with the nice one I left behind at Lake School. But there's always something that we're not happy with. My fourth-grade teacher was not only mean to her class—she was mean to her own son, who attended Kellom but was in another classroom. She just seemed to pick on him. He didn't seem to be able to do anything right or good enough to please her, and that was sad to me. Picking on him didn't seem to make her any happier. Nothing made her happy. She even spanked some kids, and frightened one so much that he even wet on himself in the hallway. I heard that his parents came up to the school and pulled him out. It wasn't long after that when my teacher left. I guess you can tell that it wasn't one of my best years.

By fifth grade I was becoming seriously interested in music. I secretly enjoyed singing opera and studying ballet—I never forgot the egging that I received when I participated in the Show Wagon. Despite the assurances from my parents that it would never happen again, I made it my business to refrain from showing off my talents in the classical arts in certain public venues again.

I was a proud aunt now and fervently tried to persuade my sisters and brothers to let me babysit for money. I wanted to buy some new clothes and new shoes for the upcoming school year.

Sixth grade was fun. I felt important, and so did the rest of the sixth graders. Even though I thought I knew everything I really didn't, and that fact became obvious when I thought I could handle babysitting two of my sister's kids at the same time. I quickly learned that my mother, who had told me not to do it, knew what she was talking about. Both my niece and nephew cried nonstop after their parents left for the show, and they didn't stop crying until they returned. I was taught a good lesson and decided that I would avoid motherhood at all costs. Even so, I continued babysitting for anybody brave enough to entrust their children to me. I used the money for clothes, shoes, and music and dance lessons. My parents knew I loved the arts. My dad said that all my life I was dramatic, so I should at least make money at it.

As the end of elementary school was approaching my father and mother were given notice that the house we were living in was being sold. We were all sad about it. I was especially sad. Where would we go? In my mind I could only imagine us going back to the projects. My dad only worked when they called him in; you might say that he worked part-time, and that wasn't good enough to move into another house. I would catch my mom sitting at the kitchen table with unpeeled potatoes in front of her, staring off aimlessly out of the window. I could feel her sadness so I would go over to her, sit beside her, and put my head against her arm, leaning securely in the crevice. She wouldn't say anything to me. She was always so quiet, keeping most of her thoughts to herself, especially about my dad, how we lived, money and the lack thereof, and the pain that never seem to entirely go away. As quickly as it began it would end. She would slowly get up, straighten out her clothes, and center the line on the back of her loose stockings. I would watch her with respect as she moved the loose hair out of her face and straightened out her glasses so she could keenly see through her bifocals.

Every weekend after dad's announcement we would pack, starting with the things that we hardly ever used. Then, as the moving date got closer, the whole family came over to help pack the items that we used but could do without. Moving day came too soon that summer. I wasn't ready to say goodbye to my friends and neighbors.

I especially hated to leave my mother's cousin Anna and her husband, Cousin Russell, and the rest of the Cook family. They owned a business, one of the first of its kind: a tamale stand and a small store. My mom was always so proud of them. It was located right in front of their house. I always thought that they were rich. Joe was my favorite cousin out of all of the people in that family. He was the one who told me who to make friends with and who the bullies were in the neighborhood. He even told me who the adults were who liked to mess with kids and said that I should feel sorry for them and pray for them, but more importantly stay away from them. When it came time to leave I wasn't ready to say goodbye to the people that I would be leaving behind on Ohio Street, and so I didn't.

It was the end of my sixth-grade year, and I was being promoted to the seventh grade. I was too old to slide down the banister. I stood at the top of the stairs, ready to walk down, not run like I usually did. I looked around at the place that I lived in, taking it all in, in a more mature way—and why not? I was going to enter junior high school soon. I can't explain what happened next. I turned around, lifted my leg up and over the banister, took a deep breath, and while holding on I slid down the smooth, dark wood with a big smile on my face. My dad met me at the end of the stairs along with my mom. I thought he would be mad, but with a grin that managed to show itself on the other side of his large, smelly cigar he made the strangest remark. "Well, Juanita, I think we can call this Cathy's rite of passage."

I was quickly approaching my teens, a milestone in my life. We were leaving our home and my parents were checking our house for what would be the last time, making sure that we didn't leave anything behind. My mom and I left a portion of our hearts behind. We loved the house at 2023 Ohio Street. Funny, although both our home on Ohio Street and the one on Seward were in North Omaha, they were worlds apart. Before the last lights were turned off I ran up the stairs and slid down the banister one more time, and then I began to cry. Why I did that I really can't say. I suppose in our hearts, a part of us tries to stay a kid forever.

Home.

Kellom School.

My home after elementary school.

Mount Moriah Baptist Church.

Convent on Hamilton Street.

The Christmas parade.

A community gathering.

10

Where Should We Play?

It was a bright and beautiful spring day. The kind of day that means you have to be outside, especially if you're a kid. The girls were all playing jump rope. The boys were tossing a ball around. A car whizzed by Thirty-First and Seward. The kids jumped back just in time. The driver yelled from his window—"The streets are no place for kids to play!" We agree, sir. Too bad City Hall doesn't.

—Undercurrents of News

The Hamilton-Lake Community Council (H-LCC) had its origins in May of 1966, when I was finishing my junior year of high school. Residents like me living in the area from Hamilton to Lake and Thirtieth to Thirty-Fifth Streets saw the need for some type of economic and social stability in our sociologically changing neighborhood. We were faced with growing poverty, substandard housing, inadequate recreational facilities, and discrimination. We requested aid in organizing our community into a structure powerful enough to begin meeting and solving our problems.

As a result, Father R. Patrick McCaslin, assistant at St. Cecilia's Cathedral Parish, and seven young women, Lois Dargan, Connie

Ellenberger, Kathy Garrigan, Kathy Jensen, Mary Ellen Kauth, Barbara McDonald, and Rita Sherman, volunteered their energies and abilities to help begin this important work. With their neighbors, they worked in laying the basis for the H-LCC.

My parents, my sister Rose Mary, and I participated in many community meetings that summer. They gave us an opportunity to express our ideas, frustrations, and hopes for the neighborhood. I assisted others in establishing recreation for the children in the community. We held a play day in June, and later in the summer many children were sent to the Christ Child Camp or the day camp sponsored by Greater Omaha Community Action (GOCA), a grassroots organization developed by the community to serve and meet the needs of the people. The Hamilton-Lake residents were finally given a chance to make known to the city our need for adequate recreational facilities. We were placed on the agenda of the city's Blue Ribbon Committee. I was chosen along with my mom, Mr. Henry Collins, and Mr. James Bruner to speak for the H-LCC. We presented specific information and requests concerning the development of various lots in the area. In attendance were thirty-five supporting members of our council.

After the meeting we held a street party to raise money for our expenses. We then began to hold various activities, asking for the participation of the entire community. In September we leased a building on Thirty-Third and Franklin from Mr. Jake Lagman of Phoenix, Arizona. With the help of neighborhood people and professional volunteers, the building was renovated and converted into the Hamilton-Lake Community Center. We held meetings to organize and develop tactics to encourage our communities to register to vote. I began to solicit the aid of high-school students from Tech and Central and college students from Creighton, Duchesne, and St. John's Seminary, and they began working with our membership. We canvassed the areas in and outside of our community to encourage black residents to register and vote.

On December 10, 1966, the community center's grand opening was held. Now we were on our way.

We had a number of accomplishments. The Hamilton-Lake Community Center leased a facility in September 1966. The following year, on February 14, 1967, we opened a Head-Start preschool program. Seventeen children attended Monday–Thursday for the purpose of preparing them for school. All of the funding to continue the program was approved by GOCA in July 1967. GOCA also approved a recreation plan utilizing vacant lots;

the plan was drawn up to develop three vacant lots into basketball courts, playgrounds for tots, and softball fields, and the City Parks and Recreation Department obtained several leases for all of the lots. Following the approval for play areas, plans for a summer youth recreation program were submitted to United Community Services for financing. These requests for funding were also approved. During this time we also pushed for a local program to be funded by GOCA. It was named the Sunshine School of the Arts. It took a while, but this program also received funding. The local television station, WOW-TV, followed our progress and failures in documentary films made by Tom Murray.

We protested inappropriate and degrading political signs that were placed in our community. A Wallace for President sign was successfully removed from our community through the efforts and protests of the H-LCC. We held parades, and lots of them. I made and sponsored the winning float, donating my award money back to the community. One of the best things that we did was to develop and publish a local newspaper called *Undercurrents of News*. It was published every two weeks and gave community members an opportunity to read local news and also a chance to contribute to the news; I finally had an opportunity to be apart of a legitimate newspaper. In the paper we announced our support for Mothers for Adequate Welfare.

We were united in support of Nebraska Legislative Bill 563, to increase Aid to Dependent Children grants, making the community center available to these mothers for their meetings. Community members used the facility to give parties for children as well as adults. We formed two Girls' Club troops for fourth-, fifth-, and sixth-grade students, totaling more than thirty-five members who met weekly.

We also held Christmas parties. We wanted to make sure that no family went without toys, food, and a tree during Christmas. Because of my family's personal and financial struggles at Christmastime, this effort became a special project of mine.

My mother wrote an article in *Undercurrents of News* that summed up all of the reasons for our push to make things happen in our community.

> *And so a white flag went up and a sign came down. I like to think reasoning and persuasion caused Mr. Murphy to draw up the white flag and pull down the sign—that it was*

not rocks, bottles, or threats. I like to think that this is the American dream.

The civilized way should be where men are able to compromise and persuade, where men learn to have a deep feeling of an obligation to their fellow man and neighbors.

I believe that it is sometimes possible to find sane answers without men giving up sane principles, by using sane tactics, without violence. I believe that the strife and conflicts now going on in the world will never be eliminated by violence but that men will eventually have to find their way to the peace tables to solve their differences. I realize the existence of terrible pressures and abuses put on certain minorities—and that there are pressures and discriminatory practices being inflicted upon these minorities, that these discriminatory practices and civil rights denials have gone past their endurance.

I realize that there are many people that would like to strike back with rocks and bottles. But this is not the democratic way as I see it. This only aggravates the situation and throws us back into barbaric chaos. I believe that the problems will eventually be solved, not in the streets, but by education and integrated groups dedicated to community action such as the Hamilton-Lake Community Council, and by certain pressure tactics such as our ability to use the polls and choose leaders that have a keen sense of dedication and fair mindedness—men of good will, character, and integrity, leaders of both races that are able to communicate with the masses—men that take pride in their responsibility to God and man to uphold the constitution: courageous men that are unafraid to demand and enforce the rights of all men, loyal men who have love and undying devotion to America so that they will speak out and so challenge the very foundation and real meaning of our constitution and democratic society.

—Mrs. Juanita Pope

A musical performance.

11

Our Sixties Facebook: Student Lockers

By the 1960s many things were happening, and I can't truthfully say that I was tuned in to any of it. I was aware that John F. Kennedy had won the presidency and was sworn in on January 20, 1961. I also knew that many people in Omaha weren't very happy about that. There were those who expected Richard Nixon to win. My mom and dad were happy—extremely happy—that Nixon didn't win the presidency. I even knew about President Kennedy. This forty-three-year-old man was the youngest man to ever serve as a president in the White House. He was always described by my sisters as the intelligent, good-looking president with all the beautiful hair and—let's not leave out—rich. He created the Peace Corps in 1961 and everyone wanted to join, even the blacks in my neighborhood. He worked hard along with his staff and others to negotiate the Nuclear Test Ban Treaty, and everyone around the country was glad of that.

By the end of 1961 I was moving on from grammar school, and my brothers and sisters were also moving on. They were marrying and looking for their own places to live. I was sad; for some reason I felt deserted, and I felt that my parents did too although they tried hard not to show it. Even though I felt left behind I had a lot to look forward to: junior high.

My first few months of junior high school went along quite smoothly.

I found my classes with the help of staff and teachers. Even the restrooms were no problem. At the start of the year I walked to school and home from school each day, but by November, as fall turned to winter, I had difficulty making the walk. My legs were always hurting me, but I never complained about it. I had done enough of that in elementary school.

During junior high I was trading in *The Story Hour, It's Howdy Dowdy Time, The Lone Ranger, My Friend Flicka,* and *The Roy Rogers and Dale Evans Show* for *The Ed Sullivan Show,* where I first saw Leslie Uggams, the Beatles, and the Rolling Stones. Then there was *Ben Casey* and *Dr. Kildare* and *The Dick Clark Show.* I can also remember *Mod Squad* and *The Monkees.*

Most of my friends were the same kids that I knew during elementary school, although several of them went to other schools. We moved two times before I landed in junior high school. The junior high school was large, but it appeared to be even larger because it was attached to the high school. Whenever we were on an outing and drove by the school I felt a sense of pride.

I was in the eighth grade when I took it upon myself to volunteer across the street in group homes that were responsible for housing special-education students. There were classrooms designed to teach them about day-to-day living: how to cook, clean, shop, handle money, and budget that money to last until the next check. Some kids worked hard to receive points for service learning by helping out in the homes across the street. It could be referred to as a kind of work study. I just wanted to help out by volunteering along with several of my friends. Besides, I grew up with some of these kids and they were just like me except it took them more time to do what came a bit easier for me.

Most kids shied away from the small, brown-framed, brick houses across the street, but not me. I enjoyed volunteering. In the evenings I would walk home alone in the twilight. Most kids left right after school, but I was determined to help the special students as much as I could even though they seemingly didn't want the help. They were proud; they always said that they could do everything on their own. I had the idea that the homes were a part of the Boys Town facilities, but in retrospect I was probably wrong. I never stayed as long as I wanted to. I would work hard and fast to make sure that they learned as much as they could as fast as they could.

Most of the time I ate my lunch at school, but when I didn't I went home and tried to eat quietly with my mom. We would have soup and sandwiches along with a fruit cup. Sometimes I didn't feel like going home for lunch, because my mom was usually babysitting for my older brothers and sister's kids. By now we were living in a wood-framed house on Thirty-First Street.

When I arrived at school one morning everyone was excited and huddled in small groups in the hall in front of the lockers. They were discussing the information posted on a large sign taped to the wall. This week there would be auditions for *South Pacific*. I tried jumping up to look over the heads of several students closer to the sign. They were looking for a lot of singers as well as leads. "Cathy, do you think you're going to try out?" asked one of the students. The question came from behind me. There were many talented students in my junior high school, but there were only a small number of parts set aside for us. Most of the parts were for the high-school students, those in grades nine through twelve.

"I don't know if I will try out," I said to the hidden voice behind me. "Anyway, do you think I have a chance?"

Before anyone could answer me, the second bell rang. Now I was late to my math class, and I still had to go to the bathroom. I finally arrived at my classroom, only to find that the wooden door was shut. This was customary. The teachers always shut the door after the second bell. Over the weekend my friends purchased the music for *South Pacific*. We knew that all of us couldn't get a part. But we were hopeful that one of us would. The school music teacher and his accompanist made sure we all knew the songs by heart. The whole thing was exciting, and scary at the same time. I worked hard to get the young girl's part in the musical, but someone else got the role. Teresa was her name; she was small, cute, and smart. After I got over it, I gladly accepted a part in the chorus, and when I got an opportunity to hear her during the practices I realized that she was perfect for the part. She did a great job. I was in the musical, along with at least thirty other students. At the end of opening night my family met me backstage and told me what a super job I did. Several people in the audience said they could hear my voice and it sounded beautiful.

The summer of 1963 arrived before I knew it. I was leaving behind junior high and entering the strange world of high school. My mom was still juggling babysitting and supporting all of my activities in and out of school. Most of my extra money came from babysitting and helping older people in the neighborhood with their housework. I spent a lot of my time at choir rehearsal learning solos for Sunday's service.

But no matter what I was doing I always made time to help my mother with the chores and babysitting my nieces and nephews. My mom loved her grandbabies and taught them throughout the day how to play games and read. Most of the time when I came downstairs in the morning they would already be in the house, sitting at the table eating breakfast. A lot of them would bring a book with them and ask my mom to read to them or tell them a story. A book in their hands was invariably her cue to stop whatever she was doing, even if it meant turning off the stove. It didn't matter what the book was about—they would all pay close attention and listen. Sometimes she would even make up stories. Ahhh! Those were the best kind. Her vocal inflection and the way she took on the personalities of her characters seemed to carry you off into her space and another place. I can remember all of the kids, from the oldest to the youngest, focusing intently on my mother's words. Karen, Johnny, Melody, Derek, Wally, Rosalind, Brenda, Francine, and Geoffrey all experienced her ability to tell stories. I would sit back and pretend not to listen, but I did. Her other grandkids, Stephen—who was born three months before she passed—and Reagan and Ryan—who were born after she passed—never had an opportunity to enjoy her gift of storytelling.

It didn't matter how many of my mother's grandkids were dropped off for her to watch throughout the years; she never complained. During the day while I was at school Mom always did her chores, ironing, mopping the floors down on her knees, and dusting all of her knickknacks and furniture. All the while she'd listen to the radio or watch the TV. Like most women, she listened to or watched the soaps during the day. *Search for Tomorrow* and *The Guiding Light* were among her favorites. By the time I would walk through the door she'd either be happy, sad, frustrated, or mad. With a serious expression on her face and in her quiet tone she would tell me about what was going on in the world of the soaps. "Why, do you know Susan is expecting another baby and she hasn't even told her husband yet? He is going to be awfully mad. He just got laid off his job. Anyway, this is going to be extremely hard on him, especially with his mother in the hospital. Cathy, what do you think? Do you think that he'll get his job back, or possibly his mother will miraculously get well from her undiagnosed illness? Iola believes that his mother is going to die. I pray she won't. Well, Cathy, what do you think?" I always tried to respond as if I really cared, all the while thinking about such things as my chances of getting a good part in the next school play.

"Momma," I'd say, "don't worry about everything and everybody. You know how Daddy feels about that. Besides, they're not any of our relatives. It's just *As the World Turns,* a serial on television." She'd reluctantly go back to ironing, and we'd both laugh out loud.

My mother always found things to laugh and joke about. Her humor was not always embraced by everyone in her small circle, but it was infectious. I believe if there was one thing that I got from my mother, it was her seemingly strange sense of humor. But her humor was only one side of her. She often appeared out of nowhere at demonstrations. She took the time to formally sit in and stand in whenever and wherever she found injustice. What amazed me is she would usually be home in time to cook our supper.

We didn't have a formal graduation from junior high school. That summer I spent my time babysitting for my siblings and their friends, working odd jobs, having fun with my friends, and along with my mom carrying protest signs throughout the streets of Omaha as well as attending meetings at City Hall and the Omaha Public School District.

One day when I was in the hallway preparing to leave the house I heard a noise outside. I stood on my tiptoes to peek out of the small window in the door and see if anyone was on the porch; maybe the milkman or the bread man was early. But it wasn't the milk or bread man. It was a small group of boys—two, to be exact—and one girl. They were leaving a small bottle of something that looked like milk or cream on the steps. I guess they decided not to come all the way up to the porch to leave it . There was a paper with it attached to the neck of the bottle with a rubber band. I couldn't understand what they were saying to each other, but I did notice that they were laughing—and laughing loudly. For some reason I was glad my parent's room and the kitchen was to the back of the house so they couldn't see or hear them. I could hear them as they ran away in opposite directions when they heard the door open. They are very lucky that it wasn't my dad who opened that door. When they left I hurried outside, picked up the bottle of cream and removed the paper to read it. "Cathy, this is for you from your friends so you can put some meat on your bones, especially your skinny legs. You look like a baby and dress like one."

During the eighth grade I had stopped wearing my special shoes too soon, and while dancing in a competition, my partner accidently dropped me. The arches on both of my feet were severely injured and fell. So first my orthopedic doctor put both of my legs in casts up to midthigh. The doctors were concerned about stabilizing my legs, because the bones in my legs were already weak.

I was out of commission for several weeks. When I went back to some of my activities I was on crutches. It wasn't long before the casts were removed and arch supports made of stainless steel were made for me and fitted inside of special black orthopedic shoes that I had to wear. I could have died. I wanted to put my whole body in one of those manholes that line the streets. Why couldn't my parents send me away to the South? I'd heard that black girls from the North who had issues went to the South. I told them that I could go to Aunt Janie's house in Oklahoma. But my dad didn't pay any attention to me and my mom, although sympathetic, told me that I couldn't run from problems and if I did I'd probably be running the rest of my life and run smack dab into myself. It was bad enough that I always had to rub smelly liniment on both of my legs. When I decided to stop feeling sorry for myself I followed the directions of the physical therapist so I could wear shoes like all the other girls. I didn't like being different.

The kids accomplished what they wanted to. I cried so hard that I almost dropped the bottle of cream. I was so upset that I didn't leave the house that day or the entire weekend. Of course my mother kept telling me that they knew nothing of me or my medical challenges. "Catherine Grace," she said, with a serious look on her face, "you should feel sorry for them. They are far more challenged than you are."

"They are?" I questioned.

"Why yes, they are, they can't even write or spell, and you can do both—and quite well, I might add."

I had the entire weekend to think about what she said. For the most part I had a hard time feeling sorry for them, because it was me that was hurting. But when Monday rolled around, as hard as it was I stepped outside beyond the security of my four walls at home and faced the world.

In late August, on August 28, 1963, I sat in the living room along with my parents and watched thousands of people on our television set as they listened to Martin Luther King Jr. give his soon to become famous "I Have a Dream" speech on the steps of the Lincoln Memorial in Washington, DC.

On November 22, 1963, someone brought a note to my classroom and gave it to my teacher. I remember my teacher's face as if it were yesterday. All of the blood and life seemed to drain from it. She walked to her chair and slumped down in it. I had never seen her lose her composure before. She didn't say a word; she just kept looking at the paper in front of her.

Finally the door opened again. It was our vice principal. "Well, did you tell them?" were his soft, muffled words. She only shook her head, still saying nothing.

The vice principal walked in front of my teacher's desk and said, "Students, the president, President Kennedy, has been shot in Dallas, Texas. We don't know his condition yet. Please gather your books and personal belongings together. When you hear the bells leave quietly and go straight home."

When I got home most of my family was there, huddled around the television and listening to the news as it streamed across every station. Later that evening President Kennedy passed away. His body was placed on Air Force One. Lyndon Baines Johnson, with Jacquelyn Kennedy by his side, took the oath of office and became our thirty-sixth president. I was overwhelmed. That night when I went to bed I couldn't sleep. All I could do was cry my eyes out. My family watched the funeral on the television. While we were watching, in the background I heard my dad sigh a long sigh. For months our flags flew at half mast. For months people walked around with looks of hopelessness on their faces. There were so many theories surrounding his death; most of us never knew what to believe.

Now about that—well, enough said.

I was supposed to go to Central High School, and I did for a few days. No one really knew that I ever attended Central. I heard that most of the kids there were white and Jewish. In the past my oldest sister Rose Mary had attended Central, and now many of my friends would be going there.

When I walked up the stairs I felt so proud. I thought how lucky I was to be attending such a prestigious school. Many of the kids who graduated from there went on to college.

Soon after I enrolled there were play auditions, and of course I was one of the first to sign up for a part. When I heard over a loudspeaker that the drama department was seeking me out—well, I was a little puffed up. Entering the auditorium I immediately went over to the casting table to find out what role that they were considering me for. One of the young women handed me a script and told me to look on the casting list and find my name. There it was, Cathy Pope. Later that day I couldn't remember my name in the play, nor could I remember the name of the play; what I do remember was I was to play a maid. Not an important maid, but a maid without lines. I immediately and without regard to protocol exited the very same door that I entered, caught a bus and walked the rest of the way in a beeline to Technical High School.

Technical High School was a fun place to be, and I was present all the way. Tech was a combination of a junior and senior high school—you might as well say two schools in one. It was also one of the largest. I always appreciated old buildings, and this building was one of the oldest. Located at 3215 Cuming Street, the school opened in 1923. I heard that it was the largest high school in Omaha, and even in the state of Nebraska. In the twenties the school even had a radio station, KFOX. Along with my classmates I used the two gyms and an indoor swimming pool. If we stayed through high school we were required to pass a swimming test that included diving from one of the tall diving boards. We had wood and metal shops and scientific laboratories as well as a greenhouse. We even had an auto shop, where I learned to change tires and even change the oil in a car. Some of my best times were learning to drive in Mr. Roy's driving class on Saturdays.

What happened in the fall of 1964 was the fact that I was a fourteen-year-old entering Technical High School through the front of the building on Burt Street. That made me formally a new high-school student. I was now in the ninth grade. I think I was supposed to feel different. I really didn't feel any different from any other time that I changed grades, but different it was.

In high school we still couldn't wear whatever we wanted to. Some of the deans checked our hemlines to make sure that they weren't too far above our knees, and as the years went on the hemline could be a little higher. In several of the Catholic schools, like Duchesne Academy, to test things out you would have to kneel down, and your skirt better touch the ground. If not the nuns would send you home. In a lot of our local schools you couldn't wear pants, and definitely no jeans, and absolutely no shorts.

It was a very conservative time in dress and also in the attitude of the adults around us. On most Fridays we would show our school spirit by wearing school colors. On PE days we would always bring our gym clothes and change at school. The boys in our school had to wear a shirt and not a tee shirt, except under their shirt, and they always had to wear a belt with their pants.

I always looked forward to the weekends, when I could wear bell-bottoms or pedal pushers. When my brothers and sisters and I went to the movies we would usually dress up, day or night. Of course all of us wore our best attire to church and special events. Whenever we shopped at Brandeis or Kilpatrick's we would dress up.

The day came when I was allowed to go shopping with my friends instead of my mom. When I went to Brandeis department store to buy my shoes I had to buy them in a bigger size, and even my bra size had increased a little. I was glad about that. I was allowed to buy two new outfits. Picking them out on my own made me feel powerful.

What was even more important was the fact that I didn't have to wear braids or a ponytail to school anymore if I didn't want to. Me, I didn't want to. And I could finally get my hair pressed, which means smoothed or straightened on a regular basis, and not in my mother's kitchen or in someone else's kitchen in front of their stove. The harsh combing, tugging, and pulling, looking up with a twisted face exhibiting horrific pain was finally over. Why? Because I could now go to the beauty school on Twenty-Fourth Street at least every other month, whenever we had the money. For the most part my mother still felt that washing and braiding your hair without any type of process was the best thing for anyone, but on the eve of my ninth-grade year I was allowed to go to the beauty shop and get my hair done.

I really enjoyed listening to all of the gossip at the beauty shop—mostly silly stuff that was passed on from person to person. In the end the information was usually totally inaccurate and deceiving. As you can imagine, sometimes the ladies that entertained me the most were the ones with the worldly experience. The local "working girls," formally called prostitutes, had to get their hair done; it was at least as important to them as it was to the church ladies. Their business required them to look good, and for the most part they usually did. Most of the time, these women of the night came into the shop with very interesting tales. "They have to get their hair done, too," I would proclaim in a hurry when the church ladies looked disgusted. Some of the church ladies just appeared to me to be jealous, because—well, they did look pretty damn good. They hardly ever whispered anything while seated in their hairdresser's chair, so it wasn't necessary for me to act like I didn't hear anything that they said.

"Girl, I need to look extra good tonight. I have a new friend, and he likes long dark curly hair—and make my bands extra tight, because you know how much I sweat on my forehead girl when I get down with someone." I always looked at the beautician's face if I was in a position to do so, and this time was no different.

"Hey, quiet down—can't you see all the kids in here?" she said emphatically, embarrassment showing all over her face.

Me, I just enjoyed watching the whole thing.

"Now keep still. You know your edges and kitchen are the hardest to press, and I don't want to burn you like the last time." I heard what I perceived to be threats, loud and clear. I continued to duck down, wrinkling my neck while making squelching sounds as I suppressed my giggles.

When I first went to the beauty shop, the individuals who worked on my hair were students, but they were the cheapest and I needed to keep that in mind. A burn every now and then on the back of my neck was well worth it. The fact that they were still learning had to remain at the forefront of my mind, so I was usually alert and vigilant. There were those times when I sat in the chair dodging and weaving like my Uncle Leonard preparing for a fight. I'm sure I made faces that could stop a clock.

This day was different! I wasn't in a student's chair any longer. I was in a licensed beautician's chair getting my hair done!

"Okay, how do you want your do? Does your mother still want you in braids, or can you have one big ponytail in the back?" I couldn't have been more embarrassed if she had said that she was glad to see me finally in some stylish shoes. There were a lot of girls in Little Fields shop that day getting their hair done, and I didn't appreciate my beautician speaking so loud. I'm sure she didn't do it to make me feel bad—but I did. The other girls in the shop turned, and I'm sure at that point they recognized me. With the young eyes in the room focused on me, I picked up an *Ebony* magazine on a small table to the side of my beautician's work station. Quickly I opened up the magazine, held it up in Beverly's face, and declared, "I want my hair done like this."

I had held up the July 1962 issue of *Ebony* with Diahann Carroll on the cover. The shop always kept issues of *Ebony*, a magazine that featured African Americans. She had a pageboy hair style without bangs, a sophisticated look among African American women. In the picture she was wearing a short-sleeved pink top with a long opening in front of her wraparound skirt. Underneath the skirt were pedal pushers, just like the ones that I preferred to wear. "See?"

My hairdresser left my side to meet another client at the door.

"Well, can you look?" I was so excited that day that I forgot my manners. "Look, please," I said changing to a more insistent tone. "Can you do it, can you make my hair look like hers?" I pleaded.

"Well, I think I can, but it might not look exactly like Ms. Carroll's. Besides, you have long hair, and hers is a lot shorter. But I'll make it as close to hers as I can get it. If I could cut your hair . . ." she said thoughtfully. "Oh well, your mom would hardly agree to that."

The younger girls in the shop laughed. The ones that knew me always felt that I was a momma's girl—not allowed to grow up. Even I felt that my parents held on too tight.

The beautician shook out the plastic coverup and placed it over my clothing, securing the top firmly around my neck. "Okay, head for the washbowl."

The shop was becoming crowded. It was Saturday, and the older women were getting ready for church. Their hats were destined to be set on top of the most beautiful hairstyles. I never understood the importance of getting your hair professionally done when you were going to put a hat on top of your head covering it up.

On this particular day, the week before school, the other half of the shop was filled with students representing my school and the schools from the surrounding areas. In my community it was understood that girls would get their hair done before school started. If you wanted to look for boys, especially the fine ones, you could find them at the local barbershops, especially the shops located on Twenty-Fourth Street.

When my beautician finished with me at the washbowl she conditioned my hair with a product that smelled like lilacs. "Your hair feels good; very little dandruff." She pulled the lever on the side of the chair and encouraged me to hold still while she slowly rinsed out my hair and then combed my hair out so it wouldn't tangle. Another worker was standing anxiously in front of my feet giving my beautician a sign to hurry up, she wanted the shampoo chair. My hair was quickly patted dry, and I was pushed from the chair. I was directed to the room with the large pink hoods. The hair dryers looked like colorful Sputniks. Under the hood I could see very little, and the motor was so loud that I could hear even less. The juicy conversations whirled around me, giving me little room for speculation. I could see the shoes passing in front of me that were worn mostly by working women.

I got hotter and hotter while sitting under that contraption. The hairdresser checked my hair several times to see if I was "done" as she called it, ready to go back to the styling chair. Next thing I knew I was awakened from a deep sleep. "Cathy! Cathy, wake up! I need to hurry up, there are a lot of people waiting." And there were. When she finished with me I looked at myself in the mirror at her work station. Then I looked at the back of my head in a handheld mirror that she held above my head. "Do you like it?" she asked.

"Yes, a lot," I said, and we both smiled.

"I think the boys are going to really like what they see."

I looked down, but my spirits were looking up. I paid her and asked her if it was the correct amount. She said yes. I tipped her and politely said goodbye. I waited close to the door and entertained myself with several new and out-of-date magazines while I waited for my dad to pick me up. Soon my dad pulled up in front of the shop. I stepped outside and got into his old, white Cadillac.

"You look great," he said as I climbed into the front seat. I was pleased with his observation, but I kept wondering what the kids at the school would think.

"Cathy," my dad said casually, "did you mom know that you were going to change your hair?"

The eighth grade was now behind me. It was 1964, and I was beginning the ninth grade. I was looking forward to it with great anticipation. There was another 1964 where everything was blowing up across the country, and Omaha was no exception. I wasn't looking forward to that.

There were so many things happening around me and even to me. My mother was involved in several civil-rights organizations, especially the 4CL. She was determined with all of her being to work for change in our city and schools, and I was willing to do whatever I could as a young person to help. I became involved in an organization called BANTU, the Black Association for Nationalism through Unity. Black students in the North Omaha high schools were determined to support the community. All of us wanted to see change. And why not? There was as much at stake for my generation, if not more.

Technical High School.

12

Peony Park

For me, one of the most memorable occasions of civil disobedience involved my entire family along with the black community. It occurred over a series of months at a local controversial amusement park, Peony Park. This was one of the places that I always begged my parents, my brothers and sisters, and my cousins to take me. At school the white kids would always share with the other students how much fun that they had there—the picnics, concerts, and plays. They would talk about the bright lights strung throughout the park and the music, sharing their experiences while laughing. I noticed that whenever the white kids talked about the park they were happy and animated.

My parents were always reluctant to go to Peony because of all the controversy surrounding the park. There were so many restrictions that my father felt it really wasn't worth it. So most of the time we would wind up at Carter Lake, where we would park and eat our ice-cream cones and watch the planes at the airport take off and land. My mom didn't like the ideal of me playing around the lake, so most of the time I wouldn't get out of the car. For the most part that seemed to satisfy me.

Whenever anyone brought up the subject of Peony Park we were all reminded of the Amateur Athletic Union Swimming Meet held in August 1955. All of us in the family wanted to attend, along with many people in our community. Upon our arrival, we could see people waving signs, and there were shouts of "Niggers go home! This is our park!" The jeers and the yelling along with the hateful signs frightened me. I didn't understand why they hated us so much. We had come to see my cousin Leonard Hawkins— our brother, cousin, nephew, and friend—compete along with another Negro boy. They were so proud. Leonard was so eager; he had prepared for years and waited and practiced for months for this event. What was wrong? Why didn't they want him there, or want us there? The boys had registered for the meet. How they got through the registration I really don't know. But what I do know is that they were not allowed to participate—not because there was anything wrong with their paperwork, but because they were black. My cousin Leonard and the other registered black swimmer were both turned away, barred from the pool area. I realized then why my parents didn't want to take me there. The park was strictly segregated. The kids in my family and the kids in the Hawkins family always considered the park off limits. Our families shared most things at one time or another, housing, food, and celebrations. Our lives were always intertwined for better or worse.

My family always said that this affected Leonard for his entire life, and by the look of things it did. With the encouragement and insistence of the entire black community, including the churches, the *Omaha Star,* the Urban League, and the National Association for the Advancement of Colored People (NAACP), the State of Nebraska took the park to district court. The suit was titled *Nebraska v. Peony Park.* It was the final determination of the court that under Nebraska Civil Rights Law Peony Park had discriminated against the African American swimmers at the Amateur Athletic Union Swimming Meet. They were fined $50 and required to pay court costs. Additional civil suits were brought and settled out of court.

Several youth organizations and activists were instrumental in changing the color barrier restrictions through protests. However, as some would say, it was a little too late. I believe that my cousin Leonard had aspirations to eventually participate in Olympic swimming competitions. Was that dream possible? We'll never know.

Later Peony Park expanded by adding an several amusement rides, and by 1970 I was taking my nieces and nephews there. For some reason I always hesitated going through the gates; in my mind I could still hear the screaming and the name calling and feel the anger. I could very clearly see the white faces and hear the word *nigger* ringing in my ears. I could visualize the signs of the protestors and the marching and the singing of old spirituals and civil-rights songs sung by the blacks in attendance.

For many people in the African American community, both young and old, Peony Park was a place of pride in Omaha, a family gathering place that would provide good memories for them for years and years. For seventy-five years the park, located for on approximately thirty-five acres, would be a place of mixed feelings. For many it would just be an amusement park, but my cousin Leonard never got over the rejection, and I could see the damage that occurred that day in his eyes, in his attitude, and in his diminished desire to move forward in his life. I think he died that day spiritually and, years later, literally—to me they are one and the same.

High-school days.

13

Technical High School

While attending Technical High School, I met a white girl named Phyllis Moberly. She became one of my very best friends. We studied together and hung out together at each other's homes. We shared our dreams and ambitions with each other. I even shared with her my disappointment in our country.

I often told Phyllis that I enjoyed watching movies with and about people who looked like me. On one occasion while Phyllis was visiting me we watched the Miss America Pageant to the very end. The 1966 winner was Debra Bryant, from Overland Park, Kansas. My mother, who sat on the couch watching with us, said, "Cathy, you should enter that contest." Phyllis, who was sitting next to me, chimed in and said, "Yes, Cathy, you should find out how you enter and submit an application."

"Both of you need to open your eyes. Do you see anybody up there that looks anything like me—even slightly looks like me? Besides, look at them. Look how beautiful they are. I wouldn't stand a chance."

"What do you mean? You're every bit as pretty as any of those girls, and I know you're just as smart," Phyllis said enthusiastically.

"Smarter" a strong voice said out of nowhere. It was my brother John. He was always in my cheering section. I told them that they could all keep talking, but they were wasting their breath. But in the back of my mind

I kept wondering what the scholarship money would look like for the winner by the time I was eligible to run. But soon the show was over, and we both had to look forward to school. Tomorrow was going to be another school day.

Phyllis shared her dreams with me, especially about going to college. She was just as concerned about money as I was, so she was always looking for scholarships and other money to continue her education. She had many dreams, among them to visit her mother's homeland, Scotland, and take her mother there on a visit.

When it came to most outside social events we went our separate ways. Her personal friends were different from mine. We lived in different neighborhoods, but even so our parents became friends. They didn't visit each other in their homes, but they spent hours talking to each other over the telephone. Over the years Phyllis and I joined every academic organization and social club that suited us. We joined the International Friendship Club, sponsored by our favorite language teacher, Mrs. Rindone. Under her I studied French, Italian, and some German. I wanted to become an opera singer, so I had to study other languages, especially the Romance languages. Both of us became forensic debaters; we shined both as partners and as individuals. We participated in the school's dance club, pep club, and beginning and advanced choir.

My instincts had been good when I made the decision to change schools. Near the end of my freshman year I was selected to act in *The Recco,* one of two plays directed by Kenneth Roy, the head of our drama department at Tech. I was so excited I could barely contain my enthusiasm. We performed the play during variety night at the school.

One of the activities that I really never wanted to be involved in was homecoming. I thought that it was for the popular girls and guys at the school, the cheerleaders and football players. Sometimes those kids appeared to be slated to win.

Believe it or not I was considered a geek, someone who kept their nose in the books all the time. In any case, I didn't understand why students made so much of homecoming. To me the football game was far more important and thrilling than a bunch of students riding around the field on the backs of cars or on flatbeds called floats—at least until my tenth-grade year. The process never appeared to be fair. If your dad had a fancy new car with a convertible hood or knew someone with one, of course you wanted to ride on the back of it—it made you look good. But neither of those things applied to me. Nevertheless, if I was selected I would of course smile until my face cracked and vigorously wave my right hand as I rode by the crowd in the stands. I was never really interested, but when football season rolled around I found myself as excited as any student around when I was selected as a homecoming candidate along with my friend Phyllis. For some reason, whenever I participated in a school event so did my friend Phyllis. Her mother described us as two peas in a pod. We were close and becoming closer.

I had several white friends that I grew up with. By the tenth grade many of them had found their way over to Tech for a variety of reasons. Some of them had a hard time keeping up in class, others said that they were excluded from the activities, but for the most part they just wanted to go to school with their friends. There were even those who didn't have any desire to go to college—they just wanted to learn a trade and get a job when they left high school.

Now I was a candidate for Tech's homecoming coronation. I had never participated in this type of event, and I had a strong desire to win. I wanted to win. It was obvious. Several weeks before the actual coronation I had my sisters help me make large posters that displayed slogans and my motto. I suppose it ended with "Vote for me!"; not very original, but to the point. Some of my few supporters helped me hang the posters around the school.

The week before the game all the students attending the school voted. My mom told me not to worry about winning, just enjoy the ride. I didn't win, but I tried to enjoy the ride around the field—as short as it was. That evening we played Ryan High School. I didn't concern myself with winning the football game. That night just being there was enough for me.

The loss wasn't as devastating as I thought it was going to be. As a matter a fact, I didn't lose one night's sleep over it. I was just fine. What put a bright shine on everything was the fact that I was among several students named "distinguished collaborators" in the annual Columbus essay contest sponsored by the village of Palos de la Frontera in the province of Huelva, Spain, and I thought that was awesome. I was invited to Spain, but my family couldn't afford to send me.

During my junior year I began taking tests and writing essays, hoping to get enough money together to attend college. I also entered singing and dancing competitions in my church as well as in school. I was a member of Junior Achievement, a local program that encouraged students to learn business skills and create products, and the National Forensic League, all in an effort to gather together enough money to attend college. Of course I worked hard on top of that; I babysat and later worked for Sears department store in the basement.

During high school I had several boyfriends.

First there was Jimmy. I knew him from church. We both sang in the church choir. His mother led our choir and played the piano for us when it was our Sunday to sing. I think that I was his only girlfriend during high school. I don't think that I was interested in the things that he was interested in. He would always talk about going steady, getting engaged, and marrying in the future. And what would I talk about? Well, I would consistently talk about school, getting a scholarship, and completing my education. I would spend a lot of our time together trying to convince him to do the same. Jimmy said that I was always searching for something. "I suppose I am," I would tell him. "I am searching—but not for a guy, and my ultimate goal is not marriage." When I would babysit my nieces and nephews, Jimmy would come over to help me after my sister or brother left. He never pushed me to go beyond a kiss or necking. I was always aware of the children being in the house. Jimmy's mother led the choir, and for some reason I had the majority of the solos—I'd like to thing that I earned that privilege. Besides it's always a privilege to sing for the Lord; at least for me it was.

Jimmy would always come to see me and support me at my events. He was an active member of the ROTC in high school, and in our junior year he took me to the Military Ball. My mother took money from a small coffee can hidden in the kitchen so she could buy me an evening gown for the ball. At the ball, some of the ROTC students presented the flag in front of the guests and parents, while others came out with rifles and twirled them like batons. Jimmy was an officer, and all of the officers marched into the ballroom forming two separate lines, removed their swords from their sides, and lifted them into a point, touching the swords on the other side. Then the music changed, and I walked out with the other young ladies in beautiful gowns, passing under the arch created with the swords. That evening we both had a great time. It was a wonderful night.

Before graduation from high school Jimmy was drafted into the Army to serve in Vietnam. He returned home safely, only to die later of a heart attack. I heard he was shoveling snow in his front yard when his heart failed. I also learned that along with several of his family members he'd had a serious heart condition for most of his life. I often wonder how he passed the health screening and was drafted into the Army in the first place.

On several occasions my mother and sisters asked me to babysit for a family friend. I noticed that whenever her name had been brought up around the kitchen table and my brother Wallace entered the room, everyone quickly became silent. I can't say what that was about. But I do remember that they had dated in high school. But now by the time I was babysitting they were both married to other fine people. My mother wanted me to babysit for her because she felt that she needed the help. Jimmy always felt concerned whenever I told him that I had plans to babysit over there, so he would ask me if he could stop by. I always told him no, because they didn't know him and besides when they had the money they would pay me. Most of the time, I walked over to her home even though it was a long way from where I lived. In the evening my dad would take me because my mother didn't drive and my friend's husband worked odd hours. I loved my sister's friend, and I highly respected her husband. Like most people during this time they married young, as did my brothers and sisters. I came to know her because my sisters at one time or another went to school with her. She had four beautiful kids: two girls and two boys. I grew to love the whole family, especially her. She was a friend to me, even though she was a little older. She was an attractive woman. She had long, naturally curly hair. Her features were keen and she seldom wore makeup—she didn't have to. She had two sisters, and it was said by some that she was really the pretty one. But to me it was a toss-up. One evening when I went to her house I called first but there was no answer. My mother asked me to go over there to see if anything was wrong while she tried to reach her husband at work. My mother always had a strong feeling whenever she thought something was wrong. When I arrived, the front door was unlocked, so I went right in. All the lights in the house were on, and I found the house in a mess—pillows off the couch, trash partially swept on the floor, papers all over the place, and dirty dishes in the sink and throughout the house. The kids were running around, and their small dogs were running loose.

I found her asleep on the couch, sprawled out with her right leg and arm dangling over the side. "Wake up, wake up," I demanded. "How long have you been asleep? Do you realize your kids haven't eaten? And your house—well, it's a mess. What's going on around here?" But my words fell on deaf ears. "Stop running around," I told the kids. "How long has your mother been asleep?" I knew she was asleep because her chest was swiftly moving up and down through her sheer gown and her eyes were closed.

The kids didn't know what was going on, and they didn't appear to be concerned. They were very young—in kindergarten, first, second, and third grade, but they were old enough to be concerned about their mother. It was as if they were used to seeing her that way. When I realized that she wasn't going to wake up I panicked. I had the kids locate the phone and then called my mom. In turn she called the rescue squad and then her husband for assistance. I hung up and also dialed for help. While the rescue squad was on the way, the dispatcher kept me on the telephone and asked me to describe her condition. I don't think that I did a very good job because I was so nervous. The dispatcher asked me if I knew CPR, and I did. I learned CPR while participating on a special swimming team. While talking to the dispatch worker I noticed that she was sweating and clammy. Her hair was wet, straight on her face and matted to her head. Her mouth was slightly ajar, and now her eyes opened and began rolling back in her head. She didn't look good. I continued talking to the dispatcher. She never asked me to perform CPR. They asked me to look around for anything unusual in the room, and when I looked down on the floor right at my feet was a pill bottle. Several loose pills were rolling around on the floor. I asked the kids to help me, and we dragged their mother off of the couch before she fell off and hit her head. We shook her and threw water on her, and she began coming around. Not knowing what was going on she began flailing her arms, and when she hit me several times I backed off. As I moved toward her again she began to calm down.

"Don't go back to sleep," I kept saying over and over again. "Don't go back to sleep, please." I noticed that the kids were now gathered on the other side of the room. They sat without moving, like mannequins, a clear sign of fearing for the safety and well-being of their mother.

When I heard the rescue squad pulling up in front of the house, I looked out and noticed that the police were already sitting out front. Before the paramedics entered they asked me to remove the dogs from the house. They immediately took her vitals and then asked her if she felt like she could stand up by herself. Even though she answered yes, they carefully placed her on a gurney and took her outside to put her into the ambulance.

My family later learned that her husband sent her to a special hospital, and I wondered if it was the same kind of hospital that my mom had to go to from time to time. But I never asked anyone in my family about that.

We could talk about every kind of illness but the Big C—cancer—and in the black community especially, the illness that could never be spoken of: depression or mental illness. It was considered taboo, and your family would sometimes be ostracized because of it. I know. I was told by everyone that our friend just had to get away for a while. I noticed that she had to get away more often as the years went on, and I would truly miss her whenever she was gone. My mother asked me to continue to babysit even when she was gone because it would be a big help to her family, and I did. I would do anything to help them. My mother was always empathic and caring when it came to my friends' personal struggles and the struggles of others in the black community.

Occasionally I was allowed to visit my friend in the hospital. I was never told the reasons they sent her there. She sometimes asked me to come back, and I did. I never told my father that I went there. I went on the city bus. The only thing that I seemed to have trouble when I visited with was the large, steel doors closing and the sound of the keys locking the doors behind me, locking me in.

On the day my mother died it was a cold, rainy October afternoon. I became despondent and confused. After leaving the hospital I wandered around the streets of Omaha with no definite destination. My brother-in-law Alvin found me sitting at a downtown bus stop. It was raining, and I was crying. Even the rain couldn't wash away my tears. I knew that I would never be the same. Alvin was going to take me home, but why would I go there? I asked him to take me to the lady that I always agreed to babysit for, and he did. That night the first person I thought of going to was her. She took me to what she called her quiet place, her attic. There she held me as I cried my eyes out. As I moaned and sighed she held me and rocked me. She comforted me and showed me love as only a mother could. There were no words between us because it just wasn't necessary. I have never mentioned her name, because that's not necessary either.

14

Yoshi

"Lastly, I thank Cathy Pope, who has politically inspired me."
—*Yoshihisa Matsuda*

In the eleventh grade I met several new students. One of those students became a very good friend. His name was Yoshihisa Matsuda, from Kōchi, Kōchi Prefecture, Japan. He studied at Tosa High School in Japan for two years. In 1966, he came to the United States to resume his education.

He decided to attend Technical High School, even against his uncle Kazuo Takechi's urging, because the school was described as being located in North Omaha. His uncle owned a jewelry store in Omaha. Without his extended family's assistance his education in the States wouldn't have been possible. He may even have worked at their store. Somehow Yoshi, as his close friends called him, persuaded his uncle to let him attend Tech High School. Yoshi became a good friend. For some reason we just clicked. After he arrived at Tech, I would watch him as he moved through the halls and up and down the stairs. I could tell that he was quiet and extremely sure of himself. Another thing: he always minded his own business, something that was often times difficult for kids our age.

Ring, ring—pause—*ring.* At the final bell, the doors quickly opened, and we began to pour into the school. It was time for classes to start. Students were moving, laughing, and talking. Out of the corner of my eyes I noticed several boys arguing. Some of the boys I didn't recognize as going to Tech High. They were loud, but even so it was difficult to understand what they were yelling about. On each side of the main hall were two large, waist-high brick dividers that separated and flanked the large open space, the main hall. Several stairs ran between the dividers. As I stepped further into the main hall I noticed one group of students quickly moving toward the other group, yelling. All of a sudden fists began flailing and punching any body or object in front of them. At that point as I tried to negotiate myself through the crowd I fell into a boy, and he immediately turned around and lifted his arm, readying himself to strike me. Then out of nowhere a voice called out, "Wait, don't hit her." The next thing that happened wasn't clear, and it is even more difficult to describe, but Yoshi put his body into a karate stance and flipped the guy over one of the dividers. Then he did something hard to explain—at least it was to most of our family and friends. He went around the wall of bricks and extended his open hand to the boy he had just hit. To my amazement the other boy let Yoshi help him up. As I picked up my books, Yoshi bent down to help me.

All the students, both those involved and those just standing around as onlookers, began to walk away. It was all over with. But Carl Palmquist, the principal, didn't see things the same way. He directed all those involved from the school to immediately report to his office. The others who didn't go to our school had to go with the police, who were called by the vice principal.

As we sat there waiting for the principal I had plenty of time to think of an excuse, and I probably did.

Yoshi finished school at Tech and went on to college at UNO. He was always very special to me because he cared about the things that I valued and he always put my interests close to his. I will always call him my friend. When he finished writing his dissertation he added a dedication page and listed several people, including me!

As the eleventh grade came to an end I was determined to study hard, making sure that I kept all of my grades up. Even though I was one of two recipients of the National Merit Scholarship, as a runner-up I hadn't received enough money to fund my entire education. I wanted to go to college, and I also wanted to be an actor who could dance and sing in musicals like my cousin Cleavon Little.

The thought of being on stage was always on my mind, even when I was a little girl. "Stop all of that jumping around up there!" my father would always say.

But my mother—well, I would hear my mother say, using the nickname his family and friends often used for him, "Shut up, Bud. Now I mean it: leave the girl alone, she's practicing."

"For what?" he'd say. "She's always practicing for something or another. What is it now?"

"Maybe it's the Ed Sullivan Show or maybe Johnny Carson's nighttime program. Only God knows, and you're certainly not Him."

And that was that. My mom had the last word, as usual.

The end of my junior year was filled with plays, musicals, and debates—and of course dances and parties.

The Omaha Links Cotillion Ball. My friend Terese is in the bottom row near the center, and I'm in the top row near the center.

15

My Senior Year

🌱

My senior year began with protests growing around the country in opposition to the Vietnam War. I was not for the war and all of my male friends didn't believe in this war, along with most blacks across this country. Some said they would leave the country rather than serve—go to Canada and never come back. Others said that they would become conscientious objectors. Several of my good friends said that they just wouldn't go; they didn't care what our government said. Things were truly a mess. The country was seriously divided, and I wanted our troops to pull out of there.

In my senior year I participated in even more activities. I supplemented my formal education with the activities that I participated in so my resume would look outstanding, which would help me get into the college of my choice even if I didn't have the money.

I began studying at the college level before graduating from high school. During the winter, along with my friend Phyllis, I was enrolled in Creighton University. We were the first Tech students to study in both schools at the same time. According to Creighton University officials it was unusual to enroll students before they completed high school, but some superior students were admitted, and I was among them. As far as I know, I was the first black student to be admitted to Creighton while still attending

Technical High School. My parents were proud of me. My mother was so happy; and I think it was at that point that she decided to do whatever she could to make sure I had an opportunity to attend college.

During my senior year I had the honor of competing for the title of Debutante in the Omaha Links Cotillion Ball. This annual event is a fundraiser for the Omaha chapter of The Links, Incorporated, a nonprofit women's service organization with 267 other chapters located across the country and in Europe. Their mission centers on quality-of-life issues for African Americans and people of African descent worldwide. The Omaha chapter provided scholarships to graduating seniors, and I was hopeful and encouraged that I could possibly be one of them. I really had no idea what that would mean. I knew that I had to have decent grades and that I would have to attend practices. I also knew that I would have to select as my escort a boy who also had to be upstanding with decent grades. There would be girls involved from upper-middle-class backgrounds—daughters of doctors, lawyers, businessmen, and politicians—and my parents were none of these. They were honest and hardworking people with few assets. During the practices I felt insecure around many of the girls who came from well-to-do families. Most of them stayed together whenever we went to functions or practiced for the cotillion. I was surprised and hurt by the fact that even though we were all black, I felt a strong and clearly delineated social divide among us. I had never before experienced black girls separating themselves on the basis of economic and social status. Most of the time, I had very few social encounters with young black women of financial privilege, who felt entitled, until the cotillion. I became more at ease as the ball approached. Many of the girls who had seemed stuck-up in the beginning became friendly with the rest of us, the girls you might say who were from the other side of the tracks.

My escort was my friend Jimmy, but the real man in my life during practices and at the event was my dad. He drove me to most of the practices, and he supported me all the way. The night of the ball was the first time that he ever danced with me. I felt like a princess, and during our dance in front of several hundred people I felt as if we were the only father and daughter on the floor. I could see my mom wipe her eyes as we twirled past her on the ballroom floor.

Then something happened: my father whispered to me in my ear. He said to me, "Cat, I've never been so proud of you. You are the most beautiful girl here." He was so handsome, so kind.

That night was also the first time I saw my parents dance together. Of course it was with my siblings' encouragement. That didn't matter, though—they were dancing. I really didn't know that either of them knew how to ballroom dance, but they did. There was probably a lot more that I didn't know and would never know about them. Leslie Taylor, a seventeen-year-old, was the 1967 Debutante. This was the eighth annual cotillion in our city. She looked so beautiful, and I was excited and happy for her. It was evident that all of us were winners. Young women who never socialized before learned to appreciate and value each other. We learned etiquette skills and we learned that even ladies need to be well educated, to value themselves and have the courage to trust others. I also learned to not jump to conclusions about people whom I perceived as being different from myself, something that I always expected from others. As a debutante I made friends that I know and love even today.

This was the first time that I didn't feel intimidated by a loss. I was always crying in my room as a child if I wasn't chosen on a track team or a softball team or if I entered a contest and lost. I had no idea why I subjected myself to things that would bring me such pain. It made me feel like a failure. I was frail and frightened for most of my life. I was always hiding my feelings under a veil, cloaked in one excuse after the other that made it appear as if I really didn't care. My parents would always say, "*Don't-care* doesn't live here and never did." But for some reason I still felt as if I didn't belong in my skin. I felt that I was unworthy whenever something good happened to me, and I believed that it would soon be taken away. My mother was the one who always reassured me. She was my personal cheerleader, complete with pompoms, who would shore me up and let me know that I could do anything that I set out to do. "You're beautiful and smart," she would always tell me. But I didn't believe her. For some reason I always thought that I fell short of my parents' expectations. She wanted me to shine, and so she pushed me—and she pushed me hard—to achieve in any and everything. Eventually my dad went along with whatever my mom did and said, except attend most of my events.

To win the title of Debutante along with its accompanying scholarship, you had to sell the most tickets. As I recall, I came in second or third place. So I didn't receive the scholarship. But what I gained from the experience was far more impressive. I became better acquainted with myself—and more importantly, I grew closer to my dad.

As the end of my senior year approached I became very concerned about how I was going to pay for college. I continued working part-time at Sears and I also babysat for my brothers and sisters and my neighbors as much as I could. Even with all of that I realized that I just didn't have enough money. Fall came early. The leaves were falling from the trees, and their beautiful colors of red, gold, yellow, and orange were quickly vanishing as they were washed away in the sudden autumn winds formed in the foreground of the sky and clouds. The leaves rustled under my feet as I walked through my neighborhood. Adults were annoyed because they had to spend the vast majority of their Saturday afternoon raking up the leaves and disposing of them. The kids, on the other hand, enjoyed piling up the leaves and falling into them. It all brought back memories.

"Twirl, Cathy, twirl. Fall into the leaves with us," my cousin Lynwood said.

"Oh, she can't do what we do. She can't get up if she falls down. Look at her—she's ugly and skinny."

The other kids laughed, but my cousin told them to leave me alone. Lynwood told them that it might take me a little more time but I would always get up, even if he had to help me. Lynwood was always ready to fight for me, and for that matter so was his sister Christine. On that particular day I didn't want him to fight for me anymore, so I fell into the leaves—and what do you know? Despite how much it hurt, I got up quickly and with a smile on my face—but not to show them: I needed to show myself.

Halloween had come and gone along with Tech's homecoming and football games. Thanksgiving gave me an opportunity to be with family and enjoy the Cornhuskers, the University of Nebraska's football team. Soon I began looking forward to Christmas, a time that I spent shopping with my mother for gifts for our family and friends. My mother loved Christmas. It was her favorite holiday and as well as mine. I always chose one Saturday during the holidays when I would take all nine of my nieces and nephews shopping for gifts for their parents, friends, and favorite teachers. We would spend the days leading up to Christmas buying and decorating our trees and baking Christmas cookies.

Soon the winter holidays were over, and I was back in school studying vigorously and relentlessly. Boys were not on my radar; I was focused on applying to colleges and landing a longed-for scholarship.

In March I took second place in the Junior Achievement Speakers Corps contest. I enjoyed Junior Achievement and won on the topic given to all participants, "Faith, Freedom, and Free Enterprise." My group, named Flake Co., was counseled by Kellogg Company.

My mother continued to struggle with the fact that I would have a difficult time obtaining the money necessary to attend college. Then the *World-Herald* announced the 1967 winner of the unusual Alice Dubler Pierson Scholarship. The *World-Herald* had decided a Tech student should receive the scholarship, and Tech officials picked my friend Phyllis. My mother didn't think that this was entirely fair, so she asked Phyllis's mother to attend a meeting with the school's principal to encourage them to also give me a scholarship. She was determined to add me to the list of recipients. The meeting was held, but the principal didn't change his mind—I didn't think that he would. My mother had fought for what she believed in for as long as I could remember. I often wondered if I had that kind of fight in me.

Phyllis always said that she wanted to attend Creighton in the fall, and so did I. She needed the $400 along with other funds to make college happen. It might not seem like much, but every little bit would help, and our parents knew that. We both worked during the summer months and like me, work would be Phyllis's main source of money for school.

The end of the school year was an exciting time for everybody. Everyone in our school was preparing for the prom. My sister made my dress, and I felt like I was the queen of the ball. Graduation time was staring me in the face, and I thought that if I looked over my shoulder I would miss the excitement, so I didn't. I was of the mind to just look straight ahead into the future.

I can't remember much about my award dinners and who came. It's even more difficult for me to remember much about my graduation. I do remember putting on my ironed graduation gown and also my mother attaching my tassel to my mortarboard. I knew my mother would attend my graduation, but when I saw my father walk in and find his way to a seat beside her in the audience I was thrilled. It couldn't get any better than that.

In June it was announced that I was among several of my peers who were going to receive the Stanley R. Osborn scholarship, which was given to deserving students who might otherwise not have the funds to attend college. I thought that it was good of Stanley Osborn to leave some of his money in a will to be utilized in this manner. I always thought that if I ever had a will I would without hesitation do the same thing.

At the end of my senior year I was still enjoying all of the activities that I experienced throughout my school life: voice lessons for five years under my teacher Mildred Slocum, five years of piano lessons with Claudette Valentine, ballet lessons for ten years, tap and modern dance for over ten years, acting lessons at the Play House Academy, modeling for Dory Passolt Models, and training in gospel music under Katie Wilson. From time to time I worked professionally in all of these areas. I continued to be a member of the Mount Moriah Baptist Church Choir as well as one of their lead soloists.

I also continued to participate in clubs and community organizations: the Wesley Women Community Center, the Boys & Girls Clubs of America, Head Start, Junior Chamber of Commerce, and the 4CL. To say the least, I kept myself busy!

Graduation from Technical High School came too soon; fall to summer came too soon. Many of my friends moved on too soon. For various reasons, some of them I would never see again. Now I was expected to grow up and become a woman, embracing all that entails, and that definitely came all too soon.

High-school graduation.

Wesley House.

16

The American Party Convention

In 1968, former governor of Alabama George Wallace was running for president of the United States of America. He was the same man who had stood in the schoolhouse door at the University of Alabama on June 11, 1963, determined to keep his promise of preventing black students from entering and attending schools in Alabama. He was considered by many to be an arch-segregationist. He stopped off in Omaha on Sunday, March 3, 1968, to gain further support for his campaign for president on the American Party ticket. White racists attacked both whites and blacks protesting Wallace's run for the White House at the open rally. Later that night a black high-school student was shot and killed....

George Wallace arrived at Eppley Airfield at 2:30 p.m. in a chartered, four-engine Douglas DC-6. I was there among the curious. It is important to know what people, even people like George C. Wallace, have to say, even if we don't want to hear it. I even skipped a few classes because I felt that sitting in a history class could not bring life to any of the events that were about to unfold.

I woke that morning with excitement, wanting to personally see this man that everyone said stood against everything that defined who I was. Many protesters were there when he arrived at Eppley, and most carried antiwar signs. I carried a black sign with colored lettering, "Is this the

America we want?" One group said that they were present to speak for the *True Voice*, an archdiocese newspaper. Wallace's many supporters carried signs welcoming him.

When Wallace arrived at the airport, 1,500 supporters greeted him. After he got off the plane, he shook many hands—several of them the eager hands of Negroes. Someone set a Confederate flag on fire and threw the partially burned flag at Wallace but missed him. After his arrival Wallace held a news conference during which he spoken angrily, hoping to provoke a large turnout at the rally the following day. According to the newspaper, he intended to collect 750 signatures to support his campaign as a third-party candidate. Wallace said that riots were "caused by militants, activists, Communists, and revolutionaries." As I stood there in back of the crowd, I thought how stupid he was. Our country was founded by revolutionaries. He then said, "Leaders and sympathizers of militant civil-rights organizations are Communists." I was left speechless.

I couldn't believe there were so many present who supported this man's beliefs. I was eighteen, but I looked around with astonishment and awe. I was with several friends, and we stood near the back watching the crowd. One individual in Wallace's party was John De Carlo, a member of his campaign staff. De Carlo was in charge of forming the American Party in Nebraska. The party had set a rally time for 8 p.m. on Monday at the Omaha Civic Auditorium. The party's headquarters had been opened at the Sheraton Fontenelle Hotel. The group had just organized, meeting the previous Wednesday at 7:30 p.m. in the hotel's West Room.

Numerous protesters followed him on Monday as he campaigned in the city. The former governor's first stop was Omaha University. Police dogs blocked protesters as he got into his car after speaking at the university.

That night at the Civic Auditorium, about 1,000 Wallace supporters were on the main floor, seated on folding chairs. My mother and I were on the main floor along with other nonsupporters, watching and waiting for Wallace to speak. When I looked up I could see that the balcony was filled with several thousand nonsupporters. We were there to protest Wallace's presence in our city.

A young man named David Rice was there to report for two local underground newspapers, *The Buffalo Chip* and *Asterisk*. David Rice and about fifty other protesters, mostly black, entered the main floor and marched in front of the podium, to shouts of outrage from the crowd. I noticed David Rice was also on the main floor. He was standing close to the media. My sister Joyce and her sisters-in-law Shirley and Eve were among those brave fifty in the front. My other sister, Rose Mary, was also in the building. While some people came to encourage hatred and violence, many others came simply to express their outrage and dissatisfaction with individuals like George Wallace and his run for the presidency.

Wallace made the crowd wait about one hour before he entered to a roaring crowd, and when he spoke, those of us opposing him shouted over almost every word. Many protesters began tearing up their signs and throwing them at Wallace. Several people approached the stage and threw raw eggs at the speaker's platform. The attention of the security personnel was drawn in another direction, trying to stop more people from entering the building. Several of the demonstrators yelled out that Wallace needed to be sent to Vietnam to experience what those Americans would go through until someone was brave enough to admit that it had to end. There were shouts that we had made a mistake to go in the first place. People were carrying signs that read "End the Vietnam War." Black people were also there to protest Wallace's position against white and black people attending school together, eating together in public places, shopping together, or even drinking from the same water fountain. My mother and I were also there to protest his views on voter rights, blacks holding public office, and his support of police brutality. He just didn't want the races to mix. I knew that if it was left up to him we'd be back on the plantation picking cotton. My father always said that *Gone with the Wind* was probably his favorite movie.

David Rice, wanting the group to send its message without violence, attempted to stop it from losing control, but it was too late. Along with others David was hit with mace by an undercover police officer. Demonstrators locked arms and surrounded David in an attempt to protect him and several of the other writers. They couldn't hold their positions for long. I wanted to get my mother out of there, but she told me that she had no intention of leaving that night until she'd seen and heard the rest of his speech and the evening's events. Things were already out of control, but the scuffle with David Rice along with others shouting and throwing things probably started the melee. Police appeared out of nowhere and began charging up the center aisles of the large auditorium. They began swinging their batons, forcing us to run into each other. I was falling into people as I tried to stay on my feet. I moved quickly, with my arms held up in front of my face trying to protect myself. My purse was knocked to the floor a couple of times. Fists were flailing violently and angrily in the air.

People were also picketing outside, and they could be heard over the jeers inside. People continued to yell, "Black power!" and "Power to the people!" Several of the picketers carried signs that said "GEORGE WALLACE BELONGS TO AMERICA." Other signs read, "PSEUDO-INTELLECTUALS UNITE! AMERICA DOESN'T NEED WALLACE!" Most of our signs read, "WHITE POWER, BLACK POWER, and HUMAN POWER."

Agitators released stink bombs among the crowd. I had no idea where they were coming from. The heckling continued. But it did not stop the invocation or those who played the national anthem. There was also a plea for money, and a collection was taken up—it was interesting how they went about raising money for his campaign. Wallace speakers asked the decent people to sit down. Microphone and television cables had been cut shortly after the convention began, but that didn't prevent the program from taking place. Wallace's speech seemed to take about forty-five minutes, although it probably ended much sooner than that.

Police continued charging up the aisles, and suddenly extreme violence erupted as Wallace supporters picked up their chairs and began to hit the demonstrators. My mother and I were sprayed with mace by police officers while dodging blows from Wallace supporters. Mom cried out and fell to the floor. It was obvious that she couldn't see as she began to feel around for her purse. "I can't see!" she yelled. "I can't see, something is stinging my eyes!"

Even though I felt dizzy from the effects of the spray I remained standing. I wiped my watering, irritated eyes and looked for the nearest exit. I bent down and carefully put my body over my mother's to keep her from getting trampled as the stampeding crowd struggled to get to the exits.

"Juanita! Reach up!" The next thing I knew my mom was pulled up off of the floor from under me. She was crying, confused, and dazed. Her saviors were my brothers-in-law, Bill and Al. They threw a coat over her and quickly escorted her from the auditorium.

I stayed behind. I saw people running and heard them screaming all around me. The arm of a small boy reached through a stampede of adults running in the opposite direction. I managed to reach out and lock his hand into mine. I pulled him toward me, managing to keep him upright in the crowd. He was young, about five. I began pulling him quickly through the moving legs around us, determined to get him to safety. We were both breathing so hard I didn't even consider asking him his name or if he could see someone that he knew in the crowd. Several other students had dropped their signs and were trying to help anyone that they could. I saw several black senior citizens being aided by white students who were there with us from Creighton University, Omaha University, and other colleges and high schools in the area.

I saw a friendly face close to an exit and immediately lifted up the boy and passed him along. He finally reached someone by the door, and they took him out. I'm sure that in all the frenzy he had become separated from his parents or whoever brought him there.

When I finally got outside, I leaned against the side of the building. I could still hear the yelling and screaming all around me. People were running out, being carried out, and even limping out of the auditorium. Some looked angry, and others showed no expression at all. By now the police were there en masse. Some entered the building with their guns drawn, and others arrived on horseback dressed in riot gear. In the darkness I looked around to see if there was any one left who could give me a ride home. My father had driven my mother and I there and dropped us off. How would I get home?

A riot was beginning, and I was scared. I start running for my life through the dark streets. I was frightened and unable to catch my breath. I saw what was happening to the people around me, and I knew that the violence wouldn't end until someone was seriously hurt. I heard screaming all around me. Then, someone yelled out my name several times.

"Cathy! Cathy, is that you? I have your jacket." I recognized the voice of Adam, a white friend from Creighton, and began to slow down. "Cathy, is this your jacket?" he asked when he had caught up to me. He said he wanted to help me get home safely, that it was too dark for me to be outside all alone walking the streets. I was grateful to have company. We crossed one street and then another, talking as we went about George Wallace and his disastrous rally. We were still several miles away from my house but just across from Creighton University when a car pulled up alongside us.

"Look here, what do we have? A nigger and a nigger-loving white boy? Now where could you possibly be coming from? Don't tell me. Either you're on a date, or you're both coming from the Wallace rally. In any case, you don't belong together."

To my horror, it was a police car. "Hey, boy," the other officer was yelling from the passenger side of the car. "Can you see you're huddled up with a nigger? We don't allow that around here, nigger-lover or not."

Adam was getting tired of them. "You'd both better leave us alone. We aren't doing anything wrong." Adam didn't realize that he had good reason to be afraid, on a night like tonight, in the streets with a black girl.

"Listen to him!" I yelled. "We have a right to be on these streets." My voice was quivering.

"They must be an item," one of the cops said.

As Adam started to talk back again, I grabbed his arm and begged him quietly not to say another word for fear of losing our lives. The cops loved that.

"You'd better listen to her. I can't figure for the likes of me why you're with her in the first place." They were laughing and shouting at the same time, a hysterical kind of anger. "Your momma must have been submissive because you look bright—not white, but bright enough. Max, just listen to the way she talks, she's not a typical nigger from North Omaha. I can tell that she thinks she's better than us. She probably goes to college or something. All this stuff going on with you uppity niggers. Why don't all of you go back where you came from? I heard that there was a boat leaving tonight."

"That's good, Joe!" They called each other by name. They even asked Adam for his name. He never told them. As for me, they had chosen my name before they stopped their car: Nigger.

"All of you talking about your rights. You wouldn't know what to do with your rights if we gave them to you. You should have been grateful, but no, not you people. You have to want our jobs, our houses, and now our women. Of course your friend here is an exception. He wants one of you."

I was scared to death when one of them got out of his car. He had his hand on his gun as he approached us, and as he became visible under the streetlight, I could see the sweat rolling down his face. He held his baton in his other hand as he brushed his hair out of his face, all the time looking at both me and Adam. He never took his hand off of his gun. I looked at his gun at least every other second as I tried to take in the situation and figure out what to do. I heard something strange, then I felt something wet and foamy hit my eyes and the bridge of my nose. Adam turned to see if I was okay. Before he could ask, an even larger chunk of mucus hit his face.

"That's for you, you nigger-lover."

"I want your name and your badge number!" I called out, frightened as I was. We were alone with them. It was dark, and there were no cars on the street. By this time the other cop was out of his car. "I'm not kidding. I have a right to your name and badge number."

Their laughter echoed. "Get a load of her. She does think she's somebody. You say another word and—well, I heard someone was shot. You could be next."

I realized that we could easily come up missing. We were just excess pieces of meat to them. I felt insecure and unsafe. I was suddenly unsure of the safety of the world around me. I liked that Adam had stuck by me. He didn't have to do that. He was white and easily could have left me behind, but he didn't. And now he was really stuck.

With that, we were taken down to the police station. We were never formally arrested or thrown into a jail cell, but we were held by the police for a few hours and then for some reason taken back to the very place, in the middle of the city far from home, where they had picked both of us up.

"Now get out of here." And we did.

We half-ran, half-walked, wiping sweat from our faces, and quickly made our way across the street to the Creighton campus. We stood beneath a security light until we were discovered by school security. As they began to approach us I stepped back, wary of another assault. Finally, I let myself break down crying. The police were no longer interested in tormenting us. They weren't around. I hoped that they had moved on to investigate other things happening in the city.

"Do you see them? Did you see them?" we both asked in unison.

I could tell by the way the guards looked at each other that they saw the police watching us from across the street. The guards leaned against their bikes and asked us if we were all right. Neither of us responded. I'm sure they could tell that we were far from all right.

I was at my wit's end. I was trying to stop crying, and I hadn't been to the bathroom. I was out of breath and short on dignity. Adam and I could no longer look at each other in the same way that we had the day before. Now we were different.

The security guards were sympathetic. "Want to come into the school and wait for someone to pick you up?" I probably should have waited there, but I knew that there was no one to pick me up that evening. I walked toward the library, where I noticed several students from my neighborhood and asked them if they were going home anytime soon. I was anxious to get home and find out about my mom. She was sprayed with mace, hit in the face with God only knows what—probably with one of the steel chairs being thrown, and knocked to the floor.

The kids at the library gladly gave me a ride home. During the ride, they stared at me. Even the driver took her eyes off the road long enough to peer at me in the mirror. One of the students asked the driver if she could stop at the filling station so he could grab some chips and a Coke. I quickly spoke out of turn and advised her not to stop. It was still too dangerous. All the while I was thinking that the police, those same horrible, bigoted cops, were probably still on the prowl, abusing their authority. "Please just get me home. I need to get home and see about my mom," I pleaded. The boy in the back seat put his arm around me and drew me near, patting me on the back and comforting me with his words.

"Cathy, I'm sure your mom's all right. She is probably already at home. I bet she'll open the door to greet you."

"Yeah," the rest of the car chimed in. "She's at home waiting for you."

When I arrived home, I had an eerie feeling. As I walked up the slippery, uneven, concrete stairs leading to the front door, I noticed that all the lights were still on. It was after one in the morning. Before I could put my key in the door, my dad opened it. He was standing there with my brother and nephew, who were now living with us.

"Be quiet," they said, as I slowly walked in. "Your mother is in bed, and we're waiting for your sisters to come over."

Then the questions and the finger pointing came at me fast and furious. "Where have you been? Why weren't you with your mother? How could you leave her like that in the shape that she was in?" My dad was furious.

"Didn't Al or Bill bring her home?" I jumped in, trying to defend myself.

"That's beside the point! Just answer me!" my dad shouted angrily. "Do you know the condition that your mother's in?"

"But Dad, I tried to see to it that she was safe, but we were separated from each other. You weren't there, how can you say what you're saying?"

My brother and nephew didn't say a word. They supported, with their crude nods, everything my dad was saying. Not that I expected them to defend me in front of my dad. They were trying to win Dad's favor. I couldn't blame them for that. My brothers and dad were always at odds, and sometimes they looked for opportunities to agree with him. Most of the time they didn't have quiet discussions, they had screaming matches, so this was a rare sight. Even though I was a little disappointed in them I knew that they loved me and would do practically anything for me.

My dad viciously came back with "I can say what I'm saying because I saw her when she came into this house."

I rushed past all of them and their criticism to go into my mom's room and see her for myself. I wasn't prepared for what I saw. She was lying in her bed, worn out from her unappreciated battle. Her body was black and blue in so many places that I couldn't have counted them. She had a swollen black eye and a cut under her right eyebrow. Her lower lip was punctured. Her false teeth were on her dresser, cracked, along with her broken glasses. Her shoulder was burned from the mace.

My father was standing in the doorway. "She still cannot focus or see very well. I told both of you not to go down there. Even your bother said that it wouldn't do any good; your presence wouldn't mean a thing. But no, neither of you would listen, as usual. Hardheaded! Your mother always trying to change the world, and you—you're right behind her. You're just like her. Can't you see that nothing's going to change? It certainly hasn't so far."

I could barely hear my dad's rant; I just kept looking at my mom, trying to figure it all out. Why hurt my mother, who always gave so much? She loved everybody. No answers came to me that night. I was so tired that I just plopped down on the other side of the bed, stretched out beside my mother and fell into a deep sleep.

When I got up the next day, the newspaper had several pages glamorizing the events, packing the pages with sensationalism: a sobbing teenager, a poor white girl trapped in the aisles among the uncontrollable crowd, a Negro girl screaming in agony while a policeman tried to peacefully move people into the lobby of the arena. The news media had difficulty getting coherent responses from most.

Although I didn't know the screaming girl's name, I reexperienced the events as I read about her. She fled the main floor as police used their clubs to disperse the crowd, landing hard blows on the fleeing people. I saw again people wearing blood-spattered clothes. The room smelled of open flesh and sweat. It was similar to an urban war zone. Threats and swearing came from all around.

People on both sides were stunned and disgusted with the events. A young girl watched people from both sides spit on one another while yelling profanities. People there were as young as nine and ten years old, spewing hatred.

Reverend Father Robert Burns, a teacher I worked for at Creighton University, and Father John McCaslin, head of the Catholic Social Action Office and the pastor at Holy Family Catholic Church, wore black sweatshirts. "Sock it to me/Black Power" was printed on Father Burns's shirt. He always gave me the power and strength to try new things, and he encouraged me to stand up for myself. He told me that no matter what individuals think, God has the power, and I could rely on faith to encourage change in order to help others.

Father McCaslin supported me and the entire Omaha community. He was very active politically. When asked on the day of George Wallace's arrival, "Why are you here? Why are you protesting?" he responded, "I don't think Omaha would knowingly put a racist on the ballot for United States President."

"I'm here to try to help pinpoint the meaning of Christianity," said Father Burns. "Racism means hatred for my fellow man. Racism and Christianity cannot exist in the same person at the same time."

Among the protesters were clergy, politicians, religious figures, educators, students, and everyday citizens. People, although it was ill-advised, even brought their children to witness the arrival of George Wallace. Hand-held signs were carried:

> WALLACE MEANS LAWLESSNESS
> ONLY BIGOTS ARE FOR WALLACE
> NOTHING DOING WITH WALLACE

More signs, though, were in support of Wallace and his run for the presidency than against him, to my dismay.

Later, following the mayhem in our auditorium, Wallace was again given the platform to speak. According to reports, he said that this was a matter of revolution. That those freedom-of-speech supporters were willing to listen to some Communist on a college campus but didn't want those who were assembled peacefully to speak. He continued on to say that the majority of Negroes were against the breakdown of law and order. He also reminded the people that they needed to thank God for the police and firemen. His supporters applauded and gave him a standing ovation. He told them, "If you go out of here tonight and you get knocked in the head, your attacker will probably get released from jail before you are released from the hospital."

It was a bloody night, and the fighting continued inside and outside of the Civic Center. The arena had over 1,200 windows broken, and before the night was over there was a riot on the Near North Side in Omaha. Thirteen people, most of them on the Near North Side, went to the hospital with injuries, and a sixteen-year-old was shot to death by police. They said that he was attempting to break into a pawn shop.

The following Tuesday, over a dozen black community leaders descended on the mayor's office to complain. That night more rioting occurred, with fire bombs being thrown at businesses. People in the black community, my community, were frustrated with the way the police had handled the riot and all of the events that took place at the convention center during Wallace's visit to Omaha. Shooting the young black man in the street sent the violence and retaliation by us to another level. Our community was demanding to be heard. We were no longer going to tolerate the way we were being treated. We were dissatisfied with the way our concerns were being handled by the police and by the city. It was later reported that we were supposed to be upstairs in the gallery, but Wallace's political-event handlers were told to let us down on the main floor. I believe that this was to encourage the unrest and later the violent outbursts that resulted in bloodshed. Since youths were arrested, including a Central High basketball star, the police were careful in handling the situation. It's unclear if any of the Wallace supporters were arrested; however, community activists and sympathizers as well as concerned Omaha citizens were being harassed and locked up around the city. Father John McCaslin was among those arrested.

Finally, after almost a week of unrest and violence the National Guard were called in to control the citizens in our community. FBI Director J. Edgar Hoover had ordered the secret counterintelligence operation COINTELPRO into effect against black nationalist groups in twenty-seven selected cities. This effort began on August 25, 1967. Hoover was taking heat for the riots and protests sweeping the nation at the time of the Wallace riot on March 4, 1968, in Omaha.

Nebraska Governor Tiemann did say several things regarding the violence that came out of George Wallace's appearance at the convention center. He felt that the disturbance would never have happened if Wallace had not appeared. He said that it was like throwing gasoline on the fire. He also said that Wallace could have made the event one of sensible dialogue, but I will always have a great deal of difficulty understanding how. He also placed the blame for the civil disorder that occurred squarely on Wallace and his supporters. He made it clear to a student audience that Wallace and his supporters had instigated the events that took place.

In the aftermath of Governor Wallace's visit there were riots, a killing, vandalism, and friends taking sides against one another out of fear. This was hardly the first time. Sadly, there are many recordings of events similar to this one taking place throughout Omaha's history. In the *Omaha World-Herald*, people willingly stepped out of the shadows to voice their opinions:

> *George Wallace will cause more hot summers in more cities than any other person.*

> *I wonder if the agitators realize the more disturbances they cause the more certain Wallace's route toward the White House.*

> *Since George Wallace professes to be so concerned about crime in the streets, riots, etc., he must be his own worst enemy. He should stay in Alabama where he belongs.*

> *Mr. Wallace seems to consider the ideal American the one who hits his fellow Americans with folding chairs.*

> *I was ashamed to read about the Rev. John McCaslin. Had his group sat down in an orderly fashion like the rest of us, there would not have been any need for police handling of this group.*

> *Priests and nuns who have so much time protesting should devote their energies to updating the Catholic Church's laws regarding divorce, remarriage, and birth control.*

For the mayor to suggest that the Wallace people might pay for the damage is adding insult to injury. Our political structure, city, county, and state, shows a lack of sound judgment in allowing anybody to promote hate in Nebraska. The law states that anyone who incites others to riot is guilty of a crime, yet two priests were arrested, not for disrupting a public meeting, as stated, but for association with colored people.

———

Since when does the concept of freedom of speech entail the right to prevent others from speaking, or involve the right to throw bricks at peaceful citizens, or include the right to destroy property, or grant the right to endanger lives? Monday, in a television interview, one of the organizers of the demonstration stated that because Wallace had the freedom to speak, the demonstrators had the freedom to speak. At the Wallace political rally, the demonstrators did not practice the right to freedom of speech, but rather substituted their own right. Although I am not necessarily a Wallace fan, I think that when rowdy children are allowed to prevent the free speech of others by yelling, chanting, and destroying property it is indeed a sad commentary.

At that time and in that space I really had no idea what the repercussions would be, because of all of the events that were occurring around me. I did know that in a few weeks I would walk onto a stage and compete for the title of Miss Omaha. If I won, I would be the first African American to win that title in the Miss America Pageant. If I was able to go all the way, and that was my intention, I would be on a national stage with the potential to make a difference in my country. But as a black teenager, eighteen years old, it was difficult for me to wrap my mind around these thoughts. Was this pageant a part of my authentic journey, or would these experiences cause my dream to collapse? How important was it really? How meaningful?

17

Miss Omaha 1968

My mother began her conversation with me out of left field. "There's a women's interdenominational religious group. I believe they call themselves the Panel of American Women. They called us and said they want to sponsor you."

I just stared at her.

"You're not saying anything. I heard you casually say that you could see yourself in this contest someday. Why not today?" She was looking at me anxiously.

"But I was just talking. A thousand girls probably say that when they're watching that show on television."

She just kept right on talking as if I hadn't even opened my mouth. "I think they see you as being much stronger than you see yourself."

"But, Mom, they don't even know me."

"Well, several of them did stop by last week to talk to your dad and me." I started.

"Before you say anything, we didn't commit you. You know, though, that one of those ladies was Susie Buffett, Warren's wife." This impressed her, I could tell. She was stumbling over her words. "They said you are a young person whom they believe stands by your convictions. One of them used the word *conduit*. That means that they see you as someone who can bring people together, creating a healing atmosphere."

I quickly opened my mouth, silently, it turned out.

My mother was truly in an excited state. I could have sworn she was talking about herself. "You will be the first—or at least they believe the first—to show young black girls across our country that they can be anything that they want to be, that they desire to be."

But a beauty queen? That wasn't exactly a Mrs. Coretta Scott King or a Mrs. Jacqueline Kennedy. My mother used the words *intentional conduit for young black girls' rites of passage*. It all seemed so strange and made me wonder, why me?

I saw my face in her reflection sometimes when I entered her room and she was looking at herself in the mirror. Sometimes I would see pain in my mother's eyes. I decided that if I learned how my mother endured the pain in her own life, I could learn how to endure any pain and anguish that I could possibly experience in my own lifetime.

Later in the week a meeting of the Panel of American Women was held at my home. There were at least nine women there, including Mrs. Susie Buffett, wife of the local multimillionaire and philanthropist Warren Buffett; Mrs. Jeri Elrod, wife of Reverend Jerry Elrod; Mrs. Fannie Lou Goodwin; Mrs. Sharon Rhodes; Mrs. Rachael Newman; Mrs. Judy Harding; Mrs. Charlene Gibson, wife of Bob Gibson; Mrs. Julie Schelger; and Mrs. Angie Wead, wife of Rodney Wead. One of the women introduced the group, and another gave their history.

The National Panel of American Women emerged in Kansas City, Missouri, in 1956. It gave its participants the opportunity to learn more about people of different races and cultures. It provided a forum to discuss how to go about desegregating schools across the state, focusing discussions around racial and religious differences. They spoke around the city of Omaha, five or six at a time—white Protestants, Jews, Catholics, African Americans, Asian Americans, and others. They assigned roles as moderators and speakers, and simply talked about their experiences with segregation when they were children. The ladies spoke about how getting to know each other had changed and improved their opinions of each other and of each other's races, creating a deeper knowledge and understanding.

They continued talking about their group and then seamlessly began to address why they wanted to encourage a Negro girl to run for Miss Omaha. To them it was very simple: it was the right time. As they began to explain why they had chosen me, I glanced across the room and noticed that my mom's face was full of worry. I wondered what she could possibly be thinking about. I wondered what caused her expression to shift from one of excitement to one of worry. I'd seen that look before on nights when my dad got paid and didn't come right home with his check. In the past she would send my sisters out to find him and bring him home before he gambled most of the check away. When I was no older than eight years old she would reluctantly send me to look for him on Twenty-Fourth Street. Most of the time I would find him at his local hangout, the Bomber, a cigar shop where they played cards and gambled in the back room. I would insist that he return home with me, and he usually did. But by the time we got home my mother would be distraught; she depended on his entire paycheck to make ends meet.

My mom knew that I was very different from the other girls who would participate, and if I won Miss Omaha, I would be the first of my race to win a local title in Nebraska. I would be alone, and sometimes I would feel ostracized. I would have to continue forward to the Miss Nebraska Pageant, and I wouldn't be able to change my mind. Even if the others didn't, she understood that this was going to be challenging and sometimes frightening. Little did I know that I would ultimately feel like an enigma, a strange creature in a strange land.

As a girl, whenever I was asked a question or presented with an opportunity, I never mentioned it to my parents—not because their opinion didn't matter, but I felt it was the coward's way of dealing with things. I was worried about their rejection. How else should I have felt when I always wanted to please people? My strong need to please and my desire to be accepted by my parents, especially my mom, became a justification for how I presented myself to others, especially the men in my life. My strong need for acceptance became an issue that would scar me. My life was not my own; it was the shadowy reflection of my mother and her mother before her. I'd be entering this contest with all of our insecurities in tow.

"Of course this won't be easy," Mrs. Elrod told us. "But I'll be there with you every step of the way."

"Don't worry," another agreed.

All of the ladies looked so nice in their dresses and slacks. They could have been leaving our house and going straight to church. They took turns speaking, and when they spoke they enunciated each and every word. They were kind, calm, and enthusiastic. As they continued to speak my fears subsided and at times even turned to excitement. Before they left they gave me some information on the history behind the Miss America Contest. I was told to take my time, but they needed to hear from me as soon as possible.

I was always interested in the Miss America Pageant. I would sit in front of the television watching beautiful, young, white women walk across a stage in glamorous gowns and swimsuits. My most favorite segment was the contestants' performances. I thought they were so talented. As the years went on, I learned that a contestant could receive a four-year scholarship to the school or institution of her choice. That really drew me in. As early as twelve, I began thinking about the competition more personally. I felt that since this institution provided young women with more scholarships across the United States than any other, I should take the pageant seriously, and if I wanted it badly enough, I could win. I was unaware of the history of the Miss America Pageant and how its history would actually affect my chances of winning. As I got older I would listen to the contestants answer questions. I wondered why the questions weren't more serious, more inclusive of the times and of people like me. I began to wonder about the chances that someone who looked like me could win a contest like this one.

The day after the meeting, I began reading the materials the group had left with me. According to the first pamphlet the Miss America Pageant began as a marketing strategy. Atlantic City needed a way to bring tourists to the boardwalk. The first event, called the Fall Frolic, was held in 1920. There were parades, and various items were shown and sold up and down the boardwalk. The most popular part of the event was the young women, who walked up and down the boardwalk. Men enjoyed watching the beautiful women display their beautiful bodies, and women enjoyed seeing them in their beautiful clothes. Later girls submitted their photographs, and that became the beginning of the contest. The contest took on many different looks throughout the years. In 1921, sixteen-year-old Margaret Gorman won the Most Beautiful Bathing Girl in America contest. She was awarded the title of Golden Mermaid, along with 100 dollars. She returned to Atlantic City in 1922 covered with the American flag, and that year they called her Miss America.

At that time rule number seven said no nonwhite women could enter: "Contestants must be of good health and of the white race." However, African Americans were allowed to entertain the crowd by singing and dancing as far back as 1923. They were cast as slaves in short skits performed between portions of the pageant. In order to make sure African Americans couldn't slip in due to a mixed heritage or simply attempting to pass for white, until the 1940s, each contestants had to complete a biological questionnaire designed to trace her ancestry.

Years later, the organizers of the pageant wanted to encourage a new type of professional woman to enter. They wanted Miss America to exemplify conservative values. Contestants were not expected to want to become the counterparts of men or to desire their jobs, and they should limit their aspirations and expectations to little more than finding a good husband to support them. Finally, at the height of feminism and the civil-rights movement, people began to protest the pageant. An organization called the New York Radical Women rallied about 400 women, and protests sprang up across the country.

Finally, the pamphlet went on to tell how the pageant benefited women through its scholarship program. About $50,000 was awarded annually. Then as now, the Miss America Scholarship Program had local and state affiliates, including Omaha, owned and controlled by the main branch of the Miss America Pageant.

Another set of papers described the specific rules that the judges followed for determining the winners of the contest in the various categories. In 1968 and 1969, we were also judged in the same five areas:

1. *Personal Interview—25%:* In the personal interview, each contestant carries on a conversation with the judges on several topics, from casual issues to more serious social and political subjects. Points are given based on how well-spoken you are, as well as your manners and sincerity. This segment of the contest is done outside of the view of the public and the audience, and most people are unaware that contestants receive scores in this area.
2. *Talent—15%:* In this area contestants demonstrate their talent and also their creative side. This includes original, classical, and generally known forms of art including music, dance, and baton twirling.
3. *Swimsuit—15%:* The focus in this category is on health and physical fitness. Swimwear has to be approved by the pageant, and it must be modest. You are judged on posture and poise. Contestants are required to wear one-piece suits that are identical. No fitted

support wear or padding can be worn under the suits. Girls are required to dress with each other in an open area.
4. *Evening Wear—20%:* In this part of the competition contestants are judged on how they carry themselves during their walk across the stage.
5. *Question—25%:* While dressed in her evening gown, each contestant is asked a question that she randomly selects from a glass bowl on stage. She must answer the question without prior preparation.

I read anything and everything that I could get my hands on about the contest: history, rules, and past winners. I wanted to find out if there was ever anyone even similar to me that tried to compete, and what happened to her. I wanted to know if it changed her life and if so, how?

It wasn't long before I made a commitment to the National Panel of American Women. Before committing, I had several serious discussions with my family and close friends. Most of them were very excited for me and thought that being asked to run for Miss Omaha was an honor that might never come again.

Mrs. Elrod contacted the local pageant committee and requested that my name be added to the list of contestants. Before long, the paperwork was in our mailbox. All of us were slow to open the oversized envelope that arrived with the state emblem in the upper right-hand corner. It lay in a small basket by the front door for several days, and before long there were other envelopes in the same basket from the Miss Omaha committee. My dad couldn't stand unopened mail lying around, so on the weekend he directed us to sit down and open the mail. It was Sunday, and like many Sundays, most of my family came over after church to spend time with my parents.

My parents read each and every page out loud. I could tell by my father's expression that he was having trouble with the whole thing.

"What's wrong?" Rose Mary asked him.

"Well," he began slowly. "I was talking to one of my friends down at the Bomber while we were playing cards, and—well . . ."

"Go on, Dad, we want to hear whatever you have to say," my sister said.

"He said that he heard that a black girl might run for some contest, Miss Omaha, and—well, most people will think that the girl is a token and that she will be used as a pawn to placate blacks."

"What did they mean by that?" I asked.

"I don't know. You asked me, so I'm just telling you what they said."

The room became quiet. My mother went into the kitchen to get her apron. She began drying her wet hands vigorously on her apron in the kitchen doorway, preparing to wash the dishes.

"Well, she's going to run, and we don't need to talk any more about what those men in the streets have to say. They don't know anything about it."

We all knew that they might not know anything about it, but they did know the word on the streets.

"Did you all hear Mama? I'm going to be in this thing. That's right, isn't it?"

Everyone but my dad reluctantly agreed, nodding their heads in a unanimous family vote. My sister Joyce was peering around her son, who was sitting on her lap. Little Johnny, my brother John's son, sat on the bottom of the stairs with one of his favorite toy cars clutched tightly under his arm, protecting it from the jealous gaze of his male cousins, Derek and Geoffrey. "Are we done yet?" he anxiously blurted out. "Some of us want to go out and play while it's still light outside." His dad moved closer to him and thumped him on the back of his head for being so disrespectful.

"Okay, but don't go out into the streets," my mom told him. The boys dashed outside, passing Mom's friend Iola coming in the door.

I was still waiting for one person to answer my question. "Dad, I didn't see you shake your head in agreement," I said. There was silence.

The following evening my mother helped me fill out the paperwork. For the most part we left my dad alone and tiptoed around him. Except every now and then we had to ask him questions about money and insurance. I thought my sponsors would pay my fees, but we didn't want to take anything for granted. The insurance was something that every contestant had to have. It was for the sum of $5,000. It was a specific loss indemnity and it covered us for injuries that resulted in any loss within 100 days after the occurrence of the accident, including the loss of limb or the loss of life.

When the word got around that I was going to be in the contest there was a mixed reaction across the city. Phone calls started coming in to our home, both good and bad. What was I getting into?

I was never one to just arbitrarily put myself out there, especially if I thought that there wasn't one possibility in the world that I would benefit from my efforts. I tried to be more calculated about my activities. I had about three months to prepare myself for the event. So in between helping my mother at home and going to classes, church, activities, lessons, and jobs, I read everything I could get my hands on to prepare myself for the contest. Because there was so much information to sort through, I wound up discarding most of it because it had little to do with the local contest.

I soon learned that getting ready for a beauty pageant is like getting ready for a strenuous, public, athletic completion. Someone takes on the role of motivator, trainer, and manager. Your name and contact information is put on a long list with names of other people you don't know and, even more frustrating, individuals that you have very little in common with. I had to decide who I would blame if I ever decided to back out of the contest.

At the same time, there were rumors going around Omaha that my four-year college, Duchesne, was going to close. I had a hard time believing it. In about a year's time, I had gone from high school to Creighton University to Duchesne College. I was beginning to feel bitter and defeated. Duchesne Women's College was one of the most beautiful landmarks in Omaha, and I was one of a handful of black girls in attendance, along with my sister Joyce. Now it was moving to Illinois, and I knew for a fact that I wouldn't be going there. But it hadn't closed yet, and I had to study hard for my finals as well as worry about this pageant business.

"Okay, stand up tall and walk with your head up. Look ahead. Now look straight at me," demanded Ms. Passolt in her usual authoritative way. Dory Passolt was my modeling teacher, and later she became my modeling agent. She was good looking and sharp, and her studio was well known throughout the Midwest. Because I modeled, I assumed I was ready for the pageant. Wrong. Mrs. Elrod and Mrs. Passolt had to explain to me that modeling was very different from presenting yourself on the stage as a beauty contestant. Both ladies had acted as judges in other pageants at one time or another so they knew exactly what they were talking about.

They laid out a plan for me. I began practicing my walk on and off the stage. I walked in my bare feet and with heels on, and I walked with quarters between my thighs and books on my head. I stood against walls while Mrs. Elrod tested my posture by trying to fit her hand between my back and the wall.

"Too much space. Try again," she would say. And I would try again and again until I got it right.

I was told I was overweight. As skinny as I was, I needed to be skinnier. There was no room for any fat handles or wobbly thighs in the pageant lineup. A double chin wasn't welcomed. My butt, however, was hereditary, and that was here to stay. And everything had to be real. No stuffing of tissue or stockings inside your swimsuit, something every young woman would do at one time or another even if they would never admit to it. So I walked around the school track and took the stairs when I would rather have taken the elevator or escalator. I ran alone and with supportive friends, and I jumped rope on the sidewalk outside of my house.

I now belonged to Mrs. Elrod. She was a Mary Kay distributor, and she took a lot of time with me to share her knowledge. She showed me how to meticulously apply makeup suitable for this competition. I was already behind many of the girls that had been in other contests. But I couldn't spend time thinking about that. This was a different time and a different contest, because I was in it. I decided I need some real practice.

I looked for other opportunities and distractions around the community. Along with other girls in Omaha I participated in the Alpha Eta Chapter of Kappa Alpha Psi Fraternity's Sweetheart Ball at the Diplomat Motor Inn. I was one of eight girls at Omaha University who were a part of the contest. We were named the Kappa Kourt. The girl chosen that night at the Valentine's Day Sweetheart Dance would be crowned the Alpha Eta Chapter Kappa Sweetheart for 1969. The judges were made up of the Omaha Alumni Chapter of Kappa Alpha Psi Fraternity. Their decision was based on personality, charm, poise, academic aspirations, civic and social contributions, and contributions to Kappa Alpha Psi. The judges spent a lot of time meeting with us individually and as a group. Although I was not chosen as the Kappa Sweetheart, I got a lot out of the experience. I needed to be able to compete with girls who grew up knowing what knife to use at the table and how to sit properly.

I was still in a fog and had not really accepted the fact that I was going to participate in the Miss Omaha Pageant. It wasn't long before the announcement was in stores and newspapers across the city. The entry forms were now available at the Jaycees headquarters. A lot of girls were interested, but most of them didn't follow through with the application process. The announcement said, "The pageant is open to single girls between 18 and 28 years of age who will have graduated from high school as of September 1970. The winner will be chosen based on . . ." All that stood out to me was the word *beauty*. Poise, personality, and talent were included, but it was, after all, a *beauty* pageant. We were required to present three minutes of talent, such as singing, dancing, playing a musical instrument, creative poetry, or dramatic reading. Just going through the list was exhausting and overwhelming to me. But I just kept thinking, "Scholarship, scholarship. That's why I'm doing all this. Keep your eye on the prize." So I just kept practicing and practicing. Even my minister supported me, praying with me after church. The Sunday before the pageant, the entire church prayed for me. I encouraged my friends to pray and to keep their fingers crossed. My sister Joyce finally finished making my evening gown for the contest. It was beautiful. Everything was coming together, and I was ready!

It wasn't very long before I heard my name announced for the second time in front of a room full of people at the Western Electric Company building. I had sailed through the preliminary portion of the contest, and now I was among ten finalists.

"Next is Catherine Pope. This evening she is doing an original reading and singing 'Exodus.'"

The crowd gave me a warm welcome. When I finished, the crowd yelled, screamed, and whistled. I suppose it wasn't very polite, but it made me feel good and I enjoyed every moment of it. Because of the strong lights it was difficult to see my mother and father, but I knew they were there.

At the end of the pageant, the judges handed the contest runner their decisions. My parents said that after that it seemed like the clocks stopped. Finally the pageant host and hostess came out on stage. Then all of us had to return to the stage. By this time my face was hurting from smiling so much, and my feet hurt from walking and standing in new shoes. But I was happy.

"The Miss Talent title goes to La Rae Koppit, nineteen. Miss Congeniality goes to Diana Ervin, eighteen." Everyone was applauding. "Our Second Runner-up is Donna Olmsted, eighteen. First Runner-up is, specifically and this is an important title, in case our queen for some unforeseen reason cannot fulfill her duties as Miss Omaha . . ."—another pause—"Catherine Pope, nineteen. Miss Omaha of 1968 is . . ."—the music began and a long pause for drama.—"Lindsey Bloom! A seventeen-year-old Central High School senior is the winner. Her plans are to become a dance instructor. She does her own choreography." All of us gathered around her, congratulating, hugging, and kissing her as the former Miss Omaha and the hostess struggled to put the sash across her body, the flowers in her arms, and the crown on her head. Then the music began again, and the new 1968 Miss Omaha began walking down the long runway waving her hand just like they taught us in our practices.

On our way home that evening my parents suggested we go out and "celebrate Cathy."

"Why, you are the first runner-up!" my mother said. "You heard him. If something happens to her—God forbid—you will be obligated to perform her duties. Anyway, think of all that you learned. I'm sure that when you enter next year you'll win. Why, you can't help but win."

All I could help but think to myself was "What in the world could she possibly be thinking?"

My dad had to respond to that. "Juanita," he said sharply. By now we were close to home. "Juanita, that girl doesn't want to do this again. Once is enough. Besides, this has cost us too much money."

"Bud, don't discourage the girl. There's next year. She'll be Miss Omaha 1969. That's a much better year anyway. Don't you think so, Bud?"

"Let me just drive, Juanita." My dad was disgusted. He couldn't believe that my mom was already planning for next year.

As time went on after the pageant things began to calm down. I was slowly forgetting about the contest. The negative calls and letters from people were dwindling and subsiding. So were the ones letting me know how proud people were of me for attempting to participate in a contest that was for whites only. I was glad that my family had now chosen other things to talk about and to focus on at the dinner table on Sunday afternoons. We were now smiling and laughing again. We weren't afraid to answer the phone or get the mail like we were before the contest. Things seemed to be getting back to normal.

To me the experience was like running a race. I stopped at the finish line but my heart felt as if I were still racing, telling me that I was still moving, still running. I realized that I hadn't come to a complete stop.

In August it was announced that I was a recipient of the Youth Incentive and Scholarship Committees of the Urban League of Nebraska Martin Luther King Jr. Scholarship for $300. When I signed the check, I proudly noticed the names on it: Jack V. Clayter, Executive Director; Mrs. Elizabeth Davis Pittman, Co-Chairman, Youth Incentives & Scholarship; Joseph A. Cowans, Scholarship Coordinator. The board was made up of prominent citizens in Omaha: Leo Daly, Peter Kiewit, Dr. Claude Organ, Dr. A. B. Pittman, V. J. Skutt, and Willis A. Strauss. The fund provided more than $59,000 in scholarships to 131 students. The scholarship was established after the North Omaha riots in response to the assassination of the Reverend Dr. Martin Luther King Jr.

That same year Robert Kennedy came to North Omaha seeking nomination for president. In his speech he spoke in support of civil-rights activists. As a Young Democrat, I met with Robert Kennedy. Along with several other students, we asked for his assistance in addressing the needs of our youth and postsecondary students in our community.

I continued to be active and involved in my community. I could tell that my mother was becoming weaker, and my family was growing more concerned about her fragile condition. But she never said a word; she never complained. Throughout my life I always thought that I was a problem for her, and this Miss America Contest and all the stuff that it involved was no different. No matter what she said to try to make me believe otherwise, I was sure I was one of the reasons for her condition. She wanted so much for me, but what did I really want for myself and what was I willing to sacrifice in order to get it?

The Top Tan Beauty Contest (second from right)

The Kappa Kourt.
(photo courtesy of Omaha Star)

Miss Omaha 1969.
(photo courtesy of Omaha World-Herald)

178

18

Can't Turn Around Now

The Run for Miss Omaha 1969

I had lost my 1968 bid for Miss Omaha, but I didn't have much time to feel bad about it or sorry for myself. I never dropped the ball in my personal life. I was working, acting, singing around the city, and preparing for my junior year at UNO. But swirling around me was utter chaos. In the midst of everything, as if we didn't have enough going on, the city was like a war zone. There were ongoing riots, robberies, and looting. Black men and women were shot in the streets by Omaha's "finest." There was a growing dissatisfaction with the Omaha Public Schools. The Black Panther Party was becoming stronger, along with other activist groups, because of the growing dissatisfaction with the leaders in the black community and white and black politicians. Groups across the city were confronting the police and making no effort to back down when looking down the wrong end of a gun. Our ministers continued to stress nonviolence from their pulpits, along with ongoing prayer and marching in the streets, hoping for a better world or at least a just America.

Mrs. Elrod called me on a Saturday afternoon to ask me what I thought about entering the Miss Omaha Pageant for the second time. Before she could even finish her pitch, I was laughing out loud.

"Okay, what's so funny?" she asked.

"Well, my mother must be reading your mind. She asked me the same thing this morning."

"To be perfectly honest," she said, "I spoke with her this morning, and we both feel that you should try it again. But to be honest and upfront with you, I have to confess, the group that approached you and supported you last year are considering putting forth the name of another black girl this year. Maybe you know her? Sharon something? And if that's the case, there would be three of you entering because another girl, Vivian, has already submitted her name."

I was proud to think that maybe because of my willingness to participate last year several other girls now had the courage to step out and put their names forward as candidates.

Jeri said everything in one big breath. "I'm noticing some hesitation on your part. You're awfully quiet. Could I come over so we can discuss the pros and cons of all of this before you make your final decision?"

Jeri was a good saleswoman, but it would take more than that to convince me to reenter a contest that had left me empty and confused. My feelings, though, were the least of it. My family had spent a lot of money on me. I didn't know what I expected to get out of this contest. So far I hadn't really won anything—especially a scholarship, the thing that I needed and would value the most. Titles didn't impress me. I valued making a difference, and if I won that's exactly what I wanted to do. I wanted to use my title to encourage young men and woman. I wanted to be a living example of what was possible, even for a poor black girl from the ghetto. But I questioned all of the sacrifices that my family and I would have to make to fulfill this dream of mine. Or, was there a greater purpose?

I looked at the phone and couldn't believe what came out of my mouth next. "Okay, I agree with you. It won't hurt to talk about it." She just didn't understand that my answer would be no. I didn't get it. Why again? Why me? I was fighting for voter rights, a community police force, jobs and decent housing, medical benefits for the elderly and underserved. I was demonstrating with groups protesting the disparities in the stocking of food pantries in low-income communities, completing my degree, and taking on more responsibility at home because of my mother's mounting illnesses. This contest had already cost my family money and time and emotional distress. How could I ask them to go through this again? If Mrs. Elrod's organization had another girl running in the contest, saying no wouldn't be letting anyone down except my own mother.

Mrs. Elrod arrived early for our meeting several days later. When she arrived she told us there were two other guests who might stop by. As we sat on the couch making small talk my mind drifted to all of the unrest across the city, the race riots. All of the distrust that existed between whites and blacks was flowing out into the streets.

"Do you think the other people will be here soon?" my mother gracefully asked while sipping on her tea.

"I don't know. We don't need to wait for them," Mrs. Elrod responded.

I quickly spoke up. "I never really understood why I was chosen to run last year, and I understand even less why you want me to try again."

"That's a fair question, Cathy. The idea was brought up by one of the ladies in our group." She answered my next question before I could ask it. "Who isn't important? We felt that Omaha never had a black beauty queen, nor did the national pageant. I think that Omaha deserves another chance, don't you?" She quickly filled the stunned silence answering her question. "Anyway, we noticed all of the wonderful things you were involved in and accomplishing for the benefit of the community, and we were impressed by your stewardship. We were also impressed with your commitment and your follow-through. Of course we know how talented you are. And smart. More importantly, you're an excellent role model for girls, *all* girls." It felt like she was reading from a teleprompter. "Another thing was several people in our group heard that you expressed an interest in this contest months ago, that you were very interested in the scholarship because you needed the money for school. Is that right?"

"Well, yes," I answered slowly.

But I was growing impatient. I noticed that she hadn't mentioned my outer appearance. "What about beauty? Isn't that important?" I suspiciously asked. I wanted to be pretty enough to win a beauty pageant while also talented and engaging enough to not have to be pretty. As a child I never even thought about something as shallow as whether or not I was pretty. Even now I think it's frivolous to be preoccupied with one's looks when there are far more important things to focus on in this world. But, like most girls and women of all ages, being the beautiful Cinderella is far more attractive than being relegated to being the ugly wicked witch, and I'm no different—although throughout my life I was never considered to be the "pretty one," a rose among thorns. I heard and appreciated compliments from others about my attractiveness, but it made me feel uncomfortable, as if they were speaking of someone else—like I was trying to get into a dress that was the wrong size. I thought I had gotten over most of my insecurities, but I guess not.

Looks and body image plague a lot of men as well as women, although most men would never admit it. But women young and old alike support a billion-dollar industry trying to reach an image of perfection. Me—well, I don't know what I think about myself, but I do know that whether I like it or not or whether people in America want to admit it or not, it is damn important.

"Of course all of us considered that, but we don't want that to stop us from putting you or someone who looks like you forward."

Wow. That felt like a slap in the face. Was she saying that my black skin and "Negroid" features stood in my way of winning, or was I just being overly sensitive? All my life my parents had told me that I was a pretty girl. My grandmother would tell me, "You're pretty, but your hair is . . . nappy." Or, "You're pretty, but—if only you were lighter, not so dark, just lighter like your sisters." Some people made me wonder if they were even my sisters. It was obvious that the light-complexioned girls got the best parts in the school plays, or at least second to the white girls. And they always got the dates and boyfriends. Darker girls got the leftovers.

Mrs. Elrod was still talking. "Your mother was casually telling Mrs. Goodwin that when you were little you told her you wanted to enter this very contest. And of course you know how things happen. Mrs. Goodwin told Susie Buffett over lunch one day, and they came up with the idea of having you enter the local Miss America Contest. Why you? Well some of us think, and that includes your mother, why *not* you?"

The stares from neighbors, the laughs coming from those who really didn't know or like me, the whispers behind my back, and the many anonymous phone calls had encroached on my family's peace and privacy. Each night I filled my prayers asking God to help me forget about the pageant. I felt like an oddity. Sometimes I felt like I needed to move away to another city or state. I wanted to be invisible. My old dreams were returning from when I was a little girl. I would see strange, faceless people standing around my bed. I didn't know who they were or why they were standing all around me. I hadn't had those dreams for over seven years, but now they had returned. I had night sweats. My legs were in pain. I didn't want to take any chances on making this all worse by participating in the contest again.

"The doorbell! Your mother's in the kitchen, Cathy, and I don't think that she can hear the doorbell."

I did not move, which confused Mrs. Elrod.

"Cathy, someone's at your door," she said, a little louder.

That time I jumped up, still thinking about faceless strangers, and went to the door and swiftly opened it. Two ladies I had never met entered.

"Hello," I said. "Would you like to sit down?"

"Thank you," one of them responded. They both sat down in the living room.

"Jeri, let's get right to the point," one of them said. "The other black girl, Sharon, decided not to run for Miss Omaha. I don't think she wants to go through all of the scrutiny and emotional distress that"—she looked at me—"that Miss Pope has gone through."

I thought now maybe the whole idea associated with putting a black girl back in this contest would be dropped, without any further consideration. But I could see that we needed to discuss this a little further. I was determined to push ahead.

"That's good," my mother said, interrupting with a smile as she served coffee and tea on an old, rusted TV tray.

I couldn't believe her. I couldn't believe what I was now hearing. I kept trying to get her to look at me, but she wouldn't even turn her body in my direction.

"Well now, what's next?" I said. I couldn't believe that was coming out of my mouth. I had no clear explanation why I gave in so quickly, except for the fact that I always welcomed a challenge, and a good fight was irresistible. Tell me or make me feel as if something can't be done, and I'll go out of my way to prove you wrong. I guess that's why I was always a civil-rights activist—I guess it's just in my blood.

"Well, this time," Mrs. Elrod began, "it's going to be a little more difficult."

"Why?" I asked.

"Well, they saw you already. The judges and the city saw you lose."

"Psychologically?" I was thinking out loud. "I get it. You think that it's imprinted in their minds that I'm a loser. That we can't, nor should we, win against a white girl." I allowed my words to sink in, as if I were physically jumping in with both feet.

"That may be right," Mrs. Elrod said. "But of course we'll never really know that for sure, especially if we don't try again. Cathy, we don't want to push you to do anything that you really don't want to do." She was smiling at me but remained very serious.

For the first time I didn't see her as just someone involved in a group. I was beginning to also see her as a new friend. Jeri was a medium-height, small-framed, white woman. I always thought she was pretty. She sometimes wore her hair curly and hanging at shoulder length, while at other times it was cut short and wavy. Her hair was usually two colors, dark brown and dishwater blonde, like she couldn't make up her mind or something. Omaha's community saw her as Reverend Jerry Elrod's wife, but I saw her as a strong community activist making a recognizable difference in Omaha. I agreed to try again. I knew that it would be up to me to win this contest; no matter how much support they gave me, the outcome would rest on my shoulders. All of us shook hands, including my mother. I wanted to win; I wanted to become the first black Miss Omaha.

Mrs. Elrod became a dear friend. As time passed, we found ourselves virtually glued to each other. We spent so much time together preparing for the contest, that one of us would begin to say something and the other one would complete the thought. We discovered that we were focused on the same issues, and politically we were on the same page a lot of the time. I began not to take her criticism personally, and she began to let up on me when I became melancholy and depressed. She sought out other people in the black community, besides my own family and friends, who would support and encourage me, like Rodney Wead, a community leader and the director of Wesley House Community Center. She also connected me with Charles Washington, a national freelance photographer and writer who also worked for the *Omaha Star*. They were just two of many individuals who helped along the way. Even though they were extremely busy, they took me under their wings. As the date for the contest approached, time just flew by.

On one evening prior to the contest my mother was accosted and robbed while returning home from our neighborhood grocery store, not one block away from our house. The robbery was even more devastating because the same thing had happened to her many years before. I heard the scuffle from inside our house and ran outside, screaming for my dad, who was out in a flash. The perpetrator had snatched my mom's purse but then dropped it while running away. My mom was knocked to the ground and groceries lay all over the sidewalk and in the street. I wondered if the attacker knew us and had targeted my mother because of the contest. On many levels I felt responsible, even though I knew it was far-fetched. The police were called, but the man was never caught.

My mother was frightened by the robber, but she refused to let that squash her enthusiasm surrounding the pageant. If anything, she put more of herself into it. It was as if she were actually running for the title. I often wished she were.

I refused to let my family, the community, or any community organizations spend more money on me for clothes, shoes, makeup, or my gown. My parents had very little money. Everything that they had and the money that I earned from various jobs while in college mostly went toward our living expenses. I became perturbed when someone instructed my parents to purchase a new gown. I emphatically told my sponsors to forget it. My sister spent months designing and making my dress and extra hours and days sewing on beads and sequins. I loved that gown. If they wanted me to walk onto that stage, it would be in the evening gown created by my sister and worn in the last pageant. The subject was never brought up again. I happily took up jogging, however, because after all my big talk, stubbornness, and threats, I had to make sure that I still fit into my gown.

People in the neighborhood decided to get into the act. Mrs. Alston, our family friend and the director of the Sunshine Cultural School, thought that I needed more dance instruction. She had her daughter Sherri work with me during her free time. My mother's other friend, Mrs. Roundtree, felt that I needed to practice answering questions about local and world issues, so she suggested I begin to pick up the pieces of the newspaper discarded by my dad close to his favorite chair. I would read the paper from cover to cover.

The person who knew me the best and the longest outside of my family was my mom's friend Mrs. McIntosh. She told my mother that I had to go to the dentist and get my teeth cleaned if I wanted an impressive smile. She thought my smile was key to winning, and she was right; my teeth were somewhat dingy and stained. I hadn't been to the dentist in years. I was afraid to go to the dentist. I always saw myself strapped into a chair surrounded by instruments, and I felt the dentist had an advantage over me. But I knew she was right; getting my teeth cleaned was a necessity. My mother contacted the dental office while I was at school and made the appointment for me, never saying a word about my fear of The Chair.

By my third visit I was a pro, the perfect patient. It took a couple of visits to get me pageant-ready, and my final visit was scheduled for late in the evening. When I arrived I asked the office manager if I could brush my teeth, because I'd had a very late lunch and had had no time to clean them. The dentist's hygienist gave me a new toothbrush and a small tube of toothpaste to use. His staff was so polite. It was nice to see a black-owned business that was both efficient and courteous. I had begun to refer my friends to this dental office. I was happy with this new young dentist.

I hung my coat on the rack in the hall outside of Room 2 and took my purse and a book in with me. I sat in the large dental chair and began looking through a *Jet* magazine the nurse had given me. It was much more interesting than the book that I had with me. I heard steps coming down the hall and noticed an older gentleman walking by my room. A nurse was giving him instructions regarding denture care. I was glad that I wasn't there yet. The nurse came in and gave me a shot, preparing me for deep cleaning on one side of my mouth and probably a filling. At some point I realized I had been there for a long time, much longer than usual. I noticed how dark it was becoming outside. My dad was going to pick me up soon, and I wanted to be ready so he wouldn't have to turn off the engine and come inside.

I was on my third magazine, and I was becoming sleepy. I no longer heard the office staff, other doctors, and patients, or the nurses gossiping. It was obvious that most of the workers and patients were gone. Then, from around the corner the nurse appeared. She had me sit up straight in the chair and straightened out the towel that was around my neck.

"Cathy, swish this around in your mouth and spit it out. Now rinse and do it again," the nurse instructed. "Relax. I'm going to give you a shot. It won't hurt."

Finally the dentist appeared. "Okay, I'll take over now. I can finish things up. You can go home. It's getting late." He handed me a small paper cup and an even smaller pill to help me relax. I could have sworn that the nurse had already given me several shots. As I listened to the low music playing, I took the pill, and began drifting off to sleep.

When I had arrived it was lightly snowing. It was really coming down now, and I was becoming concerned about my dad driving around in inclement weather, even as I slowly drifted in and out of consciousness. The lights were low, and the elevator music was soporific. The doctor began elevating the chair. I heard the nurse enter again and let him know that she had forgotten several instruments. She placed them on the small, round table in front of me as he adjusted the light. I could hardly hear her talking to him. I did hear her voice fade, as she said she was locking the front door, and then I didn't hear her at all. She was gone.

He told me to relax and lowered the chair in a deep reclining position. "Open your mouth," he told me.

I could barely hear or see him now. I was sleepy and delirious. I felt lightheaded, out of control. "Don't be so nervous; stay still."

I could tell that he was becoming agitated with me as I fidgeted. I felt him lift my head slowly as he removed the cloth around my neck. I could hear and feel the buttons loosen on my blouse, slowly, one by one. As my white blouse opened, I could feel a slight breeze and urgent spurts of his hard breath hitting my chest as he leaned over me. I was working hard to hear and see now.

"You're as pretty as they say you are. People around town are talking about you running a second time for Miss Omaha. Let me tell you, as beautiful as you are, I think you should have won the first time. If I would have been a judge you would have won." I was startled by the sound of a quick snap—the front hook of my bra coming undone. A hand wet with perspiration jostled for position between my thighs, while the other hand was fumbling, trying to caress my breasts. I struggled to move, feeling paralyzed and dazed. With everything that I had in me I sat forward, toppling over the tray in front of me and breaking the arm of the dental chair. I slammed the light while instruments flew everywhere. Now the light wasn't on me, it was on him. I was quickly regaining my bearings. Jumping up from the chair, I pushed him away from me, daring him to step toward me as I clumsily pulled down my skirt with one hand while holding him at bay with the other.

"What's wrong with you? What's going on?" I screamed, as I tried to button my wrinkled blouse. "You were touching me!" I was out of breath, tired and confused.

"Shush. Be quiet. Someone might hear you," he said as he turned away from, me fumbling with his pants while attempting to compose himself. I was getting nauseous. I hadn't noticed his pants undone before.

"What did you do? What did you do?" I yelled.

"Nothing," he snarled. "Nothing."

"Something's wrong with you! You're sick!" I cried.

He just stood there saying nothing, with a blank stare spread across his pitiful face. He was no longer smart, nice, or good looking to me. He was a disgusting man who used his position to prey on women and girls. I stumbled toward the door and grabbed my things. I was dizzy and lightheaded and had a strong headache, but I successfully opened the locked door. He was shifting back toward his power.

"You know you wanted this as much as I did, and now you're playing so surprised and hurt. I could tell by the way you came in here each visit. Smiling and talking, dressing so nice and sexy." He was talking fast and now becoming louder. For a moment he made me question myself and my personal intentions, but only for a moment. Men who committed crimes like this always tried to make the victims feel like it was their fault. I looked back at him for the last time as I ran to the door.

I hadn't heard my dad banging furiously on the other side. Maybe that's why the dentist wasn't chasing me. Right away my dad started shouting, "What's going on in there?" I opened the door to the hallway and pushed my dad backwards, stumbling over his shoes. He tried to move around me but I kept pushing, moving him toward the elevator. As the elevator went down I took a deep breath and begged my dad to listen to me without saying a word. But he couldn't wait.

"What was going on in there? You don't look right. Look at your hair." He opened my coat, which made me recoil. "Look at your clothes; they're all wrinkled and dirty. Hurry up girl, answer me."

"If you'll just give me a chance, I'll tell you. It was just a misunderstanding. You know how I am around dentists. I became frightened when I saw the needle coming at me, and I instinctively pushed over the table and broke the arm of his chair. I didn't mean to, it just happened."

"We should go back up there and see if he's all right. He wasn't hurt, was he?" My dad was suspicious, and I don't think that he really believed me at all.

"Oh, I don't think he wants to see us right now." I was still breathing fast and talking just as fast, hoping that I was making sense. I didn't know why I was making up this story. I knew I needed time to think up an even better story; because I certainly wasn't going to tell the truth.

"You're sure everything is all right? What about him? Is he okay? And the bill? What about the bill? You didn't tear up the office, did you?"

We were now on the main floor, for which I was thankful. "Yes, Dad, I'm sure. I'll explain things to you later. Let's just go home. We can discuss everything in the morning, I promise."

On the long ride home I began to compose myself enough to realize that if I told my dad what actually happened he'd probably go home, get his gun, and kill the man. This was confirmed when my dad wouldn't let up. "Why are you so jumpy, girl? Why did you run out of there like someone running for their life? I have eyes. I can see. I wasn't born yesterday. That man did something in there, and you'd better tell me or you'd better believe me he will."

Arriving home, I said goodnight to everyone, ran up the stairs to my room, closed the door, fell on top of my bed, and cried while my body shook. I had to take a shower to wash off all of the scum that tightly clung to my body. Then I took a bath to help soothe the aches and pains pounding my body. Every bone ached, every muscle was tight, and every quiet tear took something away from me. He had taken something away from me, and I was determined to get it back. Just as I had mustered up the strength to stop him from raping me, I would gather the courage to see to it that he never had an opportunity to do it again. As I brushed my hair, I noticed that there was blood caking up on my lower lip. When I opened my mouth, I saw more blood, coming from my lower gums. My gums were swollen and must have been cut when I struggled to get out from under his grip. That night when I said my prayers, I prayed for my family, my friends, the people who supported me, and—I don't know why, and I don't want to be judged—but I prayed for my lost dentist and asked for God's mercy.

The next day I got up before anyone else in the house and placed my torn blouse in a brown paper bag so I could dispose of it. My dad was still asking me what happened. I told him not to worry about it. I said I would take care of everything and then changed the subject.

It would be months before I told anybody about what happened. I probably never would have, except I read in the paper that he was being recognized for being an outstanding role model in our community. That prompted me to tell my family what had happened. They quietly notified the Nebraska Board of Dentistry and demanded that he lose his license. When it became public, other women began coming forward with similar stories.

I don't know if I was ever vindicated. He molested me and he violated me. He hurt and disappointed me, and he let down the community that he swore to serve. I don't think he lost his license. I never found out what happened to him legally. I was ultimately glad I didn't push it under the rug or hide what happened. The experience helped me to face the world without shame and with an earned sense of dignity.

Because I didn't have much time before the contest I found another dentist in town. He was thorough and efficient. My teeth glistened white; but my smile was weak, with the corners of my mouth slightly turned down. With the help of my family and my pastor at Mount Moriah Baptist

Church, I found the strength and courage to intentionally put that traumatic experience behind me, at least for the time being. I knew that I might not ever get over that experience, but I began to carry it like a badge of courage. I was determined to be a positive example for other young women who might experience the same thing.

I was walking straighter, waving better, and over time smiling wider. The word was getting around not that a black girl was running for Miss Omaha but that the same black girl was running. More advertising was popping up all around the city, and radio and television announcements let people know about the pageant.

I was ready for the Miss Omaha Pageant, but I didn't know if the Miss Omaha Pageant was ready for me.

Representing the mayor to welcome visitors from France.
(photo courtesy of Omaha Star)

19

The Semifinals

Miss Omaha 1969

It's not easy for five people to get dressed in a small house with one tiny bathroom, especially when all of them have to be ready at the same time. On this date, however, we all did manage to dress and leave the house on time, a small miracle for the Pope family. I left the house last, with my parents following close behind me, turning out the lights and locking the door.

"Do you have your dress? Make sure the bag is tightly zipped." My mother's voice was low yet steady.

I immediately turned around and went back into the house. I had left my shoes on the bed and my snug slip–bra combination in a brown bag in my dresser drawer. Everything else was now in the trunk of our car. When I returned to the car I squeezed into the back seat. From the front seat, my mother read over the list that we'd made together the night before, and my father started down the street, leading a short caravan of three cars. Looking on were many well-wishers.

It was Sunday, March 30, and our destination was the Flamingo Supper Club, for the semifinals for the Miss Omaha Pageant. As we made the first turn onto Hamilton Street on our way to the Flamingo, a place that hosted many city events throughout the years, I decided to go over my speech. I had practiced and practiced for this second try, but I guess you just can't practice enough when something means so much to you. It was then that I realized I didn't have my music. The musicians were all new to me, so to not have my music with me was not an option. Telling my dad that we had to go back to the house was something that I had to do without any hesitation, even though I was reluctant. It was always hard for me to talk to my dad, especially when it came to questioning him or consulting him on the future. His sometimes poor decision making regarding family finances often stood in the way of us seeing eye to eye. Sometimes he was a pleasant kind of man, but his entire life was spent dealing with the here and now, and he usually thought he was right without question. I suppose my father was no exception among the many Negro fathers in my community.

"Dad, we need to turn around and go back to the house. I forgot my music!" I had no intention of telling them that I had also forgotten my oration, especially since I was supposed to have it memorized. I was so worried about making a mistake and disappointing my family.

We turned the corner and silently went back to the house. Everyone else kept going. We were the only ones that went back to the house. I could tell he was seething. The only thing you could hear was the engine. My father pulled into the driveway and put the car in park, and I quietly opened the door and got out of the back. It wasn't easy: we had a one-car garage with a short driveway bordered by two brick walls. The walkway was made of uneven bricks that had been pushed out of place by the roots of several overgrown trees. My high-heeled pumps made me stumble and feel legless. It wasn't the first time that I felt that way.

After retrieving the rest of my things from my room I stopped and looked around for several moments. It was as if I were seeing my small space for the first time: the red, white, and gray linoleum floor, the black table I used as a desk that had belonged to my mother and before that to Mrs. Gooden, whom I called Grandmother. We had painted that desk a shiny black every Christmas for as long as I could remember. Before it was mine, it always had a special place of honor in our living room where my mom would put out the fruit cake, pecans, Christmas candy, and Mogen David wine for guests who came through. My record player, which stood next to the desk, was spinning without a record, and I turned it off. Then I quickly made up my bed. I turned around a second time to look back at my room as I ran down the stairs and locked the door behind me. I was very mindful that a lot of people knew that no one would be home that night, so I checked the lock several times before heading back to the car. I opened the car door and slowly got back in. I had so many mixed feelings. I wanted to hurry up and get to the contest, but at the same time I hesitated because I had no idea what was about to happen.

"We had better hurry," my mother said. "The last thing we want to do is be late to the pageant."

We talked a lot and even laughed a little on the way. I enjoyed that ride. My cup was full on that late afternoon. Our neighbors waved to us and called out good luck, casting a warm, exuberant feeling over me. My mother especially enjoyed that warmth from our neighbors. I could tell by her smile and continuous thank yous to the crowds. As we traveled through the streets, more and more people continued to wave to us. It was as if we were in an impromptu parade. My mom rolled down her window, smiled a big wide smile, and stuck her arm out of the window, waving back to each and every one of them. Even the people in the traffic didn't seem to mind. People along the way slowed down to see what was going on as we continued on our way. I believe that most of them had heard about the contest on their radio and television sets.

"Good luck, Cathy!" one elderly lady cried with pride from her doorway. She was out of breath. "We're praying for you, honey." Others stood in their yards with their small children, pointing at our car. I don't know what they were telling them, but I'm sure it was positive.

People continued to yell, "You can do it!" and "Wish we could be there!" The excitement was coming at us from both sides of the street. People we hadn't seen or spoken to in years, along with people living outside of our neighborhood, were there to support me. After all that I had been through it felt good to know that people cared.

I noticed my father as he looked through his rearview mirror. He teared up, noticing me watching him. "Seeing our neighbor's proud faces made me choke up a little."

I let the window down and began waving, but put it up after several blocks to save my makeup and hairdo. I wish I had waved all the way from my house to the event. It was respectful of those folks, and much needed for us, and they deserved my respect and more.

We arrived at the Flamingo, where several smiling people were present to greet us, all of them white and beautifully dressed in evening wear and uniforms. My father was encouraged to turn over his keys to a young man who looked like he worked for the restaurant. It wasn't easy for him to trust others with his prize possession. He loved it because he owned it outright, and he didn't trust valets. My mother whispered something in his ear, and he reluctantly handed over his keys. I looked back to make sure that I had removed everything from the car, and then we went into the restaurant.

My parents were escorted to a large room, and I was directed to go in the opposite direction, a large room being used for a dressing room. I found myself standing among a large group of young women, all of whom were smiling, laughing, and talking. None of them seemed to notice me standing there. They were focused on themselves and going over their acts, stretching and reciting to themselves. But that was quite all right with me, because I was enjoying watching the commotion and listening to the chatter. The girls began showing each other their beautiful clothing for the contest, and I finally moved to talk with several girls that I knew. The only other black girl in the contest was Vivian Lewis, and when we found each other we didn't part until forced to. Most of the girls were showing each other their beautiful dresses and teasing each other about the rollers in their hair, their makeup, and their unusual hairdos. Several times I even looked down at my own attire and reached up to touch my hair.

I suppose I was becoming a little uncomfortable with myself. I was really tired, and I felt drained and confused. At times I was up and then just as quickly I was down, almost depressed, and I didn't understand why. One of my sisters said that it was hormones, something that I couldn't help, but I knew better. I knew that I had better get hold of myself, because this was it and there was no turning back. I didn't want to become unsure of myself—that would be catastrophic—so I asked to be moved to another location. I wanted to go over my act but not publicly. In case anyone had been at the contest the year before, I didn't want them to know that I was using the same act. I kept looking around for my family, but I couldn't see them, and since none of the other girls were asking for their parents, I didn't want to appear to be silly by asking for mine. Then I heard someone say in a deep, loud voice, "Keep Miss Pope's family out of here!" I could see a large bouquet of flowers, but I couldn't see the person carrying them, nor did I know where they went.

Now the chaperones were arriving, and they began finding the young ladies they were responsible for. Soon we were all getting dressed for the first act. Musicians were tuning up their instruments, stagehands were setting up, and the master of ceremonies was looking around for direction. Extra workers were setting up the large dining room for guests, and cameras and lights were positioned around the room. Newspaper men and women were everywhere, ready to write a story.

People were arriving to enjoy the Miss Omaha Pageant. There were twenty-eight of us participating in the semifinals. We sang, danced, played the piano, read poetry, and performed dramatizations. We modeled in bathing suits, casual wear, and evening gowns. We answered questions and smiled, talked to judges and smiled, shook hands and smiled, and when it was almost over and we were brought to tears, we fought them back and continued to smile. All of us did our best, and in the end we stood together anxiously awaiting the results.

The ten finalists were announced, and one by one we stepped forward to the front of the stage as our names were called by the master of ceremonies. "The finalists are Patty Blum, Jackie Buchholz, Helen Burdick, Cissy Jacobsen, Vivian Lewis, Diane Mencuso, Debbie Sullivan, Nancy Thomas, Ila Voss, and Catherine Pope."

The ten of us would compete again on Thursday, April 10, for the title of Miss Omaha 1969.

Volunteering to help young women find careers.

Working as a speech pathologist with the Eastern Nebraska Community Office of Retardation.

20

The Finals

I only had two weeks to prepare for the finals in the Miss Omaha Pageant. There was so much to do and so little time to do it in. I was mentally distracted. Would I win the pageant and then flunk out of school because I had missed too many classes and I hadn't studied hard enough? I was preparing to start a job as a speech and language therapist at the Eastern Nebraska Council of Mental Retardation. I needed that job. I didn't want to do anything to jeopardize my new position, and that included missing work. I also didn't want to hazard my career at Dory Passolt Models, where I worked as a model around town, because of another contract that would supersede any previous commitments. And yes, there was my involvement in politics. I worked hard for the Hamilton-Lake project. I was also a part of the McGovern Commission and had become a serious member of the Black Liberators for Action on the UNO campus. For sanity's sake, I continued with all my dance, music, and acting lessons. In between all of that I volunteered at the Boys & Girls Clubs of America. Even though I was having difficulty juggling all of it, I had managed to stay focused on the upcoming pageant.

I was surprised, but happy, when the negative phone calls and the racist, hateful dissatisfaction with my desire to continue down this path briefly came to a halt. I did not know what the rest of the contestants were doing to prepare for the finals, but I knew all were working hard. I was curious about Vivian Lewis. How was she feeling, and what was she thinking? If I didn't win, I was rooting for her. Although I was curious about her, I refrained from making contact with her, because we were competing with each other for the same prize.

My journey leading up to this competition hadn't been easy. I had made up my mind that I couldn't assume anything, especially about becoming the first black Miss Omaha. Excitement was growing among my family, neighbors, and friends. I felt special, and I was humbled by all of the people around the city offering moral and financial support. I practiced my vocal arrangement and my original dramatization so much I started forgetting the words.

"Cathy, that is incorrect. You are leaving off your endings. It's important for even the people in the back to hear you—they have to understand what you are singing and saying." My vocal teacher, Mildred Slocum, was direct when she coached, but she was also nice.

Everything was hard for me now, an adjustment. I was taking science classes, biology, chemistry, and European history. Sometimes I was working twenty-five to thirty hours a week, and I had to ride a bus to get to work. I spent time questioning myself, asking myself why I was putting myself through this all over again. But in the quiet times I knew that I was now living my dream, and it was important that I enjoyed every waking moment of it. In the end I knew that the decision was in God's hands; this humbled me and gave me some comfort and pause.

As the date of the pageant got closer, I started losing sleep. I would wake up at all hours of the night. I was excited and frightened at the same time. Bags were beginning to form under my eyes. I lost my appetite, which worked to my advantage: everything was fitting me like a glove. My costume for the talent competition was a long jumpsuit that had an oriental neckline. My swimsuit was a standard, unimpressive, black one-piece. I would wear the same gown in this pageant as I had in 1968. My other outfits were the same ones I had worn the year before.

On Sunday, April 6, my mother and sisters prepared a special celebration dinner with all the extras: macaroni and cheese, fresh mustard and collard greens, smoked turkey legs, string beans, mashed potatoes and gravy, fried corn, beets, and even Mom's sweet cornbread. For dessert Mom made sweet bread, a small, one-layer cake without icing. Some of our neighbors baked homemade cupcakes and cakes. I filled up on the aromas coming from the kitchen, tasting and nibbling as bowls were passed around the dining-room table. I didn't have much of an appetite. Our door was constantly opening and closing; you would have thought it was a saloon door, it was swinging so much. Most of the people arrived after church and hadn't had time to change their clothes, so they all looked very nice. It was one of the nicest, most spontaneous things ever done for me.

I ran in my neighborhood and exercised at the local gym, attempting to ward off all of my demons and tire myself out so I could sleep well before the contest. I used the art of self-talk and even meditation as a way of overcoming my feelings of not being worthy, and I found myself fortified:—renewed, as my minister often said in situations like mine. Most of the other girls had spent years participating in beauty pageants. They studied in private schools, where they learned the art of being a lady. Some of the girls studied abroad and spoke several languages fluently. I kept telling myself that I needed to settle down, that it was practically over. I wondered how Vivian and the other eight girls were handling everything. For some reason many things were hard for me. I struggled with negative opinions about myself, as well as my body image and my reluctance to feel worthy, to accept myself, and even to forgive myself for any pain that I may have inflicted on others.

The night before the event I refused to take calls or meet with any of my supporters and friends. Like a hermit, I holed up in my house, mentally preparing myself for what I considered at that time to be the event of my life. Just to be given an opportunity to run again would give me a chance to earn the money that I needed to help me stay in school.

That night I sat quietly at the dinner table. I pushed the meat around the plate with my fork and moved the potatoes and broccoli from one side to the other. All my uncertainties were causing me to lose my appetite the night before the pageant.

"Are you finished? You know tomorrow will be a long day, so you should eat. You didn't put very much on your plate," my mother gently nudged me. "I've watched people pass out in the choir because they got woozy—you know, they didn't eat and thought coffee or water would get them by. Oh well, scrape your plate and put your dishes in the sink if you're done. It's getting late, and you still need to roll your hair and prepare yourself for tomorrow."

Quietly and respectfully I excused myself from the table. My legs seemed heavy as I ascended the stairs. I went to my room, rolled my hair and wrapped it in my favorite scarf, removed my shoes and clothes, and entered our one and only bathroom in my robe. This evening I poured foaming bath salts into the water and ran a hot bath, as hot as I could tolerate. I kept thinking as I soothed myself in the tub that it was obvious to anyone who knew me that I had been hurt and my heart was broken. As I lay there I couldn't help but think back on my awful experience during my visit to the dentist. I was still frightened by the attempted rape, and in the still of the night I was haunted by his voice, his touch, and his insidious expression. I had been vulnerable, and he had tried to take advantage of my trust and in some ways had stolen my belief in him and others. Dr. Gooden would call it an open wound. He would say, "Be careful. Give your heart time to heal or it could leave a permanent hole."

I mused about all of the pain created in me and my yearning desire to be more, to expect more of myself and of others. With those thoughts, I closed my eyes and sank peacefully down into the billowing suds. I spent the evening soaking in my tub under the magical illumination of the moon. Finally I went to my bedroom. I was where I wanted to be, in complete and utter solitude, contemplating the upcoming events with definite resolve. Nothing could take God's gift away. Soon I fell asleep.

The following morning I emerged as myself, a fearless, black princess in a famous fairy tale. Not a damsel in distress, but a kick-butt princess rescuing the serfs and common people from the grips of the wicked queen. Where was the prince? He was waiting to be rescued by none other than me. That's how good I felt: totally and completely removed from any and all confusion surrounding me.

That evening as we left our house, I heard no car horns or screams of excitement echoing through the streets. I could only hear the voices of passersby, the screeches of fast-moving bikes stopping in quick spins, and sounds of kids taking in the final moments of street games under the shadowy lights. There were no neighbors waving banners, and there were only a few well-wishers who stood happily as we rode through the streets of Omaha on our way to the Flamingo Supper Club. It didn't bother me that there weren't people in the streets. Most of the community had my back; they had showed their support by attending the fundraisers held on my behalf. Many people in attendance had little to give, but when collection baskets were passed or envelopes were handed out most of them gave, and all together it was enough to help finance my second run in the pageant. But I was just happy that people called out to me and even smiled at me when they passed on the streets of Omaha. I felt their love and support. In that thought I had a newfound peace.

It was obvious to everyone who really knew me that I was hopeful, delirious and overwhelmed with expectation. I knew, however, because of my faith in both things that I could see and understand and things that were beyond my understanding that the winner had already been decided or chosen. I believed that God always knew what was going to happen. It was a part of his plan. To me there was a subtle comfort in that thought. I also knew that in support of all of those who had helped and encouraged me I had to do my very best. Someone else could have been in my shoes, and for them, I planned to radiate from the inside out.

Several of my friends and family wanted to be with me backstage, but they would have to be vetted by Mrs. Elrod and the police. The police were there to watch the public in case anyone was unhappy or disappointed with the decision. The police were also there for Vivian and me because several calls had been made to my home and answered by my mom just before all of us left for the event. My mom didn't want to upset me, but some of the calls that had come to our home before we left for the pageant really concerned her.

No one volunteered any information, but I overheard several sponsors talking about it behind a sheer partition separating all of us from one another outside of my well-lit dressing area.

My mother filled me in earlier, before we left the house. "Cathy, I have to tell you something. I don't know if you know it or not, but a detective came over today to ask your dad and me some questions."

"What kind of questions?" I continued focusing my attention on my last-minute additions to my suitcase and makeup bag. "What did you say?"

"Are we still getting those calls? When we leave here are we going directly to the pageant? Is your dad driving? You know, they went on and on. He even wanted to know what time we were leaving and the path we were taking. We got a few calls that were a little different than the ones we got before."

I hesitated, took in a deep breath, held it—and asked how the calls were different.

"He said a nigger wouldn't walk out of that club wearing their crown."

"Oh, Mom, we can't let a racist nut like that stop us from going. Besides, if I win I'll carry the crown out in my hand."

"Your humor, Cathy, isn't appreciated at all—at least by me."

I explained that I didn't mean anything disrespectful by my comment—I just didn't want these people to feel that they could intimidate me.

I began thinking about Vivian Lewis. I knew her, but not very well. We would smile at each other walking across the campus, and I would sometimes see her at dances on and off the campus. I always thought that she was as pretty as any of the other girls, black or white.

At the backstage entrance, several reporters wanted to speak with me, because of everything that was being said in the news. Some were black reporters from the *Omaha Star*. They spoke with other contestants, but I seemed to be the center of their attention. I can't say why, but they asked me a lot of questions, ranging from my acting and dancing in plays to my volunteer work in the inner city and across Omaha. I noticed by their press badges that they came from as far away as Chicago and as close as Council Bluffs, Iowa, and York, Nebraska, where this year's Miss Nebraska contest would take place. The police sent them away with stern words, pointing to the signs that said no one other than authorized individuals involved in the production had permission to be backstage. Even if the police hadn't been in the area to send them away, I had no intention of speaking with the reporters, or for that matter anyone else.

I stepped abruptly into the dressing room, canvassed my surroundings, and found an end seat in front of the mirror. Without help I managed to touch up my makeup, including repairing an eyelash that had come unglued. I put on more eye shadow and relined the black around my eyelids, removing the smudges. I resisted the overwhelming urge to put more makeup on my face. I suppose I just wanted to occupy myself, stay busy. Some people might call it fidgeting, or even messing around, for lack of a better word.

People were behind the stage, hurrying around and making sure everything was ready for the program.

"Okay, girls, hurry! It's almost time for the curtain to open. Get on your marks! Remember, we're doing this just the way we rehearsed. Don't forget to smile. Now, are you all ready? Smile! The curtain is opening."

We performed the opening dance number just the way they taught us. My mother later told me that she could tell that all of us were having fun.

When our opening number was over, the master of ceremonies took over. "Ladies and Gentlemen, one of these young ladies tonight will be chosen as our 1969 Miss Omaha."

There was tremendous applause as well as yelling and whistling. The lights above us were hot, and the room was packed to standing-room only and filled with excitement. Throughout the evening audience members cheered and shouted and left nothing to the imagination whenever their favorite contestant or family member performed alone.

My turn came quickly. "Next on our stage is Catherine Pope, and she will perform an original dramatic interpretation and sing the song 'Exodus.' " In this interpretation I spoke about some of the controversial things going on in the world: "war and people's disbelief in God and in each other." I followed with a dramatic vocal presentation of the theme from the movie *Exodus*.

We moved through the other phases of the contest: an off-stage interview with a panel of judges, the bathing-suit competition, the evening gown portion and an on-stage interview. When I walked out in my bathing suit, the master of ceremonies announced, "Miss Pope is 5'5½" and her vital statistics are 36-25-37." The paper later said, "There is no need to describe her bathing suit and evening gown appearances. They were, to put it mildly, 'uptight and out-of-sight.' "

For my on-stage interview I picked one question out of a fishbowl. The question was "What would you think if your date showed up wearing unmatched stockings?" My reply was later described as witty: "I would think he was very excited about taking me out." I received an enthusiastic response from the audience during my on-stage interview.

Our names were called for the last time. One by one, we stepped forward. When my name was called, I moved off my mark on the stage toward front and center, and then slowly turned so the judges could look at me from every angle. As I started to step back, I heard my stomach growl and remembered I hadn't eaten all day. I wanted to laugh, but I didn't. That was probably the first time that I wanted to laugh all day.

"Yes? Did you say something?" the announcer asked.

I had hoped I was the only one who'd heard my stomach's demands. "Oh, no," I quietly responded with a fixed smile, not wanting to be heard by the judges. After the final girl's name was called, we walked around in unison and exited the stage. It was almost over. We followed each other around the stage, each of us pausing briefly so the judges could get one last look, looking and smiling from one judge to another, not giving any one judge more time than the next.

It actually seemed like hours before they gave us our final call in preparation for the results. We were given one final lookover from our assistants and sponsors. They left, and the stage crew asked us to reattach our numbers to our dresses and smile again as we paraded ourselves for one last time onto the stage. As we walked out on the stage all of the judges smiled at us: Jack Claytor, Marlene Staenberg, Art Raglund, Christy Brehm, Roger W. Morgan, Ron Kaplan, James M. Henderson, Bill Larson, James Dunn, and City Councilwoman Betty Abbott. They were composed and seemed to be happy with their final decision.

The audience began moving forward so they could position themselves to get a better look, but they were told by the ushers and police to return to their seats. Only individuals displaying badges, reporters, and cameramen were given permission to be front and center. It was all overwhelming and fantastic. The floodlights were turned up. I could barely see the audience of over 700.

"Judges, may we have your final decision?"

One of the judges handed their decision off to the assistant, and in turn the paper was given to the master of ceremonies. He didn't open it. All of us stood in our gowns with smiles plastered to our faces. I thought changing my expression would probably crack my face.

"Ladies and gentlemen, last year's Miss Omaha, Miss Lindsey Bloom." While she made her final walk, the audience rose to their feet, cheering. Lindsey was beautiful. "Lindsey represented our city with elegance. She has made appearances all across Omaha. This will be her final walk," reported the master of ceremonies. She stood at the end of the catwalk while photographers took pictures. The flashes were blinding.

As she walked back toward us, I was thinking how important this was to my community. So many of them were there for me and for what this win would represent to our community. It was a positive and a first. I felt hopeful, even scared, and I also felt that it was important for me to make every effort possible to knock down those walls and barriers of exclusion for woman and children of color.

"Ladies and gentlemen, it's time for me to read the results. Before I do I would like to say that every young lady on this stage is a winner, and we would be proud for any one of these young ladies to represent our city." Lindsey Bloom stood by the master of ceremonies as he opened the first envelope.

"The second runner-up is Debbie Sullivan. She is the eighteen-year-old daughter of Mr. and Mrs. Danny L. Sullivan of Omaha." She was given a trophy. She composed herself and cradled the trophy in her arm. We all stood side by side, grasping hands as the next name was read.

"The first runner-up is . . . this is a very important award because if for any reason the winner cannot carry out her duties, the first runner-up will step in and carry out her duties. . . . Ladies and gentlemen, the first runner-up is Helen Burdick of Bellevue." She was also given a trophy. I kept looking around the packed auditorium. I knew my parents were there, but I couldn't locate them in the room.

The master of ceremonies asked for quiet among the crowd. There was silence as he opened the final envelope. "The winner of the 1969 Miss Omaha Beauty Pageant is . . . "

All of us held our breath. I was a bundle of nerves.

"Miss Catherine Pope!"

When my name was announced, I felt a squeezing pain in my chest and even became a little lightheaded. As he continued speaking, the girls on either side of me let go of my hands, and I moved up toward the master of ceremonies. I thought of my teeth, strangely, wondering if I had lipstick on them—something that occurred frequently whenever I applied the stuff to my lips. I slowly moved my tongue across them so that when I smiled I wouldn't have red teeth. Then I smiled a great big smile. I felt the tears roll down my cheeks, and I sucked in a large gulp of air in an effort to steady myself. I stopped right beside the now former Miss Omaha, wondering what it felt like to give up the crown as well as receive it. I would know that feeling next year when the new winner was crowned.

A sash was carefully placed over my head and under one arm. I adjusted it across my body. Next a bouquet of flowers was placed in one arm and a large trophy in the other. Finally the crown was placed on my head, and I began my walk. The judges as well as the rest of the audience stood and continued applauding as I walked across the stage from one side to the other before traveling down the catwalk. I stood on the end as photographers took my picture over and over again. Then I looked out across the excited crowd, and my heart seemed to stop beating when my eyes met my mother's. My next smile was meant for her alone.

When I walked back the other girls ran up to me, held me, and congratulated me. All of them seemed very sincere, but I could tell as they approached me that they were really disappointed—and they had every right to be. They had worked just as hard, had wished just as hard, and even dreamed about this night just as hard. I cautiously glanced over at Vivian as she left the stage along with the eight other young women. We smiled at each other. Most of us had very little contact during the contest. Photo ops, meet-and-greets, and several planned social events including dinners formed the extent of the contacts for the majority of us. We were worlds apart when it came to our day-to-day lives. I even had very little contact with Vivian, even though I liked and admired her. Immediately after I won I felt a sense of relief. I had crossed that bridge with the necessary space to prepare for crossing another.

As I descended the stairs from the stage, I was stopped by the reporters. I told the first reporter who stopped me that, "This was my biggest challenge." Then I was asked how it felt to be the first Negro selected as Miss Omaha. My response was "I think it's good, a beginning. I hope it encourages black men and women to aspire to higher things. I hope that it won't be considered my day, but a day for all young black people." I also told them that "I once considered not entering the contest, since I was first runner-up in 1968. But because I have very good parents, and very good friends, I was encouraged to enter the contest again."

One of the reporters spoke to my mother, who was standing with other members of our family in the lobby. According to the reporter she was very excited when he interviewed her. "I'm so proud, so proud," my mother said. "Now all the little children of the ghetto will have inspiration." My Aunt Lucille said that she was so excited when I won that she tried to go into the men's restroom!

I remained at the Flamingo for about one hour after the event was over, thanking all of my family and friends for coming out and helping me backstage and the entire community for their ongoing support. I also thanked everyone else who helped me get ready for the event—the ones in attendance and those who could not attend, especially Mrs. Jeri Elrod, Mrs. Fannie Lou Goodwin, Mrs. Susie Buffett, Mrs. Sharon Rhodes, and the other women from the Panel of American Women. I hugged those who were able to attend and sent my words of appreciation through them to the other women for everything that they were doing and did for me.

The next day the newspaper gave an account of the previous night's events. The following week I met with members of the Miss Omaha Committee, a part of the Omaha Junior Chamber of Commerce. Right away they began to help me set my agenda for my year as Miss Omaha. We set a later date to discuss the upcoming Miss Nebraska Pageant. The *Omaha Star* described my win. The lead was "Black Beauty Miss Omaha." The article began with "Glory came to the Black Ghetto Thursday night. She achieved the highest possible ratings in recent contests!"

There were a lot of folks excited about my win. I received letter after letter congratulating me. I waited for all of the appearances that were supposed to go along with my win. I made quite a few public appearances, but I noticed that most of my appearances came about through the efforts of many people in the black community. Most of them who had businesses let me participate in their bipartisan social and political activities. Citywide, I opened new businesses and I even opened a new auto speedway, arriving to the opening in a helicopter. It was my first helicopter ride.

It was my understanding that I would receive a car for at least one year, but for some reason that never happened. I did, however, receive several small scholarships from individuals and organizations. I was thankful—very thankful—for any and all educational contributions that I received from my city. I continued participating in local charity events, including raising money for the Project HOPE floating hospital, a ship that provided medical help to people around the world.

I tried to ignore most of the negative, hateful mail that continued coming to my home. Most of it came from people who really didn't know me, so I kept that in mind. It was coming from people who felt that I was a token, that I didn't deserve to win. In an odd sort of way I was becoming used to the threats, and I tried to put most of them out of my mind. But now they were even more serious than the threats during the previous pageant held in 1968. However, I continued to hold my head high; I continued to smile and carry out my responsibilities as Miss Omaha. At the end of the day I knew I that I was being tested in preparation for a greater test: my entry in the Miss Nebraska Pageant.

The duties of Miss Omaha: Picking winners . . .

Accepting trophies . . .
(top photo courtesy of Omaha World-Herald)

Cutting ribbons . . .

Receiving awards . . .

—World-Herald Photo.

The Bridal Suite

The Howard Johnson Motor Lodge, Seventy-second and Grover Streets, was opened formally Friday, although the five-story 213-room motel has been partly open for business since last October. Catherine Pope, who took part in the opening ceremony as Miss Omaha, is shown in the bridal suite.

Attending opening ceremonies . . .
(photo courtesy of Omaha World-Herald)

Standing next to cars . . .

Mingling . . .

21

The Journey

Threats and Intimidation

❦

As the Miss Nebraska Pageant came closer, so did the violence. I'm sure most people in my community thought I would back down when several misguided individuals tried to discourage me. I was confused and rightly so. People worked so hard throughout the years to better the relationship between whites and blacks in our city, and yet little was changing. My sleep was disrupted with frightening thoughts of losing my life. I couldn't shake the fear.

It reminded me of my childhood, spending hours in my bed unable to move due to the irons on each leg. All I could do then was think about my life and dream. The medicine used to stop the pain caused me to dream terrible dreams over and over again. Even now when I take medication for the old pain in my legs, in my dreams I feel myself drowning, falling, running lost through doors, searching for a way out.

For most of my life I kept a secret, and it manifested itself every now and then when I was faced with things that were out of my control. I was afraid of abandonment and being alone. Ironically, I would then spend even more hours alone, going to bed early. I remember in my teens overhearing my mother say to my dad that my behavior looked like depression. He told her that wasn't true, but then we saw throughout my mother's adult life that her sadness was not fully diagnosed. She was never given the understanding and care that could have changed her life. She wanted better for me. But I dealt with my anxiety and bouts of fear by sleeping a lot and staying to myself whenever possible. In my late teens I wanted to control this thing, whatever it was, but I really couldn't. So I began to control what I could, and that was my weight. I thought I was winning my own personal war against my insecurities about rejection. I controlled my food intake by taking laxatives and even throwing up if I overate. Like a magic trick, people began to notice me more. To my family, I was thin already, but now I was given more parts in plays—speaking parts—and singing and dancing parts in musicals. There were more requests for me to model around the city and in magazines. I was taking control of my life and loving it. I was selected again to do something that I always wanted to do, to try to become Miss America. But now because I was being held up as a role model by parents in my community I didn't like how my dirty little secret made me feel. I didn't want to tell anyone else, and I told myself I didn't have to—it had nothing to do with the contest.

Then the inevitable happened: I began losing control of my appetite. I didn't want to eat, or I wanted to eat too much, and my parents, especially my mom, thought I was getting too skinny. But I continued to get positive external reactions from this demon that was still controlling me. My bouts of euphoria were waning.

And now, people were trying to intimidate me as they had in the past by threatening me and my family. I worried about the fear it would create among my friends, supporters, and community members. Would they want to distance themselves from me, turn their backs because of the threats on my life? People who didn't want to see me participate in this contest made attempts to discourage me. It was rumored that in the early hours of the morning the custodial staff had discovered a noose hanging inside the student union in an undisclosed area outside of the women's restroom. I later heard that someone had informed the administration, but they attempted to hide what happened. I also heard that the noose was removed before most students had an opportunity to see it. However, news like that always gets out.

"Juanita, are you still outside? You should get back in here. It looks like rain, and I can tell by the clouds this morning that a terrible storm might not be too far behind. Forget about hanging the sheets and bedspreads out to dry. The man from Sears is coming sometime this week to fix the dryer." The wind was picking up, so my dad went out the front door and carefully made his way through the small side yard to the back of the house. He thought my mom needed help bringing the laundry back into the house. As he turned the corner he saw her rocking back and forth, with the sheets held tightly to her face. Mom pointed at the old oak tree in our backyard; the tree that could be clearly seen from my bedroom window was a fixture in our landscape.

"Bud . . . why? Bud? Why in 1969 are we still dealing with this?"

They both stood looking up at a noose hanging menacingly from our tree. Now he heard her cries and gut-wrenching sounds through the wet, white, cotton sheets. Her cries were soon audible from inside the house; I could hear her struggling to catch her breath.

Holding her up through the moans they shared, my dad said, "We have to get that thing down. Do you hear me, Juanita? We have to get it down before anyone sees it, especially Cathy."

I'll never forget that Saturday morning. My brother John and my father took the noose down from its low-hanging branch while several of us looked on. That large, thick rope, tightly knotted and secured on a limb, was meant as a message—threats—to me, just like the noose that was rumored hanging in the university.

The noose hanging outside my home was quietly removed, but if the other one really existed it would soon set off a tornado in the community. I knew that both were a clear warning to me because what I was again about to embark on would disrupt and challenge what the white community held dear and what they seemingly valued without question. Their view of beauty was described by an unnamed caller to my home as white, pure, pale, straight, blond hair, a European face, and blue eyes. Not even all of their own young women could pass that particular test. I would have told the caller that, but I wasn't given an opportunity. I knew my ancestors died for me to have the right to run in this and any other contest, and I wasn't about to let them or myself down. I was adamant about that!

The threats left on the phone made my father angry. Several of the calls were made by black folks who were frightened by all of the attention being drawn to our community. They made themselves very clear on each and every call. Whenever I answered the phone I tried hard to figure out who they were, but I didn't recognize their voices.

"Who do you think you are? What are you trying to do? White people don't want us messing around with their traditions. Your participation is causing too much trouble, and someone is going to get hurt. Why can't you Popes let things be?"

It was several days later when Charles Washington—Charlie, as he was called by most of us in North Omaha—came by the house to take pictures of me for the *Omaha Star* and *Jet* magazine. He spoke with me before he began taking pictures, asking me about my goals and dreams. He was such an intelligent and knowledgeable man that I felt comfortable speaking with him.

"Mr. Washington."

"Oh, call me Charlie please."

"Well, Charlie, did you know about the noose that was hung outside of my home the other day? I really don't understand why anyone would do something like that to me. I'm not important in the big scheme of things."

Responding thoughtfully, he said, "I can only guess based on our past history."

The noose's history in America dates back to the early 1820s. It was used to instill fear in African Americans and to symbolize that southerners still had control of the South and of blacks socially, politically, and physically. The noose is an ugly reminder of America's evil and unjust history when it comes to prejudice and discrimination against the African American race.

"Cathy, can't you see that they probably don't want you to inspire people to rebel? You've dared to attempt to cross over class barriers. You had the audacity to run."

What was he saying—that I was seen as an uppity nigger?

"Cathy, the noose is symbolic." I tried to understand him, but the more he tried to explain the more I questioned what it all meant. I just couldn't see how what I was doing fit into the bigger concern.

I was stepping into a taboo arena. Was I attempting to change the status quo? Was I changing society, or was I being punished for loving myself? Was it an evil thing that my parents had instilled confidence in me? Was I just a beautiful, uppity nigger trying to force myself into an environment where I was not welcomed? Did it haunt the minds of white women to think that blond hair and blue eyes might not be the only example of beauty? Would it be a strange thing for white women to take their daughters to the mall to get autographs from an African American beauty queen representing the entire nation? Was I a threat for entering this competition? Courageous, yet naive? Could I be the first African American woman to change and inspire a whole generation of girls?

I looked at the noose as a threat to myself and my family and a warning to all Negro girls and boys that dared to want to achieve the same things as their white peers. I was punished and threatened that day for loving myself and having the gall to try to make things change. I was committing a rebellious act, and they didn't want me to inspire other people.

This wasn't the first time that such a thing had happened in my community. I had no answers then, but I needed answers now. One of my dad's older friends took time to talk to me one night while he was visiting our home. "Although it's a threat, can't you see that they don't want people like you to rebel? How dare you cross over class? Can't you see, child, that God is using you? How dare you have the audacity to run? Don't you know what that noose represents? What the white folks are saying to you? Your ancestors would. It's a warning not to try to move into a different class, to stay in your place. This contest is for white folks. Think child; think about what you are embarking on. Are other black girls going to get inspired?"

Most of the time, my dad had wanted me to give up the idea of running for Miss Omaha. Whenever the subject came up, he usually said I should quit. When I had tried to become Miss Omaha in 1968 and lost, he felt enough was enough. "They have no intention of letting you win this time either." He said it many times, hoping I would see things his way and then reluctantly and sadly concede. But as tough as he could be, he hated to see the disappointment in my eyes. He was always seeing disappointment, especially when he had difficulty providing us with day-to-day necessities, and it was taking its toll on him. I often wondered why he didn't leave home like so many beaten-down, discouraged Negro men did. His eyes were narrowing, the thick folds of his upper lids hanging over yellowing whites. His face was tired and drawn. He had watched his children have their dreams crushed time and time again, and he could do nothing to stop it. There were times when he did not reach out and try to help. We yearned for the times when he felt he could help and therefore tried. Anything he actively did was better than when he pretended he didn't care. Most of the time the burden and responsibility of raising us was left with my mother. She enjoyed teaching and nurturing us, but it would have been nice for Dad to give more of himself to us. Most of the time, I could see that he gave all that he had, that he had been taught to give.

Dad knew that my victory would be a victory for the entire Negro community, and that made him frightened for me. He realized that there were people living in Omaha who were determined to not let that happen.

My mother would always say that I could and would continue with the contest, but only if I wanted. And then she would give her quiet smile to both of us. I knew my dad was proud of me, even though he never said it. My father made sure the police knew about the threats of violence toward us. At night he would walk around the house a couple of times. Then he would come in and lock the doors, front and back. My mother went behind him and again checked the locks before heading toward a worried sleep.

Most of the citizens of Omaha were gracious; they told me that they were glad that I was in the contest. People gave up their seats on the bus for me, and when they saw me walking, they stopped and asked if I needed a ride. Sympathy was the last thing I wanted, but some people felt sorry for me. They told my mother that it had to be hard for me to face people and smile all the time, especially when they didn't smile back. Still others looked at me with disdain, disgust, and out-and-out hatred. I can see those faces even now. But I didn't give up. I refused to give that kind of person—a person who would throw stones—the time of day. What hurt the most was that I knew that my family and friends were subject to the same awful treatment on my behalf. I had a lot of support, though, and that gave me encouragement and some peace of mind.

Words to discourage me from running even came from some of my own community leaders. On one occasion, several preachers, business people in the community, and politicians met with my parents to persuade them to talk me out of running. We saw this as my personal decision, so what concern was it of theirs anyway? I felt they should have had more important things to do, like improve the schools and housing conditions so families could live in safe homes in safe neighborhoods. We spent some days talking about that visit, and I soon came to the conclusion that most of them were doing what they thought was right. My parents explained to me the reasons for the community's concerns, but that didn't stop me from being angry. We were a community already in turmoil; they didn't need to cause further rifts. They were simply afraid of what would happen if I continued to run. They thought there would be more violence in an already-devastated community and a greater dislike for people of African descent. I began to spend more time in church, on my knees in search of answers. I became unsure of myself and afraid.

It became clear that I had no idea what I was up against. My clothes for the contest went missing after they were dropped off at the cleaners, not just on one occasion but several times. Sometimes we were asked if we were sure that we took them in, or if maybe it was a different cleaner. So we had friends take the clothes to cleaners in other neighborhoods. Supportive white and black businesses had purchased a new wardrobe for me, determined to make this contest fair. This generosity renewed my faith. Because the evening gown was so important, and the most valuable piece of attire in my wardrobe, my sister kept the dress at her home. Right up to the night of the contest, everything was handled with secrecy, from where I exercised and practiced my talent, to what people assisted me, to where and how I traveled around the city of Omaha. My parents began to make sure that I was escorted to school and picked up, and although I didn't want it, it was necessary. It made me feel like a prisoner who had yet to be convicted of a crime.

I now realized that some people wanted me to just disappear or go missing. One evening I saw the look on my mother's face when we received one of those awful phone calls. The phone stand was by the stairs. I used to come running happily as a teenager when I heard the phone ringing, hoping it was a boy calling, asking for a date. These days I recoiled when I heard its accusatory ring.

It interrupted an eerie silence that night. When my mother picked up the receiver, I froze on the stairs and watched the expression on her face. At first she was smiling, maybe expecting a call from one of her friends, but as she listened her face turned to fear. My mom feared for me, her youngest child, and her family. I never knew what to expect from all of this, but I certainly didn't expect violence. The phone was frozen in my mother's hands when my father approached from behind and pried the phone from her fingers and away from her. He yelled and cursed into the phone, but the person on the other end was still saying vicious things. Long after my father hung up the phone, my mother was still hearing the words.

My mother was ill most of my life, enduring so much pain and disappointment. In spite of poverty and a tumultuous, sometimes unstable and unfulfilled relationship, she gave me more love and support than most people give their loved ones in three lifetimes. At times I felt insecure, wondering if I was an added burden.

One evening while quietly watching television, rocks had crashed through our living room windows, thrown from cars as they sped down the street, the passengers shouting expletives. We endured the broken windows, the noose, the stares and discouragement. But that phone call seemed to be a breaking point.

My parents sat me down in our small, unpretentious living room and were very open and candid about the journey on which I had embarked. They were never vague when they spoke to me about serious matters, and what their words didn't say, their tone and facial expressions did.

"Well, Catherine, it's up to you. Where do you want to go from here?"

I could unequivocally answer, but I paused because I had been taught that anything worthwhile was worth thinking about seriously. And so I did. What could happen if I were to continue? How would they feel? What could be the effect on my family and on me?

I answered that I had many reasons for continuing in this race. I was always up to a challenge. I was the dark horse. (At this I laughed out loud.) Could the dark horse possibly win? It wasn't just about me; it was about the greater good. This was a human issue, a human-rights issue. I was running for the right for all children to dream, even for a little Negro girl to dream bigger than her small world.

Some people felt that my win would stop other Negroes from rioting—that my win would show them that if they only worked hard, they could do something besides destroying the areas where they lived. But my family worked hard. I saw people going to work every day, working hard for their families. I saw other strong, black people who were tired of being disenfranchised and minimalized by being put on the fringes of our society, not counting, never to be taken seriously. We were angry. Because of everything happening to me, my family, and my community, I felt that I was being pushed away by the very same people who wanted to take away our freedom. I knew that I could make a difference. That's why I wanted to continue in the pageant.

My parents always felt that it was important to make a difference, to reach your goals, to desire a fulfilled life. They also felt that if you fell down in life and made mistakes, you were entitled to a second chance—an opportunity to try again. After my little speech, my parents looked at each other with tears in their eyes. I guess they thought that they were keeping me safe by giving me every advantage that they could and because of this I would be safe from the attacks that so many public people were going through. As hard as they tried, they could not protect me from the pitfalls of poverty, urban living, and my black skin.

My mother turned to me and then turned to my father. She spoke slowly and deliberately. "Well Bud, I just don't know what we can say to discourage this girl. We can't know what's in her heart."

My dad smiled at my mom, something that I really wasn't used to seeing. "I always told you she was stubborn. When she makes up her mind there is nothing else left to say."

My thoughts were swirling around in my head as I climbed into bed. The tree outside my window that used to torment me with shadows dancing around my walls, the tree that a horrifying rope had once swayed from, suddenly seemed to reflect my strength. That tree had endured years of tornados, hailstorms, electrical storms, and neglect; yet it still stood, bearing beautiful leaves that provided shade for us, shelter for birds, and protection and food for God's small creatures. That night as I closed my eyes, the shadows coming from outside my window brought a strange kind of clarity to my life. Winning the beauty pageant didn't matter to me anymore. What did matter were my intentions. What was my purpose for entering this contest in the first place? How important was it for me to win? I would have to walk through the darkness in faith. I know now that I was put in this position, a position that would require commitment and courage.

Miss Omaha 1969.

PROGRAM OF PRELIMINARY COMPETITION

"On the Other Side of the Rainbow"

OVERTURE
    Pageant Orchestra
    Ed Coleman, Conductor

"ON THE OTHER SIDE OF THE RAINBOW"
    Betty Louise Fox, Mistress of Ceremonies
    The Pageant Chorus
    Vic Michel, Director

THE MISS NEBRASKA GUEST
    ENTERTAINERS
    Phyllis Grabenstein, Miss Arapahoe, 1968
    Elizabeth Upward, Miss Arapahoe, 1967

PARADE OF CITIES

"LOOK AT HER"
    Dan Smith, Soloist

THE PAGEANT CHORUS AND
    MISS NEBRASKA, 1968
    Diane Boldt

INTRODUCTION OF JUDGES

"COLOR"
    Betty Louise Fox
    and
    The Pageant Chorus

CONTESTANTS IN SWIM SUIT
    Thursday — Group B
    Friday — Group A

"IN PHANTASMGOUCAL PHANTARY"
    Betty Louise Fox
    Phyllis Grabenstein
    Elizabeth Upward
    and
    The Pageant Chorus

CONTESTANTS IN TALENT
    Thursday — Group A
    Friday — Group B

INTERMISSION

ENTR'ACTE
    The Pageant Orchestra

"WHO IS THE NEW MISS NEBRASKA?"
    Dan Smith, Soloist
    The Pageant Chorus

CONTESTANTS IN EVENING GOWN
    Thursday — Group B
    Friday — Group A

DIVERTISSEMENT
    Donna Olmsted, Miss York, 1968

"THERE'S GOTTA BE A SOMEDAY"
    Betty Louise Fox
    The Pageant Chorus

REPRISE:
    "On The Other Side of The Rainbow"
    Entire Company

GROUP A
Kearney State	Ainsworth	North Platte
Broken Bow	Omaha	York
Oxford	Falls City	Nebraska City

GROUP B
University of Nebraska	Bellevue	Superior
Norfolk	Kearney	Chadron
Auburn	Scottsbluff	Arapahoe
Kimball		

1969 Miss Nebraska Pageant opening night program.

Preliminary winners, Miss Nebraska Pageant opening night.
(photo courtesy of York News-Times)

The talent contest.

22

Miss Nebraska 1969

Excuse the pun: I was the dark horse. No one expected me to win, especially since this was my second try.

I suppose my choice of words would seem offensive to some people, but as the only black girl making it to the Miss Nebraska Pageant, even after two tries I would honestly have to be considered the underdog as well as the dark horse. Looking at the facts, I was not offended in the least when I heard from some family and friends that there were those who did not think that I would win. However, most of my family felt that I couldn't lose. I can't say why they felt like that; I can only say that's what supportive families do. They have your back.

Although congratulation letters were streaming in, there were other letters that weren't as positive or encouraging. In one letter from a man in Nebraska City, he began by wishing me success all the way to Miss America.

He began by saying, "I'm white, but I don't judge people by their color but rather what they are or can be." Then the letter took a sharp turn. "I believe a Negro woman is a much warmer and finer mother and wife and also sweeter than most white women." He went on to describe his family and congratulate me again. Then he said, "If they get out and work, study, and learn they too can earn respect and praise. They have burned and been shot and torn up. Congratulations and best wishes always, Your friend and booster."

The contest finals would be held on June 14, and I knew the date was getting close when someone delivered my accidental-death policy from the contest organizers. The effective date was June 10, 1969, the effective hour 12:01 a.m. The policy was good for five days. In May I also received a congratulations letter from the local York pageant committee welcoming me to their town along with instructions and directions. The pageant seemed days away, but in reality I had to wait at least a month.

May was a long, hot month. I seemed to be struggling at every turn. I had a difficult time focusing on my studies. I was preparing for finals, and what used to come easy was now difficult for me. I worked harder at my job for several weeks before I asked for two weeks off, hoping that made it easier for them to say yes.

As the pageant date came closer, my sister volunteered to go to the cleaners to pick up my clothes that had been sent there to be cleaned the week before. She remembered the people behind the desk staring at her. It was the same cleaners that we were accustomed to going to over the years, the small corner cleaners located on Thirtieth and Hamilton Streets. This cleaner was used by most people in the area for miles around. The workers were usually courteous but never went out of their way to be overly friendly; they just appeared to do their jobs and nothing more. While looking over my clothes I discovered that some of them were missing—as a matter a fact, some of my nicest dresses. My mother sent my sister back to see if any of the items showed up. Of course my sister felt bad and went back right away. Maybe they had been given to the wrong customer, and they would surely notice and return them as soon as they discovered the mixup. My swimsuit wasn't among the items lost at the dry cleaners. I never liked anyone handling items that I wore close to my body, so I always washed it myself in my bathtub and hung it out over the tub to dry. My costume, for some reason, had been sent to a different cleaner with a separate batch of clothing that included the family dry cleaning. Nothing happened to any of those clothes. My evening gown was sent to a cleaner that specialized in expensive clothing—evening wear, tuxes, and even furs. At first they couldn't find my gown, but the next day for some unknown reason the gown showed up. They called us and we picked up the gown. I wish that I could say that for the other clothes at the other cleaners. Those clothes had to be purchased all over again. At the time we didn't have the extra hours to legally deal with the drama. My shoes had to go to the shoe shop so my old heels could be replaced. The few clothes that we did manage to get back were in an almost indescribable condition. Some items were too small and others too large. Some clothes were cut and torn, and others had been worn. We replaced some of the clothes, but the nice outfits were irreplaceable.

Well-wishing calls were coming in by the truckload. On occasion, when the phone rang in my presence, I asked who was calling. Sometimes I was ignored and told, "It's not for you. Don't worry about it," code words for *it's starting up again*. I knew all the signs because I had seen them before, and my parents knew what to do because they had protected me before.

There were the disgusting calls: "You'd better watch your back, niggers!"

And the hate mail: "Why can't you people have your own? This is for our girls, white girls." I'm glad my parents destroyed the hate mail before I saw it. It was so negative, so destructive. Even though I didn't see the hate mail or listen to the calls I could tell by their actions, the fear in my mother's eyes and the way both of my parents were becoming overly protective, that things were becoming worse. Fear has crippling effects.

One evening on my way to the kitchen I answered the telephone. "I guess some of your men would love to get a hold of you." I listened to the caller, and I listened hard. The palms of my hands began to sweat. I wiped each hand, one after the other, down the sides of my cotton pants, switching the phone between them, trying to wipe off the grime. I struggled to hold the receiver tightly to my ear without dropping it. I turned my back to the main part of the house hoping no one would see my face as I recalled the frightening attack and the disgusting touching and grabbing by the crude dentist. Like a dripping faucet I began crying. I hung up the phone as I wailed and moaned, collapsing on the floor. I was finally letting go my pain. My dad came running and scooped me up as if he could shield me from it with the sheer presence of his body. He touched my arm gently as he helped me up. I quickly jerked away. In that moment, I didn't want the hands of any man on my person. He eased back, and I stood to my feet somberly. We looked at each other, and I knew he understood, so I drew closer to him.

For this contest, I was again provided escorts to school and practices. Our local police volunteered to escort me all the way to York, but Mrs. Elrod and I didn't think that was necessary. My parents thought it was a good idea, but I didn't want to show up with police escorts, like I was afraid or something. Besides it would make all the other girls uncomfortable.

As the time drew near, I experienced a strange feeling, like when something exciting ends and you are anticipating, waiting for something new to begin. It seemed to take forever; but I had to quietly wait amid all the uncertainty to see what would unfold. Our clocks seemed to slow down. It was apparent to me that some of the girls in the pageant would think that there was something different about me. I couldn't imagine what, but to be a part of this contest demanded that you should belong to an exclusive club, a social order; you should meet a standard set by God knows who and that standard would qualify you for the title. The title that demanded decorum, respect for just the label—Miss America. The fact that I required protection would leave me out.

I don't know why I waited so late in the month to talk about anything that would cost money, but I did. While my parents were in the living room watching television and waiting for our dinner to warm up I decided to ask for a new evening gown. I felt strange asking my parents for a new gown. But wearing the same gown in three different pageants, 1968 and 1969 Miss Omaha, and then 1969 Miss Nebraska, seemed to be a little much. The gown was worn out. The beads were loosening up, and some were even falling off of their thin, knotted threads, along with the small pearls. Because several organizations had asked me to wear my gown during presentations around the city, the sunlight had caused a small amount of yellowing, even though it would not be noticeable to the average person. But I knew. So I got up the nerve to ask my parents for a new gown. I was surprised at my mother's response. It wasn't at all what I expected.

"Cathy, we can't hurt your sister's feelings. She has really been looking forward to you wearing your gown, especially since this is the most important contest." To my family, each and every contest was the most important contest.

Like a lot of things in my personal life, I let it go and decided not to hurt anyone's feelings. I decided to clean the dress one last time and wear it in the Nebraska pageant, knowing that if I were given the chance to compete in the Miss America Contest my entire family would have a fight on their hands if I were refused a new evening gown! Now each night would be spent preparing for the next leg of my adventure. I also spent time in my bedroom experimenting with new hairdos, especially since I would be wearing the same evening gown.

I was closely watching my parents throughout the day and into the evening. Usually whenever my dad drove my mom and me to the store he waited in the car for us. The Saturday before we left he came inside the store with us. "They're shopping together," I thought, as I followed closely behind them. "And he's pushing the cart. He never comes in, let alone pushes the shopping cart."

They talked quietly to each other without regard to my presence. Up and down the aisles, my mother reached toward items on the shelves and on most occasions refrained from placing them into her basket. When we met at the meat counter, they stopped and my dad began his ritual of examining the tough cuts of beef, as he carefully made his selections. My mother didn't say a word. Her look of disappointment was written on her face.

"I know you want something else, Juanita, but this will make a nice stew. It'll go a long way—last us throughout the week."

"I know Bud, but I just wanted something special, you know." Further down the aisle was a variety of chickens. My mom reached into the meat bin and picked out two large hens. Dad smiled, and we proceeded to the fresh vegetables. We didn't stop long. My dad always had a garden that produced fresh vegetables.

At the checkout stand I watch my Dad remove his wallet carefully from his back pocket. His messy handkerchief fell to the floor, and I inconspicuously picked it up and slid it into his pocket closet to me. Mom pulled out her coin purse while fumbling with the cash that she had removed from her wallet. They leaned their heads toward one another and when told the amount owed for the groceries each began to put various dollar bills and coins into the grocer's hand. It took a little while, and I watched the people behind us become somewhat impatient. I was now very aware of their financial situation.

I kept thinking, "I'm the first black to participate in this contest. It's an honor." But in another way I realized how much pain I was subjecting my parents to and the heartbreak that they might experience. All I could think was "Why or how can I be putting my family through all of this again, and why does it matter to me so much?" I always did most of my thinking in the quiet of the night, but this month was different. I had more to think about than winning a contest. I was now thinking about the impact that my decision to embark on this journey had made on my family. Each night when I weighed myself I noticed that the arrow on the scale was beginning to move. I was losing weight. Not a planned thing; it was just happening.

Sitting alone in the living room of my home I spent my quiet time anticipating what was about to happen at the pageant. I made up scenarios so I would be composed no matter what occurred. I was anxiously awaiting my long ride to York, Nebraska.

The night before I left for the Miss Nebraska Pageant I was scheduled to have my hair done in the kitchen of a home in the projects not far from where I lived. It was in the home of the mother of John Beasley, who would later become a famous actor. Through the large windows of her well-lit kitchen I could see people watching as she worked her magic on my hair. All I did was describe how I wanted my hair, and from there our conversation changed to where I was going and what I was going to do there. That was done so she could make sure my hair would hold up in the heat, during all of the rehearsals, and until the close of the pageant. She even spent time showing me how to work with my hair from day to day.

The next morning there were long goodbyes, hugs, and kisses from everyone around me. We were all gathered on the porch. It was June 10, eleven days before the beginning of summer. Several members of my family and close friends were there to see me off. As I waited for my ride, I noticed my parents exchanging short glances with each other. They approached me, looked me in the eyes, and began sharing their wisdom, serious words of advice telling me what to do and what not to do, to watch my back and act like a lady. There were even tears offered up by my mother and father as they wished me the best, knowing that in this world at times you had to anticipate the worst. Both of my parents were very serious that morning. My mother, in her favorite worn housedress, wiped her hands on her apron and then leaned over the open part of the porch at one end, looking down the alley like she knew something was going to happen. I watched her open her right hand and then examine it with the help of her left. Her fingers were turned up toward the sky as she looked at her fingernails. Then, inconspicuously, she put the side of her thumb into her mouth and nervously removed a hangnail. Or so I thought. I can't say what she was thinking, but I had watched her in the past do the same thing. She walked back over to me.

"Cathy, we're proud of you. Whether you know it or not, you're breaking down barriers." I smiled at my mom and dad. When I left it was a somber morning. The trees were quiet and the grass did not move, even in the hot wind. The tree out back that had caused me so much concern now appeared strong no matter how frightening it had looked before. As we pulled off I looked out of the rearview mirror, smiling and waving, knowing that whatever happened they would never look at me the same. Things would never be the same.

Mrs. Elrod picked me up that morning. She looked happy and pleased to see us, standing at the door waiting for my departure. Everyone had other places to be, but they waited with me to show me their support and love. Most black people in Omaha had never heard of York, Nebraska, let alone been there. Their experience with communities like this in Nebraska was to hear a news report about a tornado touching down leaving devastation behind or a crop failing and causing prices to rise in the grocery stores. Other than that some felt that most people in small Nebraska towns really didn't want us there. That's what most of us knew about small towns in Nebraska, true or not true. As for me, this was going to be my first visit. I wasn't going far, but to people living in a small black community like North Omaha I might as well have been traveling as far away as New York City.

The drive through the streets of Omaha was long. I had passed through these very streets taking very little notice, but today was different. When we left the city, the freeway twisted and turned as we passed one exit after the other. We chose one and straightened onto a two-lane highway. The land was no longer hilly; I could see ahead for miles, but mostly I saw wheat and corn. Wheat sheaves drying in random bundles and unharvested corn checkered the landscape, surrounding farmhouses with attached porches. Silos were sparsely placed and tractors peeked through partially open, red barn doors. Horses gracefully rested behind the fences created by the labor of hard-working farmhands. Cows grazed passively and freely in lush pastures, sharing without shame their pungent aromas with any and every passerby.

It all reminded me of the poem that my dad used to recite to us by heart, "The House by the Side of the Road" by Sam Walter Foss. I wondered if it was written in a place like this, so full of life yet so lonely.

I began counting fence posts, wondering what the digger's life was like. Did he realize his importance, that he counted and made a difference in the lives of others? Each fence was the same as the one before, although I knew that they had to have been built by different farmers. Although she was driving and focused on the road, Mrs. Elrod took every opportunity to distract me and entertain herself. We sang gospel songs. I was surprised by her vast mental library of songs.

Coming upon the final small town before our destination, we chatted about the varying sights as we lurched between stop signs on every corner. We stopped to fill the car up. People coming out of the grocery store adjacent to the filling station stared, making no excuse for giving us their undivided attention. The gas-station attendant seemed to be reluctant to give us the type of service that we were accustomed to in the city. By the time he was finished checking our oil and putting air in our tires, the small-town machine had been started: lines of people—men, women and children—watched us as we passed through the town. We were many miles from Omaha, but it felt like another planet. And we were the aliens. Or at least I was. I had to face the fact that I was a nineteen-year-old Negro girl in uncharted territory.

Even though we felt like outsiders, we decided to stop and visit an enticing antique shop and a nearby soda fountain. The shop had used miscellany and old furniture. Odds and ends were randomly displayed on shelves, in cabinets, and in large woven baskets placed in the middle of walkways. Lying among the piles in one of the baskets was a small, black mammy figure overstuffed with cotton. She was dressed in red, covered by a white pinafore. She wore a red-dotted scarf tied into a knot on her forehead. On a shelf above her were two old mammy-and-pappy salt-and-pepper shakers, remnants of the past.

"Want to buy those? Ten dollars for the pair," a man standing behind me asked.

"No, I don't need anything like that right now."

We grabbed a quick drink at the soda shop next door and walked to the car for the last leg of our journey. As I turned to take a picture with my Polaroid, I saw people in the street pointing at us and whispering. Even a policeman was among them. It was almost as if we were dolls in a display case, fixed smiles on our faces, being looked at as if we were hard and cold, without any feelings on the inside. As we left the town, not a word passed between us. I immediately regretted not purchasing all three items in the store so no one else could have. I would have put them in a place of honor.

As we headed out again I noticed I was biting my nails. The car backfired, and I jumped out of my seat. I flinched from embarrassment and tried to force my body to calm down. We both laughed nervously. It was getting hotter outside, but Mrs. Elrod insisted that we keep the windows rolled up. She said she didn't want to overuse the air conditioning because the car might overheat. Written on her face, however, was a different story.

"Cathy, are you okay? Maybe we shouldn't have taken this scenic route, going through these small towns. I just thought that this would be fun, and we'd have a little more time to get to know each other." The tone of her voice communicated concern and caring. I knew that it was important to stop and relax along the way. Besides, both of us had needed a bathroom break and something to drink.

"Yes, I think so." I was twisting my hands nervously in my lap. "To be honest I was scared at that last town."

Finally we drove into York. "Look!" I yelled out without thinking. "I think we're here." York didn't look or feel anything at all like the last town. It was a city like Omaha, only much smaller. We drove down the main street. There were banners welcoming us and people moving about through the streets focused on nothing but their day-to-day business. Others smiled at us or waved and threw kisses. It was obvious that they knew who I was and why I was there.

When we stopped at a light, a man in seersucker ran into the street, rushing toward the car. I recoiled, scared, hoping the light would change quickly. Reaching us, he removed his hat and extended his hand. As I slowly rolled down the window, he blurted out his name.

"Welcome! We're glad to have you both in our city. I hope you'll enjoy your stay here."

Mrs. Elrod reached across me and took his hand with both hands warmly, so I extended mine.

"Thank you," I responded with a relieved smile.

He stood in the street, still smiling, as we slowly crossed the intersection, passing under the green light.

We took our time driving around the city to familiarize ourselves with its streets and neighborhoods. We found a parking space outside the City Auditorium and went inside to begin the registration process. I would stay in a local home during the pageant; that family would provide my chaperone and hostess for five days. Once Mrs. Elrod was sure that I was okay she would go back to Omaha, and return later for the pageant.

Part of the registration process was reading over the regulations for contestants and parents. We weren't permitted to enter a bar or smoke in public places, and if we did we would automatically be eliminated from further judging without notice. We weren't permitted to speak to any man, including members of our own family, unless a hostess was present. We also couldn't appear with or speak to any judges except at scheduled events. We weren't allowed to have interviews or pictures, incoming calls except to our hostess and at the home of our hostess, and we also had to remain with our hostess at all times. Rehearsals were off limits to the public. If we had brought any medication with us we had to turn it in. It had to remain with the nurse on duty at all times. We would eat lunch in the auditorium and dinner out, and then we had to return to the auditorium to rehearse. We were required to wear our banners in public and our numbered badges on stage. Hairdressers were assigned to the dressing rooms. I didn't think about this before I came to the pageant, but even so it was a problem for me because these beauticians had no idea how to fix my hair. So I asked to have my own beautician to care for my hair.

There was an invisible line between me and the other girls. I saw it in some eyes as I waited to sign in. The stakes here were higher than they'd been at the local contest. Girls were sizing each other up, and they had already categorized me. But I couldn't change the color of my skin. They were losing an opportunity to enjoy a relationship with someone different from themselves. They never approached me, never introduced themselves.

I tried to make excuses for them, but I didn't approach them either. Instead my eyes swelled with tears as I watched the other girls begin to get acquainted. They smiled, talked, and laughed. Now and then I would catch one of them looking toward me as if she wanted to come over and talk, but she wouldn't. But there were a couple of other girls that also seemed to feel as awkward as I. Our eyes connected, and we smiled conspicuously at each other. That gave me some comfort.

"Well, you must be the girl from Omaha."

I had reached the front of the registration line. I smiled. "Yes, ma'am, I am."

The registrar kept talking without looking up at me. To me she was being rude. I could hear my mom's voice in my head: *Anything worthwhile takes time, and you have to be tolerant.* Patience and tolerance were always challenges for me, but I took a deep breath and kept the smile on my face. After the paperwork, we were told to go to another line to meet our chaperones. By this time I didn't want to stand in another line; the girls were watching me and whispering while they stared. For some reason I already had the name of my chaperone in my purse, so I asked Mrs. Elrod if we could just head for her house. She agreed with me, and we left the auditorium. All the while I was feeling like I was in the second act of a badly written play.

It was around noon, and the sun was beating down on us when we arrived at my chaperone's house. Mrs. Elrod and I were anxious to meet my host family. I stood at the door, dripping in sweat, waiting for someone to open it. We rang the bell a second time. No answer. I kept wondering if we were at the wrong house. Or maybe the doorbell wasn't working? Jeri went back to the car to get her address book. She stood there for a while and looked up at the numbers on the small, wood-framed house.

"I'm certain that this is the right house!" she called out to me, loudly enough to be heard inside.

The family who had agreed to house me and keep me safe and secure for one week had backed out in a most cowardly way. What more did I need to know? Mrs. Elrod came back to the door, and this time she knocked while I rang the bell. All the while I kept thinking, "Am I dreaming, or is this really happening to me? If I'm dreaming, I need to wake up right now!"

Finally, someone appeared. "Yes, may I help you?" A small-framed lady presented herself on the other side of the still-closed screen door. Her hand was raised, shielding her eyes from the glare of the sun as if she were saluting a high-ranking officer. "Who else is out there? Is anyone else with the two of you?"

It was a memorable moment. I felt as if I were looking up at her from the bottom of the steps even though I was right there at her door. I observed her awkward, superior stance: hand on one hip, adjusting her weight from one side to the other. Her eyes were tightly squeezed together as she pulled a handkerchief from the deep crevice between her breasts. It emerged like in a magician's trick; as she removed the final corner, she dramatically lifted it to her wet brow as only a heroine could. She seemed like a villain to me.

She stood in the door as if she were protecting her nest. "Why are you both here?" Before either of us could answer her she blurted out, "You must be the people from the contest. I don't understand those people. I told them a few days back that I couldn't have you staying in my home. They were too busy to listen to me."

Now I was more frightened than sad. I began to wonder what other problems I would run into and whether I be able or even want to handle them. Sweat and mascara were running down my face. I felt the thick, black eyeliner on my lips, and tried to lick it off inconspicuously. I didn't blink; I just stared straight ahead. I was wearing a blue, cotton coat dress with a small, white Peter Pan collar. In one hand I carried a small clutch bag. My stockings felt pasted to my thin, wobbly legs. My knees knocked as I attempted to hide how overwhelmed and sad I was. I felt as if the ground were rumbling under my feet. And suddenly I was weak with hunger.

Our would-be hostess noticed none of this. "Well, since you're here, I guess that I at least owe you an explanation. Let me step outside. My kids are at home, and I don't want them to hear any of this."

I could see her better now as she stepped through her protective barrier. She was middle-aged, and she looked like a smoker, like someone older than her years. I could tell she'd spent most of her life working tough jobs and long hours. Her face was weathered. Her tawny, wrinkled neck was dotted with freckles that were fading with age. Her were eyes dim behind her cat-eye glasses. I'd seen that look before in my neighborhood, and I knew what was coming.

It was obvious that she didn't want us as asking her any questions. The yard was in need of mowing, and the flowers lining the broken concrete walkway were in dire need of watering. I noticed how passing cars slowed down in front of the house as we stood awkwardly among the mess.

"Anyway," she continued, "I have two young sons—teenagers—and we only have one bathroom. . . . Well, you can understand."

Mrs. Elrod and I looked at each other, confused. Then we turned and focused on this lady directly in front of us. "We don't get it," Mrs. Elrod said with a stern voice.

"Well, my husband and I aren't rich. We just thought it would be nice for us to give to our community by volunteering our services and that it might help our small business. . . . But my husband and I thought that the girl would be white. My neighbor showed us your picture in her newspaper the other morning. We only have one bathroom, and the room you would have to sleep in is right next door to our sons' room. What else can I say?" She wasn't looking at either of us as she turned and walked back inside her house. I expected something else, so I stood there quietly, unable to speak or move.

I had expected some civility, a hint of humanity. She never asked us in, didn't offer us a glass of cool water, didn't even ask us if we needed to use the phone. I had a feeling of emptiness deep down in the pit of my stomach.

By the look on her face, I knew Mrs. Elrod was ashamed of her own race. As we were walking back to the station wagon, I doubled over, almost falling to my knees. The tears finally came. For months they had been almost coming, but I would fight back the tears. Now I wailed, crying out loud, without shame, "Oh God, did you leave me out? I feel lost."

Mrs. Elrod wrapped her arms around me and lifted me up to steady me. Looking in her eyes, I pleaded for comfort and answers as salty tears gushed from my eyes. I was in a great deal of pain. I obviously knew about racism and bigotry; it had even come to my door. But this time, it caught me off guard. It came out in the open, out in the sunlight, and it struck me down.

I can now understand a white woman wanting to protect her family, especially her son, from me—as if I would do them harm. She also wanted to protect her home from all of the bigotry, racial hatred, and ramifications she anticipated from welcoming me into her home. Maybe it wasn't her personal preference, but she did let the prejudices and the pressures of living in a racist society affect her decision to welcome me in. I can only imagine the kinds of things her friends and neighbors said to her to make her change her mind at the last minute. She missed out on the opportunity to have been considered brave, a Good Samaritan, a beacon of hope and courage for the future. I thought I now understood how Mary must have felt being turned away at the inn. Only I wasn't Mary, and this old Midwestern house wasn't an inn. I was a Negro girl, and I was turned away because of it.

"We're going back, Cathy!" Mrs. Elrod snapped me back to life.

"Going back? For what?" I was dumbfounded. "Those people don't want me staying in their house."

She looked at me wearily. "I mean we're going back to the City Auditorium."

I told her that I had no reason or desire to go back there either. I knew unequivocally that I just wanted to go home, and I didn't want to take the scenic route. When I got home, I would tell everyone what happened to me. They'd understand why I left, and that would be that.

Understanding how I felt, Mrs. Elrod spoke gingerly. "I know how you feel. At least I know that I can't possibly walk in your shoes, Cathy. But you have to go back, you just have to."

I was feeling belligerent. She didn't know how I felt. How could she? How could anyone know how degraded I felt? The way that woman looked standing in her door, the way she spoke to us? I will never forget it. But I knew what Mrs. Elrod wanted me to do, and I also knew what I had to do, not only for myself, but for my community and, more importantly, my race.

We decided to return to the City Auditorium to let them know that I had been rejected by my host family. The ride back was stressful. I was asking myself if everyone knew about me and the lady that sent us away. Were they laughing at us behind our backs? Were they wishing that we would just turn around and head back to Omaha, defeated long before the contest even began? Was I an unwanted situation to tolerate?

"Cathy, I wanted you to believe, and I wanted to believe, that everything involved with this pageant would be a positive experience for you."

"I know Mrs. Elrod, I know."

When we got back to the City Auditorium, a few people were left lounging around, but the majority of the contestants had already gone. I pictured them in the homes of their host families, sitting around large kitchen tables, smiling, laughing, and eating while they got acquainted.

All nineteen of us were determined to receive the crown before 2,000 people. One of us would be given the right to represent Nebraska in the Miss America Pageant in Atlantic City, New Jersey. I was looking forward as Miss Nebraska to winning the $1,000 scholarship, a new automobile, a $500 wardrobe, and gifts given by local merchants. The Miss Congeniality award would be a special tribute to one of us from the rest of the girls. Crowning the new Miss Nebraska would be Diane Boldt of Omaha, the retiring Miss Nebraska. The mistress of ceremonies for the second straight year would be Betty Louise Fox, Miss Kansas of 1966, who was now a music teacher in Pennsylvania.

We headed to one of the tables still showing some activity. One of the organizers was ending a pleasant conversation with some of the workers. "May I help you? Is there a problem?" he asked as he looked down at the badge still pinned to my dress. "Oh, you're Miss Omaha," he clumsily continued, while appearing to be more concerned about the paper in front of him than about us.

"Yes, there is a problem. I need another place to stay this week, another host family."

"Weren't you happy with your assignment?"

Mrs. Elrod spoke up, "I don't think that you understand. The host family, they weren't happy with her. To be quite blunt, they turned her away. Without retelling the disconcerting events of the day, it just wasn't a fit."

He was clearly not hearing us. "What? We just can't move people around. It takes us a lot of time to arrange things."

He was quickly interrupted by a woman seated nearby at the registration table. "What happened, young lady? Miss Pope. You're Miss Omaha, aren't you?" She was soft-spoken and looked at me with kind eyes.

"I was turned away by my host family." People standing close to us stopped laughing and talking and moved closer to listen. The room became still. "Ma'am, she didn't want me staying in her home for reasons that I'd rather not talk about."

"Anyway," Mrs. Elrod interrupted, "Miss Pope needs another place to stay. She's not going home."

I would pick up the baton even if I had to sleep in the City Auditorium.

I felt uncomfortable and unsure of myself, just like those fish in my kindergarten classroom. I needed air, and my chest was pounding.

"Oh, I don't think that's going to be necessary. I would like for you to stay in my home, if that would be all right with you? Mr. Witham and I would be honored. Besides, that's why I'm here. You're scheduled to stay in my home." Mrs. Jerald Witham asked me to stay in her home without regard to what the people around her thought. There was some shifting going on around her, but she just smiled sweetly. Something unusual had taken place, but I was too tired to deal with it.

"Thank you," I said, so relieved I could have cried. "I don't want to cause you any problems."

Mrs. Elrod jumped in to save us both the awkwardness. "How do we get to your house, Mrs. Witham? Is it far from here?"

She smiled and spoke in a soft voice. "Let me get my purse and gather my things, then you can follow me."

I gave a great sigh of relief. I didn't have any idea where I was going, but I knew it had to be a thousand times better than where I had been.

Driving down the street on our way to Mrs. Witham's home, I remembered the sign we saw as we drove into the city: "Welcome to York. There Are No Strangers in York; Just New Friends."

For the first time that day, I honestly felt I had met a friend.

The Withams were as nice on the inside as their home was beautiful on the outside. Even their cat, Pamper, was happy I was there. Mrs. Elrod and Mrs. Witham hit it off right away. They helped me unpack, and I could tell that Mrs. Elrod felt comfortable about leaving me with them as we later said our goodbyes at the door. I had very little time to relax that evening because I was scheduled to eat with the rest of the girls. I was gradually feeling better, beginning to put aside my feelings about some of my initial interactions on this trip. Food has a way of opening your spirit. A nice meatloaf and mashed potatoes with a small tossed salad is a way to encourage people to get acquainted. This meal was served family style; I was familiar and comfortable with this style of dining, so I let down my hair and had a good time. By the end of the evening there were three or four girls talking to me more than the others. It's impossible to tell who began the conversations—the important thing was that we were talking. Not about the pageant but about our schools and our majors. We even shared a little information about our favorite songs and movies. It was a pleasant change from the silence that seemed to pervade most of the time. It was becoming a little more relaxed and open. But I couldn't say that the word *trust* could be added to my list. Most of the time I listened, and on occasion I said something and smiled. I began to feel that these eighteen girls were more like me than not. I knew this was not going to be perfect, but I also knew that nothing in this life is. I knew that I had to ignore some things while I was here. I also knew that my faith would be tested and my mantra for the week might have to be forgiveness and charity.

The next morning I had breakfast with my host family. I packed my makeup bag and left for the City Auditorium. Now I had a new opportunity to learn more about the girls, and of course I wanted them to learn more about me. I have to admit I was nervous.

This was very different from 1968. That first time, most people didn't even know that I had run for Miss Omaha until it came out in the newspaper the following morning. There was so much going on that year—the riot caused by the assassination of Dr. Martin Luther King Jr. and the George Wallace political visit. People had mixed feelings when it came to accepting a black Miss Omaha. So my obscurity was expected when I became the first black runner-up. When I became Miss Omaha, everyone zeroed in on that win. It was in the headlines for days and in follow-up news for weeks. I was on the front page of the *Omaha World-Herald* and the *Omaha Star* and later in *Jet,* the national black magazine. Family and friends and even local schools and churches scrambled to get the news. It was a first, and beyond that it was a novelty to find this crown firmly seated on top of the head of a black girl from North Omaha.

Upon my arrival at the auditorium I learned that flowers had been delivered to me at my original host's house; they never got to me, and I had no intention of asking any questions surrounding their disappearance. I had packed the things I would need for the day into a smaller bag; everything had to be checked out by the contest committee. We couldn't have anything with us that wasn't on the list or okayed in advance by the pageant organizers. To follow all of the rules wasn't going to be an easy task. The pageant officials didn't want outside beauticians, and that's exactly what I needed. I understood that the first crown that the audience would see would be your hair, and without my personal beautician, by Friday, the last night of the pageant, my hair would probably be a mess. We would be there for three to four days, and it was hot and muggy.

I don't know why I hadn't thought of it before, but I needed to have my hairdresser come to York to assist me in maintaining my hair. June was one of the hottest months in Nebraska, and I had to look my best during the entire week. I didn't have my hair permed or processed straight, so the care and management of my hair was going to be a big problem in this weather. It took an act of Congress for the committee to give permission to Mrs. Elrod to bring a beautician to the Withams' home. This was the most important pageant so far, and because I was so far away from home I needed help from those who knew me and understood my circumstances.

This pageant demanded a lot of rehearsing at the auditorium before the preliminaries. Each group practice was better than the one before. I spent every waking moment preparing for what I hoped would be my best individual performance. Because the City Auditorium was cold most of the time, I would stretch my legs before I arrived and I would exercise my vocal cords in the Withams' steamy bathroom before I left their house each morning. Even their cat got in on the act; Pamper would bend with me, stretching backward on his hind legs and opening his back paws wide. It was as if he knew what was at stake, so he went out of his way to help me win.

On Wednesday, we were allowed to socialize at the meet-and-greet. It was the time to get to know each other. The meet-and-greet was something that took me a little time to get used to. We were told that it was going to be a casual occasion and to dress appropriately. I had no idea what we were going to actually do there. Most of the time people were just standing around or coming in the door and going out of it. I found a comfortable place to stand, by the food. An important-looking man walked over to me and introduced himself. He was one of the pageant organizers. We shook hands, and then he was soon introducing himself to another girl. Most of us were slowly mingling. I walked over to several girls standing together and introduced myself. I felt a little silly saying that I was Miss Omaha since the pin I was wearing said it. Again I shook hands and moved on. I was impressed with how the room arrangement encouraged interaction.

Several candidates did ask me unusual questions from time to time. One young woman asked, "When this is over do you think you will take your place in public life?"

Another asked, "How does it feel not to really be a part of us here? Does it feel funny, awkward? And why is the FBI here asking questions about you? My mother says that's strange, but of course I think it's exciting." Until then, no one had approached me to let me know that they were being followed or asked questions about me. I never had any idea that I was being watched by others, let alone the FBI. Like the others, however, I saw strange men and women moving among us. The difference that became obvious to me was that none of these men or woman ever stopped to talk to me in private or in public places, as they did with others.

As several girls got a little more comfortable they began to ask a few personal questions. I would describe some of them as ignorant questions: "How does it feels to be a Negro—I mean, to have black skin?" I was waiting for someone to ask me a question about my hair and sex. Thankfully nothing was asked of me about either one of those things.

It really wasn't unusual for girls coming from different backgrounds or races to be curious about one another; I had been asked a lot of questions when I attended Duchesne College. One girl asked me if I tanned and how I got my hair straight.

I felt that it was strange to answer those types of questions, so for the most part I ignored them. I was hurt, but I had to be careful so that I wouldn't become paranoid and further isolate myself. I felt frustrated and angry, and I began to turn inward as if I had fallen down a rabbit hole. Now I had to dig my way out. I told myself I would climb out utterly knowledgeable about each and every contestant, turning that frustration and anger into self-confidence and pride. I had to keep my wits about me in order to keep my confidence in myself, pulling my strength from deep within me and from those around me who honestly cared about me: my family, my friends, Mr. and Mrs. Witham, Mrs. Elrod, and even supporters like two brothers, eight-year-old Kent and five-year-old Rex Pettygrove of York.

I would watch the other contestants perform like I was a talent scout. Rather than reading magazines or gossiping like some of the girls, I spent my time during the preliminaries observing how they walked, talked, smiled, performed, and interacted with each other. I studied how they put on their makeup, did their hair, and wore their nails. I even watched what they ate during lunch and dinner. They started off wanting to learn everything they could about me, even questioning me to my face, and I was determined to turn things around; I refused to be seen as a victim or a stranger in a strange land. I would practice and practice. I was determined to win.

Preparing for the preliminaries wasn't easy. Each leg of the contest was more difficult than the last, not because we had to do more or because the events were harder, but because the environment in which we had to do it was tougher. I wanted to be perfect, but because the stakes were higher every one of us was determined to win "the pot of gold."

Participating in the swimsuit competition made me the most nervous. Our one-piece swimsuits were the same, but the bodies inside of them were very different. All the suits had to be solid colors. My black swimsuit looked like leather. It was low-cut in both the front and back, accentuating my curves. All of us lined up in a long, open stall. We were instructed to strip down. All of us were somewhat shy and appeared to be a little annoyed, although no one said a word. During the preliminaries none of us had to totally remove our clothing in front of anyone. I could tell by the looks on their faces and the way they attempted to use their hands to shield private areas that disrobing wasn't easy for anybody. We were not allowed to wear false breasts, hips, butts, body makeup, or stockings. As we quickly looked each other up and down, I realized that nineteen pairs of eyes were fixed on me as if I displayed something different to them. It was impossible to ignore the differences in color between us. Most of the girls were fair, pale, or slightly tanned, while I stood brown with shadows of black outlining the curves on my body. For many of the girls it was their first time being in intimate quarters with a Negro.

"Do you think she's got a tail?" Someone said it, and I imagined others were thinking it. The long, open stall was cold and echoed, so it wasn't hard to hear the cruel, unkind words and laughter coming from the opposite end of the room. I leaned over and looked annoyed at the ones talking about me. I wanted them to see me. Perspiration began to accumulate on my face as I struggled to maintain my composure. I quickly used a small towel lying on the table in front of me to wipe away the sweat and tears.

"Anything wrong, Miss Omaha?" one of the ladies asked. Everyone else stared at me. All of us were shaking in the air-conditioned room, which was creating goosebumps on our bodies.

We would eat together, share rest areas, and use the same restrooms. Some of them would step outside of their comfort zones and share personal stories and concerns, even laugh out loud with me every now and then. They appeared to be as confused about me as I was about them. None of us really knew each other or had the proper time to get acquainted. We were in a tough situation, trying to be nice and cordial, all the while knowing that we were there to compete against each other. We were all there to win, and that left very little room for developing friendships.

"Okay, girls, back on stage before lunch. Let's hurry up please," one of the coordinators called out. "By the way, tonight we're having dinner at the Legion Club. The address is 225 West Fifth Street, so don't forget to tell your chaperones and give them the address, even though they should already have it."

Mr. and Mrs. Jerald Witham smiled at me each and every morning at the breakfast table. I always left their home with a positive attitude, and they filled the ride to the City Auditorium with positive stories of hope and success. No matter how I felt after a day of preparations, I left their home the next day headed for the City Auditorium smiling and upbeat. The morning of the start of the preliminaries was no different. I was prepared for the day, and I began it with a positive attitude and a great big smile.

Earlier that same day, June 12, the judges, Col. Price, Mr. Badders, Mr. Williams, Mrs. Fox, and Mrs. Cauble, asked us questions as part of the official judging, to test our knowledge of our communities and civic and social issues, and learn our future plans. Each of us was given ample time to think about the questions so we could answer with care and serious thought. The girls around me were smiling as they answered their questions easily and quickly. My questions, on the other hand, were awkward and generally uncomfortable. One of the judges, Col. Mercer Lee Price, a "colonel from the South" went out of his way to inform me that he "just loved black people." Then he went on to ask me how I felt about civil-rights activists H. Rap Brown and Stokely Carmichael and all of the unrest in Omaha. I don't think the other contestants got that question. I answered as honestly as I could. I told him that there were all types of black leaders in our country, and their contributions, though radical, made me proud to see young men and woman stand up for our civil rights. I could tell that he didn't feel the same way. His face turned beet red, and I was happy to move on to the next seat. The next judge informed me that he didn't "hate black people, but . . ." I learned later that the other girls answered questions about school, home, poor people, sewing, and what they liked to cook. Not one judge asked me what I liked to cook.

We practiced our acts and routines for the contest all day. Then we had a filling lunch, practiced some more, signed autographs, and prepared for an early dinner at the York Country Club on West Elm Street.

I was excited about and looking forward to opening night. When I arrived back at my chaperone's home after a long day, Mrs. Elrod was waiting for me with my beautician. Right away she began working on my head in the kitchen. That process made me feel beautiful and ready to compete with the other girls. Now I was ready. I was overcome with excitement and couldn't wait to see all of my family and friends at the City Auditorium. I wanted to ride with Mrs. Elrod, but I was required to ride with the Withams. Looking at everyone that evening, I could tell that they were just as excited as I was.

The contest opened officially at 8 p.m. that Thursday night at the York City Auditorium. The preliminary competitions would take place on Thursday and Friday nights. Contestants were separated into two categories for each night, A and B. Because I was in group A on Thursday night, I performed my talent; on Friday I would compete in group B, in the swimsuit and evening-gown competition.

Someone brought copies of the programs backstage: *The Other Side of the Rainbow*. Girls were running all over the place making last minute adjustments: making sure everything was in the right place, putting on their makeup, warming up their bodies, practicing their routines, humming, singing, stretching, dancing, and tuning up their instruments.

And then the lights blinked, signaling that it was time for the show to begin. If you squeezed past the stage managers a little you could see the curtains as they opened; the orchestra below; and the mistress of ceremonies, Betty Louise Fox, as she entered the stage.

Then the stage producer and manager, Dick Wood, wearing a large headset, and his assistant Judy Townsend began directing us. "Okay, girls, it's time! Take your places. Remember, you're all winners! Now smile!"

The overture began with the pageant orchestra, conducted by Ed Coleman. They played "On the Other Side of the Rainbow."

"Quiet girls! I can't hear Betty speaking."

The pageant chorus sang, directed by Vic Michel. Special guest entertainers Phyllis Grabenstein, Miss Arapahoe 1968; Elizabeth Upward, Miss Arapahoe 1967; and Donna Olmsted performed. Then it was our turn in the "Parade of Cities." All of us uniformly glided out onto the stage from both sides of the auditorium to the song "Look at Her," sung by Dan Smith. When we were all on stage, Miss Nebraska 1968, Diane Boldt, was introduced to the audience. I couldn't help but notice how we all looked at her with envy. All of us wanted to be her, even me. And why not? She was cordial, beautiful, graceful, and fun. And she was the reigning Miss Nebraska, if only for two more days.

All of us came from different parts of Nebraska, but we assembled with one desire, one hope, and one dream: to become not just Miss Nebraska but

Miss America—heck, why not Miss Universe? Daring to look beyond the footlights, I could see the excitement and the pride in the faces across the audience. Little did I know that many of them were there to record a first in the history of this contest: me. The first African American woman to enter and win any local title in the Miss America Pageant was now vying for the Miss Nebraska title. I have to admit I felt the pressure.

All of us left the stage to prepare for the swimsuit, evening-gown and talent competitions. While we were gone, the judges were introduced. Each one stood up as his or her name was called, turned toward the audience, and waved or took a bow. Then Betty Louise Fox and the Pageant Chorus performed the song "Color."

The contestants in the swimsuit competition walked onto the stage as their names were called. Following that they returned in their evening gowns while the music continued playing in the background. Finally, it was time for the talent competition. When it was my turn, I felt like I gave the best possible performance of my dramatic oration I could give before singing my heart out to the music from the movie *Exodus*. The competition was fierce: four vocal presentations, an illustrated reading, a piano solo, an acrobatic jazz dance, and a clarinet solo.

When the evening was over, the judges would determine the winners for Thursday's preliminary competition. We waited. Like each time before, it seemed to take hours and hours for them to reach their decisions. Then the results were announced: Miss Kearney State, Vickie Annette Gardner, nineteen, of Arapahoe and Miss Kearney, Jackie Louise Pahl, nineteen, had tied for swimsuit honors. Miss Omaha, Catherine Grace Pope, twenty, had won the talent preliminaries along with a morale boost in this competition. On Friday night we would repeat the preliminary competition all over again in reverse. This time I would appear in a swimsuit and an evening gown.

I began Friday filled with excitement and enthusiasm. Everyone arrived at the City Auditorium earlier than expected, so we found our individual spaces and practiced our routines. We had been given our instructions for the day and came prepared for the autograph signing and parade. The parade in York was small as far as parades go. The midmorning sun was somewhat unbearable as we located our positions in the assigned lanes and were helped onto the backs of cars with our city titles displayed on both sides. We rode down the streets waving; because of the heat it seemed like it took forever.

I was surprised by the number of families and community members that turned out. Most of the buildings were small businesses and storefronts. I enjoyed watching the kids wave and waving back at them with the "beauty queen" wrist roll.

After the parade, we were assigned tables so that people could talk to us and get autographs. Signing an autograph usually meant that we wrote our name on our picture. Sometimes someone asked us to say something special to them. I tried to accommodate each and every one, even when I didn't have time. Whatever I did, I did it with a smile. After most of them stared at me for a while I would move or say something like "I look forward to seeing you again at the contest." That would snap them out of their trance; they would smile back at me and move on so the next person could meet me. I believe they stared because most of them had never been up close and personal with an African American, let alone carry on a casual conversation.

I wasn't concerned about whether things turned out well or the way I hoped. I was concerned about what was going to happen to me in the long run. Was this going to be beneficial to me, or would I have to constantly raise the bar, in pursuit of the crown?

The Friday-night preliminaries program was the flip side of the Thursday-night event. Miss Arapahoe, Ona Mae Hays, twenty, won the talent award by singing an operatic aria. Miss York, Jane Briggeman, a twenty-one-year-old student at Concordia, won the swimsuit competition. Miss Chadron, Clarise Wallingford, nineteen, received a morale boost, the same vigorous applause and strong show of approval that I had received on Thursday night.

The newspaper said, "Miss Omaha could reach even more by winning the converted crown. The petite University of Nebraska at Omaha junior, majoring in speech pathology, is the first Negro to compete in the state finals." They felt that I had a chance to win the Miss America Pageant.

When asked I said, "I'm glad the preliminary talent is over. But I know that it all has to be done over again. I'm not really too nervous. It's all been fun and I'm enjoying every moment." I was a winner, but it was now time for everything to start from scratch on Saturday night.

On Saturday night the competition began all over again. With each tone and each note I tried my best. Throughout the night people clapped and cheered for their contestant or city. When everything was over it seemed to take hours for the judges to reach their decision. All eyes were on them. The audience was tired, and some of them even left, planning to read the results in the morning newspaper. People began whispering, wanting to know what was taking the judges so long. They were seated in front of the audience so I really didn't know what was going on. What I did know was that it was taking them a very long time. All of us were waiting backstage for their decision, and the wait might have well have been days. You could hear the people out front begin talking to each other. Several times you could hear raised voices, almost arguing, among the crowd. I was wondering what was going on out there. Then out of nowhere they asked the assistant to collect the results. It was almost midnight. Everyone was exhausted. There were no words, only sighs and yawns. We all waited backstage for the results to be read.

The mistress of ceremonies returned to the stage with the results. I held my breath. This was it.

"Ladies and Gentlemen, I know that you have been waiting a long time for the results. Miss Oxford, Catherine Loewen, seventeen, First Runner-up. Linda Ann Hogel, twenty, Second Runner-up. Miss Superior, Sally Yvonne Abelbeck, seventeen, and Miss Kearney, Jackie Louise Pahl, nineteen, complete the top four finalists."

It was now over for me; I had lost. As I stood in the background on the stage after the question-and-answer segment of the contest, I waited for the results along with everyone else. Then I heard them announce the winner: Jane Deliese Briggeman, Miss York, a student at Seward Concordia College. She was crowned and presented with a large bouquet of flowers, and a large cape was draped over her gown.

I was stunned. I just have to say it. I knew there was a remote possibility that I wouldn't be selected—well, because of events occurring like the personal interview, in the back of my mind I guess I knew that there was a more than remote possibility that I wouldn't be selected. But I really wanted fairness; I wanted these individuals to take the high road. That being said, I felt miserably let down, even devastated. I just couldn't believe the whole thing. But it was true, and I had to accept it. I lost!

Like the other girls I quickly embraced and congratulated Miss Briggeman, the 1969 Miss Nebraska, and then I congratulated the other winners. That's right—I didn't even place. I was there, but I felt as if I was viewing the celebration from a distance. I watched the new Miss Nebraska walk the runway and fought back the tears.

The *Omaha World-Herald* said, "There was surprise along press row and in the audience that Miss Omaha, Catherine Grace Pope, 20, daughter of Mr. and Mrs. John Pope of Omaha, and Miss Arapahoe, Ona Mae Hays, 20, daughter of Mr. and Mrs. Thomas Hays of Edison, did not make the finals. Miss Omaha, the first Negro to compete in the state pageant, and Miss Arapahoe had both won talent competitions."

It was over. I watched the girls move gracefully around the room. They appeared distracted and unattached as they packed up their things. In their street clothes, they didn't look like beauty queens. I was congratulated by everyone there, and I was grateful. I didn't want anyone to feel as if their efforts had gone unappreciated. I gathered up my things at the Withams' house and then insisted that we drive home right away. I didn't want anyone at the City Auditorium or at the Withams' see me cry, not even Pamper.

There was controversy following the pageant. My mother spoke to a reporter and said that she wasn't certain that Miss Briggeman should have won the title. I don't understand why they decided to interview her when there were so many other girls' parents around to interview, especially the winners. I was asked to comment on my mother's comments. My comment was that I wasn't sure that Miss Briggeman was the best person for the title. Mike Nolan, who was the director of the Miss Omaha Pageant but was not an official at the York competition said, "I thought the winner was a very qualified candidate, but I was disappointed in the results after that." People from York as well as Omaha contacted my family and supporters, expressing their disappointment with the final results of the pageant. Some of them came right out and said that they felt the contest was rigged. For some it appeared through telephone calls that the pageant "wanted to make sure that the right kind of girl won."

I also said, "I'd like to be able to enter a contest where it could be fair for everyone in it, no matter what color she is. But if the contest is going to be exclusively for white Anglo-Saxons, it should be said that it is going to be whites only so someone who is maybe, for instance, Jewish or Indian or Negro, won't even have to bother to enter." When I was asked about the questions during the preliminaries, I responded, "The preliminary questions that the judges asked me all seemed to be preceded by something about race." I went on to say, "It was as if they felt they had to establish some kind of rapport with me and were trying to say, 'Now I don't hate you because you're colored, but . . . ' The judges seemed to think they had to break down some sort of color bar before they could talk to me. None of the other girls had questions like this asked of them."

My mother said, "We realize that somebody's got to lose and somebody's got to win, but it looked a little bit too obvious when five blondes made the top five when these two girls (Miss Pope and Miss Hays) didn't." We both won talent, and most people in the audience as well as the media that attended the pageant felt that one of us should have won.

On our way home my mom didn't say a word about the contest. The silence made me feel uncomfortable. Whenever my dad started to say something my mom quickly changed the subject. It was really strange. "You know you have a lot of things to do when we get home. You still haven't completed fall registration for school. How many classes are you going to take? Do you think you'll go back to any of your old jobs? I'm sure they're waiting to hear from you. And there's no telling what they're expecting of you back in Omaha. Remember, you're still Miss Omaha." That was the first time my mother mentioned anything to do with the pageant. I know what she was trying to do, but I just wasn't ready to hear any of it.

"Do you want to stop and get something to take home to eat? We're coming up on a restaurant."

"Thanks, Dad, but I'm not hungry. But maybe mom wants something." My mother didn't answer. I'm sure she was heartbroken. But as she lived her life, she kept her personal grief to herself. We pulled into our driveway. We were home.

I had no idea about the explosion that was about to take place in Omaha around the selection of Miss Nebraska 1969. We woke up to our phone ringing in the morning and went to sleep to calls at night. A lot of the calls were positive. Many people said that as far as they were concerned I won. That was nice, but it really didn't change anything. On several occasions when I was in the living room and the phone rang, I picked it up and heard disgusting comments and even threats on the other end. There was one in particular that will always haunt me. "Well, nigger, first you! Now your mother. She had no right to say what she did, calling our contest a fraud. Both of you will get what's coming to you." He didn't even attempt to disguise his voice. I couldn't hang up the phone. I had to listen. It was important, necessary. I needed to know what was being said about me around the city—the good as well as the bad. But that wasn't the end of it. There was more. I was in the *Omaha World-Herald*'s Public Pulse, a segment of the paper that allowed for public comment on issues of the day. It was difficult to put out the emotional fires. It was clear that an elephant was in the room and no one was willing to talk about it or even acknowledge it—racism.

The judges' interview.

Break time.

Jeri Elrod, Miss Arapahoe, and my mother.

23

Beyond the Rainbow

With this loss, there were no words. We rode home in silence. The next day, I received a letter from Susie Buffett:

Dearest Cathy,

I'm sitting here wishing I had some magic words of wonder. But I don't—besides, the fact that I'm an old lady leads me to suspect that as deep a disappointment as this is, your life may hold heavier ones. We sure aren't living in heaven—we're right here on earth!

But what's beautiful about living in this crazy world is that life itself is contrast. It refuses to let us hold on tight and be secure. We reach out and in our reaching often find what we wanted at the first step is not what we want where we turn another corner. If we look only ahead we don't see what's around us.

If we grasp too tightly to what we love it will not love us—nothing can live that way. The struggle for balance in all we experience seems so different at times—when others seem to care so little for us as for what we care about. But Cathy you cannot live anyone else's life—only yours. No matter what cruelty others possess, if you become cruel will you be happy being like that? If no one else ever loved—would you be willing to go through life unloving? I know you couldn't. Because that is why you are beautiful to me. And why you will be beautiful as long as you live to whomever your life touches closely.

I see in you a need to give—to reach out and love not afraid to feel and react. Some people are. Too many people. I pray that you will grow as a human being with every experience. That's the most life has to offer. And being open to all possibilities happens to enlarge life at any age or any place. And you will find such excitement—happiness—and treasured people tucked in among the devastation and hurts that you'll make a kaleidoscope of your own life pattern. And you'll weave it into beauty you can't yet imagine.

The enclosed gift is something I had framed and put in my closet to be given to someone special someday. Today seemed the day—it comes with genuine affection from someone you have touched more than perhaps you knew—
Mrs. Buffett
June Fifteenth

On June 17, 1969, I received letter from Mr. and Mrs. Witham and Pamper their cat:

Dear Cathy,

I don't suppose that many of your feline friends write letters to you, but since you're so purr-fect I wanted to let you know how I feel.

I'm lying on Mrs. Witham's lap, and I know she is writing to you because I heard her say "sure miss that sweet Cathy who brightened up our home for a week."

I've tried to get into your bedroom to see if you are sleeping, but Mrs. W scats me out when I get as far as the bathroom. It's so quiet here, so I believe you must have taken your bags and gone home.

Do you understand children's ways? Mrs. W's grandson, 4-year-old Scott, used to grab my tail and chase me all over the kitchen. And Mark, 1½ years, really has to be watched cause he likes to eat my cat food. Now is that any way for kittens—I mean people babies—to treat a friend? When I got on your lap, you let me turn around and find the right spot to lie down. Then you scratched my head and under my chin. Oh Cat, did that feel good!

Don't mean to sound gossipy—or as you'd say, Catty—but I heard Mr. W tell Mrs. W that lots of York people have told him that they can't understand why you were not in the final five in the pageant, with all of your talent. See, it isn't just your own Pop and Mom who think nice things about you. Other people can't understand why judges do certain things either. But then I guess we can't all be pageant judges.

Mr. and Mrs. W and I sure hope you will come see us sometimes if you're all dressed up. Mrs. W has an apron she will lay on your lap so you can hold me again. Mr. W has a fit when my long white hairs get on his clothes and he says, "Someday I'm going to kill that cat." That must be the reason we have nine lives. I've enjoyed "mews-sing" with you but now I must close.

Love,
Pamper

———

Dear Cathy,

It was so nice having you in our home last week. We really enjoyed getting acquainted with you in spite of the rapid time schedule you had to keep. We pray that you will remember York for all the wonderful memories and associations of friends that you made during the pageant. As our Methodist Bishop N. Moore has said, "When one door closes in your face, other doors are opened to you."

During June, July, and August our church choir disbands and we have soloists and small group specials for *our 11 a.m. church. Would it be possible for you to come down and sing for us July or the final part of August? Who brings you down we would like to have you eat dinner with us at noon. We don't pay for our special numbers, but Jerry and I will be glad to give you $5. Or whatever you feel your car expenses would be. You didn't mention your plans for the summer, so I don't know how free you will be.*

Naturally I'm busy serving on the dresses for our niece's wedding in Denver on Saturday. I have the pink dress trimmed with matching lace almost finished for my mother. Now I'll get to work on the green brocade for myself. So far I haven't been able to find green shoes. May have some dyed to match the dress.

Do hope to hear from you sometime.

Love,
Mr. and Mrs. Witham

The following week people across the state began to let their views be known in the *Omaha World-Herald's* Public Pulse.

June 21, 1969
Even Beauty Is Imported
Kearney, Nebraska

It is no wonder that Nebraska is such a backward state. We can't even seem to come up with a homegrown girl to represent us in a contest of beauty and brains (the Miss America Contest).

Steve Curtis, Jack Battershell

——

Miss Omaha to Go Far
Columbus, Nebraska

The people of Omaha deserve a round of congratulations for selecting an outstanding young woman to represent them at the Miss Nebraska Pageant. Catherine Grace Pope is a talented, intelligent girl. Nebraska could have been equally proud to have her represent the state in Atlantic City. But apparently the judges in York were more concerned with color than with qualifications. We sincerely hope Miss Pope does not let this disappointment dim her aspirations. We are sure she has what it takes to succeed far beyond many of the rest of us.

Mr. and Mrs. Ivan Milbourn,
Susanne Vlach

— —

Tuesday, June 24, 1969
Talent Worth 50 Pct.?
York, Nebraska

If the Miss Nebraska Scholarship Pageant is misrepresenting itself to gain dignity in contrast with the common swimsuit beauty contest, then I feel we have a right to question that agency. We are repeatedly told that talent is worth 50 per cent. Many in York felt that Miss Omaha, Catherine Pope had one of the outstanding talent presentations in the 1969 pageant. Where were the judges when the final five were chosen?

Mrs. Gerald Witham,
Hostess to Miss Omaha

— —

No Restrictions
Omaha, Nebraska

The Miss Nebraska Pageant has absolutely no written or unwritten restrictions as to race, religion or color. I know, because I was a finalist last year, and I am Jewish. Mrs. Pope stated the top finalists were all blondes and that this was an obvious slam against her daughter and Miss Arapahoe, both brunettes and talent winners in earlier competition. If she would glance at the list of Miss Americas, she would see the majority of them are brunettes. When Miss Pope was crowned Miss Omaha, she was selected because of her beauty, talent and poise, not her color.

Nancy Aronson Breslow,
Miss University of Nebraska, 1968

———

Talent Is Not All
Lincoln, Nebraska

True enough, Catherine Pope may have won the talent contest. This earned her enough points to become one of the 10 finalists. But winning one portion of the contest does not assure anyone high enough rank to become one of the five finalists. If the girl chosen Miss Nebraska was also selected Miss Congeniality by her fellow contestants, then her ability to be a winner lies not only in front of the judges but also offstage. The true winners in many of these contests, it seems to me, are picked from the "real them" that appears behind the scenes.

Miss Hazel Hoff

On Friday, June 13, while I was riding on the back of a convertible in the Miss Nebraska parade, a lady had slipped a piece of paper into my open hand and politely folded my fingers around it. I was unable to read the note while riding through the streets of York, but several weeks later I found the note tucked away in the bottom of the handbag I had carried that day:

Miss Omaha Queen, my name is Sara and I'm seven years old. My sister is thirteen. She wants to wear makeup but my mother won't let her until she is fourteen. We look just like you because we are colored brown. I want you to win for me and my sister and my mother. We want you to win because you are smart and pretty. You make us feel smart and pretty too. My teacher helped me write this letter. I hope she will give it to you.
I Love You,
Sara

On June 24, 1969, only ten days after the finals of the Miss Nebraska Pageant, a young fourteen-year-old Negro girl named Vivian Strong was shot in North Omaha.

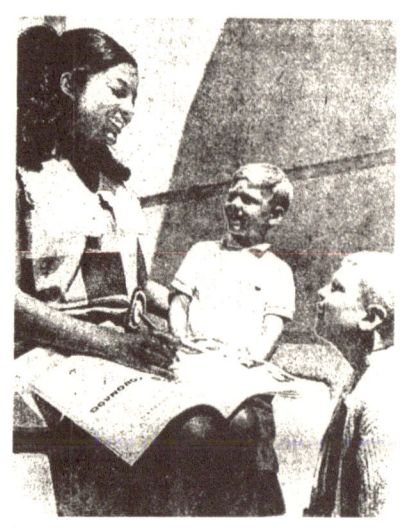

Signing autographs for Rex and Kent Pettygrove.

Jeri Elrod and I write thank-you notes to supporters.
(photos courtesy of Omaha World-Herald)

Vivian Strong.

Firemen protected by police as they put out the fires.

Police response to the rioting.

24

Taking Back Control

Courage is accepting the truth when you hear it and acting upon it with no inhibitions.

In one horrible moment it was all over for a young fourteen-year-old girl in the inner city. It was unexpected, and I was surprised. In the heat of that long, hot summer in Omaha, violence would erupt and continue to spew through the streets.

As Ryan A. Ravelomanantsoa said,

People feel the need to riot and loot for many reasons. When it happens, society flips its head and people get real. The ultimate reason groups of individuals collectively hit the streets and commit crimes in the name of protest and moral rebellion can be summed up in one phrase: to take back control of their lives. Control, frustration, and the sense of invisibility boil down to the perception of powerlessness, as well as emotional, public outrage on the surface, but in reality, it becomes just the straw that broke the camel's back. The fact is that it has more to do with being unconscious, spiritually blind, mentally asleep, or deliberately shunning the grievances of those at the bottom. Rioting is the last effort, after being ignored or morally denigrated, whether in perception or reality, by those who don't care enough to even investigate whether those people's pain is even legitimate.

In Omaha, on Tuesday, June 24, 1969, those with no voice pulled back the curtain and saw the wizard sitting there. . . . Well, that's when all hell broke loose.

What do you do when you're trying to have the best year of your life, and you find that due to circumstances beyond your control it's impossible? The year I became Miss Omaha, 1969, was the best of times for me, but the senseless killing of a young black girl in my community also made it the worst of times. Most of us grow from our challenges, mishaps, and mistakes. I've always considered challenges more of a blessing than sheer luck or boring complacency.

On that hot summer Tuesday in 1969, fourteen-year-old Vivian Strong was shot and killed at 1708 North Twenty-First Avenue Plaza. According to reports, the police said that they responded at about 10:25 p.m. to a break-in in progress a few doors down, in the public housing project. One white and one black officer responded. The white officer shot the innocent girl once, hitting her in the base of her skull and killing her. I was about two months into my reign as Miss Omaha.

At the time of the shooting, a babysitter was watching Vivian; her mother was not at home. The police were investigating the call that came into their station regarding a burglary in progress. Several kids were playing records in the alley when the police arrived, something the kids did frequently. In the group was Vivian. When they approached the area, the kids were frightened and caught off guard by the police officers. The kids took off running, thinking they were in the wrong place at the wrong time. Running away from the police was not unusual in our neighborhoods. There was a shot. Vivian didn't holler or shout when she was hit; she fell to the ground and died. People began to gather after the shooting, and a three-day rebellion ensued.

I was at home with my family that Tuesday. It was late when our downstairs phone began ringing. My father answered the phone, listened for a bit, and said, "Yes, we used to live in the projects." I stood on the stairs listening to my dad's conversation, watching his demeanor change as he listened and responded. His brow furrowed as he slowly hung up. He saw me watching him, so I carefully approached. He described the shooting as calmly as he could. Stunned, not knowing what else to do, we quietly went to bed.

While we slept, violence erupted all across the Near North Side—looting, fires, and shootings. People were in the streets throughout the night, and police were everywhere. The next day, Wednesday, the county attorney said it appeared that the officer had overstepped his lawful authority. There were rumors spreading through our neighborhoods that because he was a police officer—a white police officer—there would be no justice. He would not go to trial. The thought of that set off more violence in the streets.

On Wednesday night the rioting continued. I received a call asking if I would agree to be picked up and taken to a local television station to go on the air and ask my community to stop tearing up the city and go home.

It was an ironic request, because as Miss Omaha I hadn't been asked by our city officials to do much of anything. I assumed they thought I wasn't good enough or qualified to represent their city. But now they needed me.

I struggled with the thought of telling people, who had insurmountable struggles piling up, to stop and just go home. I couldn't ask them to go home. I was one of them, and I understood the pain. What tore at my heart the most was the death of a young girl, a girl about my age, who had been shot in the back of the head by a police officer.

It was easy for me to respond to the request. "No. I can't do that. I just can't tell them to go home. We are long overdue for justice for so many wrongs."

The night following the shooting, grocery stores and shops across the city were being looted and some of them even destroyed. People were yelling and shouting in the streets.

"We want every white man off this end of town!" and "Build it back, and we will blow it up again!"

My own church, at Twenty-Fourth and Ohio Streets, was open to crime, burning, and even bombing. The night was full of smoke and despair. Buildings were scorched. People worked around the clock looking for something—who knows what? People walked, even ran, looking for something to take their anger out on.

More police were called in, armed with shotguns and ready to eliminate the violence. Everything seemed to go on for days. Streets were closed, and the police remained to maintain order. But they weren't the only ones on the streets. Youths were angry and yelled and threw things at the police, running into the darkness and hiding in alleys.

On June 25, the day after the senseless killing of Vivian Strong, manslaughter charges were filed against one of the patrolmen involved in Strong's shooting. After the announcement, city officials met with community members in an effort to prevent further violence.

The days of violence left destruction in their wake. The utility company had to dispense crews to tear up streets in order to shut off the gas lines that fed the burning buildings. Businesses and small stores were broken into, vandalized, burned, and destroyed. The local post office closed. Firemen were dispatched to my burning neighborhood and surrounding areas by security to control and put out the fires. The National Guard was briefed on what was happening and made ready to enter the city when and if instructed by the governor.

By Thursday night of that same week, citizens were meeting across the city in an effort to find a peaceful resolution to a very complicated problem. Susie Buffett was one of many individuals who formed Community Organizing for Justice, which worked to build trust throughout the city during this rocky time in Omaha's history.

Most of the violence was subsiding, but it could flare up at any time if something wasn't done and done right away. In the aftermath of the shooting, it was evident that tension was rising on both sides. Everyone was interested in no one else getting killed. Among those who took action was the director of the Nebraska Urban League, who help initiate such things as training students to be calm when stopped by the police, and not to reach for their driver's license or registration in or out of the car, but to make sure their hands could be seen at all times. The Urban League director was also interested in the city developing a barrier between those who could kill and those who could be killed. Profiling and being stopped by police without cause had been an issue in the black community. Young black males and females were taught by their elders not to act suspiciously or talk so as to anger officers and not to run when asked to stop. In contrast, officers were instructed by their commanding officers and city officials not to fire out of fear. Even the Black Panthers assisted with maintaining order in the streets. They did not want any youth or adults gathering in crowds or running from police. Most of them tried to make sure that the people in the community were home by nightfall.

Omaha was seen across the country on television stations.

As each article appeared in the newspaper, I couldn't help but think about my personal needs and my responsibility to my community along with what that should look like. What could I do? Was I afraid to do anything? I continuously questioned myself and my personal motives surrounding these events that were taking on an uncontrollable life of their own. The FBI had already appeared in my life; I had no idea why, but those closest to me informed me about their presence. All I could think was why would the country be interested in me? Ever since my first run for Miss Omaha in 1968 the FBI had made brief appearances in and out of my life. It was a little disturbing and very creepy. I didn't know if their appearances meant protection for me or if they were merely tracking my movements and actions and possibly my family. It made me extremely uncomfortable, because of everything that had happened to me in the past. The police accosting me in the street and of course the comments made by several of the contestants in the Miss Nebraska contest were always lurking in the back of my mind.

During this time, there was a short article about a personal appearance I had made. On June 26, 1969, I remember reading all of the headlines in the newspaper. One in particular stood out. The title was "Miss Omaha to Be Honored." The text related that "Catherine Pope, Miss Omaha, is to be honored at the United Methodist Community Centers field center at 1:00 p.m."

I found myself on the streets of North Omaha with my friends and family members, walking from corner to corner, trying to find out what was going on, trying to make sense out of the senseless. Feeling depressed and at times frightened as I moved through the neighborhood, I knew that if nothing was done we would experience this type of violence again and again. Any fear that I felt soon turned to a feeling of hopelessness, so I had to do something. I couldn't let the events occurring in the street—in my streets—go on without my presence, so again I stepped outside of my house.

Although I didn't go out until dark, I heard that there was blood everywhere. People were falling in the streets. Those standing were confused and staggering on and off the sidewalks. It was difficult for most intelligent-minded people to understand or believe, but when people are scared and full of hate, they will place the blame on anything and everything except their own past and present behavior.

I understood and felt the anger that they felt, the same anger that was now playing out on the streets. They were only acting out our collective frustration with a system that time and time again had turned its back on us. I was afraid to be out there in the streets of North Omaha, but where was I supposed to be? This was where I lived, and the people in trouble were my family and friends. I was in trouble. The shopkeepers, the people who worked in the stores, the ones who had to go to work, like my brothers and sisters—all of them knew that they had to be in the streets in spite of the fighting and the chaos. We didn't want what happened in Watts or in other parts of the country to happen where we lived, and if it did we wanted it to make a difference.

Since I was the reigning Miss Omaha, whenever I made appearances around the city people asked me questions about what was going on, as if I held the pulse of every living African American in Omaha. "Why destroy your own neighborhoods, your homes, the only stores that you can utilize with little or no transportation? The community post office?" (Because of the damage to the postal station on North Twenty-Fourth Street, postal service in that location was temporarily suspended.)

After thinking over the questions for a while, I began my response with "I can't answer for everyone, but as the reigning Miss Omaha I will try and answer you. I've learned that people always take anger out on the people and things closest to them. We do what we have been taught by others, including the ones who cause us the most harm. What else can we do except that which is immediately available to us? When you feel as though you have always been hated for no reason, you become very frustrated, and you have to do something. But this violence comes because of real events. People are saying we're tired of it your way. What you're seeing is just a symptom of the real illness, racism."

The local newspaper was full of news regarding the riots, but nowhere in the paper was there news of my social endeavors and philanthropy. That was all lost to the sensational, tantalizing reports of ongoing violence in my neighborhood. It was reported that no firemen were injured, even though there were reports of thrown rocks and bottles. All emergency procedures were followed, and a task force was formed to follow emergency procedures for going into areas as fires broke out. That meant units banded together and met at certain points and received police escorts. It was their effort to move things back to normal.

I can't begin to describe all of the events that took place during those hot days and nights in June of 1969. Men were pulled from their cars and beaten. Many innocent bystanders were among those arrested. One man was beaten for one dollar and suffered a fractured jaw. Most people had cuts and bruises from thrown bottles and bricks. Some reported that they were chased by cars. The newspaper reported that their car struck a telephone pole and then they were beaten by Negroes. One individual said that he lost his glasses and money. Police officers reported sniper fire. One patrolman lost control of his car while in pursuit of another vehicle. He said that he heard several shots so he ducked, and in that second he ran head-on into another car. People were arrested. Blacks and whites were assaulted. Many people went to the hospital, and some remained there throughout the night. Dissatisfaction was expressed around the city, in the churches, businesses, schools, and public buildings. There was plenty of blame to be shared. It took 180 riot police to calm the crowds and settle them down. That night forty Negroes were arrested. Thirty were booked on suspicion of felonies, most involving looting. Those arrested ranged in age from twelve to sixty-one.

The police told their story, and that was what was being broadcast across the news. They showed pictures of the violence and destruction occurring in the streets, but nothing was said about the black communities' mistrust of the police and city officials. Nothing was said about the despair and hopelessness on the faces of black citizens. They were expressing themselves, not in a way that would ever be accepted by either side, but they were demanding to be heard.

The Black Panther Party, armed with rifles, stood guard in front of the Greater Omaha Community Action Office, protecting the black-owned business. They said the building provided sanctuary for Negro children, that it would provide a safe place for children to go if it became necessary. They were not the only black group on the streets on the night of June 25. There were also NAACP officials walking through the neighborhoods where most of the rioting took place, committed to "quieting the outburst from the youths in the neighborhoods."

By June 26, the streets were mostly quiet. City officials surveyed the damage. Although there were several fires set, no firemen were injured. Overall the city officials and many of its citizens said that they were proud of its police force and fire department. Of course they took a very different view of things from those individuals residing in the black community. The murder of Vivian Strong left a lasting stain on the department, one that could only be removed if the officer involved was found guilty of murder.

After the city officials walked through the area they met in a closed session. Another group also met, the American Civil Liberties Union. They called for changes to rules on the use of firearms by the police. There was also a rumor control established to help answer questions.

While driving to the store to get some odds and ends for my mom, I spotted several of the armed Black Panthers on the rooftops of businesses on Twenty-Fourth Street. It's hard to admit that even in the midst of the fear and people running in the streets, I was thinking about the Miss Nebraska Pageant. I was distracted by everything that had happened the night of the pageant and was lost in thought, probably trying to avoid thinking about what was going on all around me. Suddenly, I had to slam on the brakes to avoid hitting someone. A young boy about twelve years old ran out right in front of me. He looked straight into my eyes.

"Hey! What are you trying to do?" I yelled. I was frustrated, but mostly with myself. How could I be so selfish, thinking only about myself, feeling sorry for myself? I leaned over the steering wheel right in the middle of the street and began sobbing out loud. I didn't even ask the boy if he was all right. I just couldn't stop crying. Why was I consumed in self-pity?

It was dark, and people were all around me. A few of them started rocking my car, thinking that I'd almost hit that boy on purpose. I started yelling at them, pleading for them to stop.

"Watch where you're going!" someone yelled back.

I was becoming concerned for my safety and very frightened. I frantically tried to open the car door, but there were too many people leaning against it. I just wanted to get out and run down the street to my church, where I would at least feel safe. I knew that they weren't trying to hurt me, but I also knew that when people are mad and tempers flare, anything can happen: innocent people can get hurt and even killed. Vivian losing her life in such a cruel and brutal way brought out the anger and the desire to make others, anyone, pay.

A policeman finally walked over—they were everywhere those days—and signaled me to move on, to get out of the way. "Roll down your window! Pay attention, and move your car!" The officer was as frustrated as I was. But I was afraid and didn't trust the cops. I wouldn't roll down the window, in any case. Water was shooting up into the sky; it was everywhere on the streets. Clearly a main had broken, causing the boy to dart into the street. I might have noticed had I been paying attention. I wiped my eyes so I could see, took my foot off the brake, and slowly left the confusion.

On Wednesday, the day after the shooting, a small group of people were scheduled to meet in the Fontenelle Projects to express their dissatisfaction and frustration with the Omaha Police Department. By the time dusk fell, over 1,000 people had gathered on the ball field near the projects, in the area where Vivian Strong was killed.

Many of my friends wanted to go down to the ballpark, but we knew that our parents would never approve. Then I received a call from a very close friend who was an activist. Her brother, who for some reason never talked about it, was a Black Panther, and she kept me informed so I would know what they were up to. He told her she could borrow his yellow Volkswagen, so she picked me up along with several other students from the university. It was our intention to meet up with another group of friends and listen to the speeches by our community leaders. There were so many people milling around, however, that we never found the rest of our group. At one point we even lost track of each other.

As I stood there in the crowd, I almost couldn't catch my breath. As more people arrived and the crowd grew I began to feel like a pebble on a beach: obscure and indistinguishable. Right before the speeches began a hush fell like a calming breeze in the night air. All of us could feel the intense pressure coming from the crowd as the first speaker took the stage. Out of the corner of my eye I saw men walking swiftly through the crowd with rifles, and then I saw police steadily arriving onto the scene. I was anxious for them to get started; I had to get home soon, and my friend had to get the car back to her brother. He was somewhere in the crowd and probably keeping an eye on us.

Ernest Chambers, a civil-rights activist and a member of our community, was about to speak. He strongly expressed his concern for the black community, especially the children of our community. We began to slowly walk through the crowd. One of my friends spotted a leaflet on the ground advertising the meeting. The headline read, "Let's Do It Now," and asked the community, "How many black children have to be murdered by cops before something is done?"

We hung around for about an hour listening to the speeches and to the people in the crowd talking amongst themselves. It's difficult to describe all the tension I felt that night. People always say that it is tragedy that brings people together. Some reacted with outrage. Demands were made for justice. As the violence subsided and the angry citizens were allowed to express their dissatisfaction and concerns, they began to quiet down, feeling heard. The more I listened the more I realized that we weren't going to solve all the problems that night. I began to think that at least we should develop better avenues to address individual and community grievances.

As I was on my way home my mind was spinning. My Miss Omaha title had to mean more than it had so far. Is that all the city officials—the mayor, the city council, the chamber of commerce—wanted me to be, a pretty face that would appear in public once in a while saying to the outside world, "Look, we're not prejudiced in the Midwest. Our doors are open to everyone. We even chose a Negro girl to represent us in the Miss America Contest"?

When I opened the door back at home I was confronted by angry, disappointed faces glaring at me.

"Where have you been?" my dad demanded. "Don't you know that you worried your mother to death?" He had a frown on his tired face. "Remember there was a girl killed the other night. Where is your common sense?" He didn't pause. "That could have been you. It still could be you. To the rest of the world there's no difference between you and her." My dad kept talking and I stood silently, knowing he was right and there was nothing I could justifiably say in my own defense. As he continued to speak in an angry voice, I no longer heard what he was saying. I began to focus on the last words that I had heard. "The rest of the world sees no difference between you and her." Maybe he thought that they should. I'm sure that some people, mostly bigots, thought that we were just alike, niggers! I didn't see myself in that way, but we were both poor black young women who were thought of by some as lesser—not worthy of respect, justice, and equal rights. She was fourteen, I was twenty. She was a poor Negro girl growing up in the projects. I was a beauty queen living in a single-family home. I was, however, a Negro girl and had spent most of my early years growing up in the projects. She didn't live long enough to have an opportunity to experience college. I was in my second year of college. I drew very different conclusions in a seemingly very fair world. I could see how we were different and, yes, very much alike; but when you view people through a lens clouded by racial biases it's hard to see people as having more similarities than differences.

My dad had stopped talking and was walking toward his bedroom mumbling and slowly shaking his head.

"Dad, Dad," I said in a soft, respectful voice. "With all due respect, Dad, I feel that we are alike, more alike than different. And you're right, Dad, that could have been me. That still can!"

He gave me a hug, which was rare. "I'm glad you realize that," he responded with a look of concern on his face.

"That's why I feel a need to do everything possible to change things in Omaha. To do what I can to help to make it a better place for us."

He just quietly closed the door behind him.

I decided to go into the living room and turn on the television set. I brewed water and fixed a cup of tea. I sat in my dad's favorite chair and watched the cloud of steam float and evaporate in the air like puffs of smoke from my dad's cigar. The lead story on the news continued to be the fires and looting and the Vivian Strong story. There were flare-ups occurring across the city and disrupting the day-to-day calm—confrontations with the police, political fights in and out of city hall. As I got up and turned off the TV, I thought, *I'm not at all surprised at what has happened.* It had all happened before. It had all happened a year before when George Wallace came to town, to be exact. The news media would try to make you think that things were better, but they were just smoldering under the ashes waiting for someone to discard a lit match.

There was nothing left for me to do but turn off the lights and go to bed. As I walked past my parent's room I heard my mother whisper, "Cathy, I know that this upsets you, but there is nothing you can do tonight." Tonight, I thought. Tomorrow there must be something that I could do.

The Parks and Recreation Department announced that its programs would continue throughout the summer. Even the Show Wagon would operate. The show must go on, I thought to myself. They decided to keep the pool open. The destroyed post office was temporarily closed. Churches canceled revival services, banks closed for obvious reasons, grocery and clothing stores suspended operations briefly, and preschool programs were moved to safer neighborhoods. Many people called GOCA to see if it was safe for them to go back to their homes.

On Friday, June 27, the executive director of the United Methodist Community Centers made a statement in the local paper that Vivian Strong's life was worth no more than a loaf of bread or a stolen car, referring to the bail of the officer who shot her: 500 dollars. Black youth arrested for suspicion of stealing routinely had their bonds set at 300 or 400 dollars. The director worried that all the hard work we'd done building community relations was gone in the instant Vivian was shot by a policeman. Most members of the black community felt that it was futile to try and talk to anyone affiliated with Omaha's police force. Members of the white as well as the black community instead spoke out publicly against the brutality.

The newspaper was printing the names of Negroes accused of multiple crimes. I kept thinking that this was the fifth incident in two years, with Vivian's name now among them, and I felt hopeless. I was surprised at the number of people arrested, so many people that they had to set up a department to provide them with legal advice. I wanted to do something to stop the senseless violence against blacks in my community, but I felt hopeless. I was sad, and my sadness was hidden behind a smile that I continued to wear long after I was crowned. As a human being I felt disillusioned and humiliated. I wanted my role as Miss Omaha to make a difference, but as time went on I only felt vulnerable. What could I honestly do?

At the time of Vivian's shooting, police had the right to use a gun when an individual was fleeing during a misdemeanor, only being expected to exercise caution so they wouldn't strike an innocent bystander. James Loder, the police officer who fired that fatal shot, was confronted with several charges that the jury would have to select from: first-degree murder, second-degree murder, and manslaughter. First-degree murder involved premeditation; second-degree was deliberate without premeditation, and manslaughter was killing another while engaged in an unlawful act. Loder received $1,756 to help defend himself, mostly from his union. Other donations came from Washington, Florida, and Kansas. He was dismissed from the Omaha Police Force and charged with manslaughter in the killing of Vivian.

Vivian's mother began getting letters of hope, apology, and concern from around the city and across the country. Most people wrote letters of sympathy. Mrs. Strong appeared in the newspaper sitting beside one of her sons. It was difficult to look at the sadness on her face. I saved that newspaper to revisit the picture of Vivian's mom and brother reading the many cards and letters that were sent to them. The rest of the world might be moving on, but I was determined not to forget. I had to get used to the fact that everything would continue on, except the life of Vivian Strong. That was a hard pill for me to swallow.

My mind continued to search for solutions to the problems that plagued our communities, but I knew that the problems were much too complex for there to be simple solutions. As far as I was concerned, despite what others may think, to me there were 400 years of slavery not dealt with at the root of our ongoing problems.

Days, weeks, and months went by while I performed my duties as Miss Omaha. I made public appearances, participated in ribbon-cutting ceremonies, hugged and kissed babies, and continued to work and volunteer. I went back to school, working hard for my grades as usual.

My mom and dad were focused on my mom's health. Her blood pressure remained a concern, but no one could hold her back. She was continuously worried about all of the events occurring in our community, including the threats that were still being made on my life, about which most of the family remained silent. My mother preferred to answer calls when no one was around, especially me. She talked about the peculiar, nonsensical, disrespectful calls far less than she had in the past. At times when I did catch her huddled over the stairs speaking or listening to what might seem a hateful, small-minded individual, I would sometimes see an expression of familiarity as if she recognized the voice on the other end. On one occasion she spoke right up in defense of her position. "I don't care what you or your supporters think. My daughter has every right to attend any event that the city asks her to. And another thing," she continued as her voice deepened and her eyes widened, "we will not be threatened or intimidated by you or anyone else. Do you understand?" and with those last words she slammed down the phone.

"Mom, who was that?" I asked.

"Some people, some people," she kept repeating herself. Then she turned her head away from me as though she had no knowledge of my presence and went into her room.

Shortly after, there was a knock at the door. When I opened it there was no one there, so I quickly shut the door and locked it. A little paranoid, I went back and checked the lock to make sure that it was secure. I went back and checked it again. That night a large rock came through our side-yard window. Next you could hear the sound of speeding cars and their squealing breaks as they made quick turns in the street.

"Get away from that window and get down!" Dad's voice came out of nowhere, and it was welcomed. Whoever they were, they might come back, and they could have a gun. I looked up from the floor and saw the gun in my dad's hand. He always kept guns in the house, a handgun and a shotgun. We never talked about those guns either.

"I'm going to call the police," my mom said, waiting for support from my dad.

"No, what are they going to do? No, if they come back, I'm waiting. Now turn off the lights and go to bed."

Mom's steadfastness was catchy, but she was constantly worrying about my safety. She knew through the anonymous phone calls and letters without return addresses that there were those who blamed me, loosely connecting me to everything that was happening that year, including Vivian's shooting. People said that the black young people including me were troublemakers. Always wanting more, never satisfied, didn't know how to stay in our place, and even if we did somehow deserve anything we weren't patient enough to wait for the right time to receive it. There were those who needed someone to blame for the destruction and continuous unrest in the city. The police were no longer looking out for my safety because they were tied up in all of the issues plaguing the city. I understood that they weren't just there to protect me and my family. They were there to serve and protect the people, the businesses, and all of the communities in Omaha. But I lived in the black community, and whenever anything went down on my side of town, it's sad to say, they were slow to respond. I always kept this in mind because I was a public figure, and I was very much aware of the fact that there were individuals who were angry and frustrated by my rhetoric and even my physical presence. When I was given a platform to speak or asked for my opinion on what was happening in the city I spoke about the injustices in the work place and in the schools. I described the unacceptable conditions in the Omaha Public Schools: old buildings, poor teachers, old books, disproportionate funding, as my mother did and continued to do. I spoke about the lack of jobs and poor housing conditions in the projects and the lack of housing for the black working class. I voiced my concerns for women's rights and equal pay. And lately I was commenting on the lack of black professors and classes on African American history along with the insufficient recruitment of black students. My opinions were out there and I was given a stage, and when given the opportunity I intended to speak my mind.

I still cut ribbons, opened new parks, rode in parades, opened businesses, and made public appearances to raise money for worthy causes. I focused on all of my duties while remaining resolute in my role as a committed activist for civil rights. Of course this made some people uncomfortable and uneasy, even downright angry. But I knew that it was up to me to walk in my own truth whenever possible and wherever it led me.

A few months after Vivian's shooting, a grand jury was convened investigating the Black Panthers and their sympathizers like Ernest Chambers, who would later become a state senator. The "Panther Party" was opening a school in memory of Vivian Strong—the Liberator School. They planned to teach at least twenty students. We began to worry that any black who spoke out against injustice could lose his or her job or be considered a Black Panther and targeted. I was becoming even more fearful and frightened.

The report that came out of the grand-jury investigation told the story from the perspective of the white community with regards to integration, specifically white churches. Most of the people were good, solid Christians, only looking out for the safety of their neighborhoods and neighbors. They wanted a good education and fine Christian values from their own schools and churches. They were fearful of what would happen if they stood up for justice and equality under the law for everyone, including people who looked like me. Things hadn't changed much. The report lacked a thorough and critical investigation of the information, questions, and answers provided by the black community. The black community felt that the grand jury was using the Black Panther Party as a distraction to keep from focusing on the real issue, the unjust killing of Vivian Strong by a white police officer, James Loder. Over the years Omaha never fully dealt with the problems existing in the city between the white and black communities. The city always tried to put out fires, but never addressed the ongoing concerns of the people.

One day after arriving home from a Miss Omaha event, I ran upstairs to make a quick change. I had a date, and I was looking forward to an evening of fun. I removed my sash and then slowly removed my crown. I looked up at myself in the mirror, examining my face. My crown looked dull and tarnished. I placed it back on my head. I looked at my face again in the mirror, trying to smile but unable to. I should have been beaming. Someone that I'd wanted to ask me out for a long time finally had. I think he hadn't asked sooner because he didn't want to be in the limelight. He was really concerned about his own future, and he had a right to be. He was on a full scholarship to a prestigious university. He didn't need anyone to be concerned about or suspicious of him being involved with an activist who really didn't know that she was one. I knew I had accomplished something no other black girl in the city had, maybe even the country, but I still couldn't smile. I had lost my bid for Miss Nebraska, but I was still Miss Omaha.

Whenever tragedy enters people's lives the last thing they want to consider is race, but race is at the center of everything, at least in my world. It's not that I want it to be, it just is. It was at the center of all that surrounded the Miss Nebraska controversy. I couldn't hide or escape from that fact. The most I could hope for were parades, celebrations, and maybe some adoration coming from members of my own community. No matter where my head was, the truth was that most people, both black and white, weren't even thinking about beauty pageants or who won or lost. I found myself in the midst of riots set off following the local killing of a young girl, Vivian Strong, and an unjust war a world away in Vietnam. I thought about Black Panthers in the city—faces and names that I knew. Some of these young men and women in the very near future would be sought by the FBI, arrested for a bombing that killed a police officer. Several would be incarcerated in a Nebraska state penitentiary.

In my sleep I continued to see the destruction, the fires. I could see the deteriorating neighborhoods, my neighborhoods that were going down long before the fires and years before the riots. It wasn't the first or the last time that my neighbors would envision the uncertainties of their future. I felt as if we were struggling to move forward like our fathers and our fathers before them—moving forward, back at times, and then moving ahead, but always somehow on a treadmill.

I wanted to be seen as somebody different, someone special. I had just lost the Miss Nebraska title on June 14, but I was still Miss Omaha. Didn't anybody care? On June 24, a fourteen-year-old black girl was shot in the back of her head and lost her life to a policeman's bullet. Didn't anybody care? Didn't anyone notice how much our people were hurting?

During that summer of 1969, with injustices prevailing across the city, I wondered if peace could ever be found. Police officer Loder was ultimately acquitted. Even though he was acquitted, somewhere deep within me I found the courage to hope for a better life for my people, and I knew that I had to be among those individuals fighting for it. I had no choice but to step out in faith.

President Naylor delivers his statement.

BLAC President Robert "Jericho" Honore responds to President Naylor's statement.

25

Before the Demonstration

Across the country in the 1960s, students were demonstrating and at times rioting to express their dissatisfaction with the status quo. The restlessness stemmed from their intolerance for America's ongoing behavior in dealing with civil rights, freedom of speech, and the Vietnam War.

One evening in November of 1969 while waiting for my friend Frank to pick me up to attend a meeting at the Wesley House Community Center I read the newspaper headlines: "Militants on Campus Maintain Pressure." United Press International wrote about a Negro student sit-in that took place at Hampton Institute to suspend classes. The article told how blacks and Puerto Ricans had kept classrooms empty at City College of New York. The threat of a court order had ended the occupation of a George Washington University building. At another university anti-ROTC students gave up a sit-in at the school's student union. At the eastern Ivy League schools, protestors began to ease up on their tactics. Most of my friends began to hear of more peaceful approaches being used at schools like Cornell and Harvard. Friends, like Terese, began telling me about growing disagreements with the methods of the militant groups and demonstrators.

I had read in *The Omaha Star* that at Hampton University in Hampton, Virginia, the extreme step of suspending classes indefinitely was taken after

100 students took over the school's administration building. In this case state police were alerted but were not used because there was no violence. In Washington, DC, The George Washington University threatened to seek a court injunction when members of the Democratic Society occupied the Sino-Soviet Institute building.

In Queensborough College in New York, students took over the administration building and demonstrated for three days. Black students across the country were being expelled for participating in sit-ins. Students were making their demands heard all across the country, even in Whitworth University in Spokane, Washington. At Grinnell College in Grinnell, Iowa, students flew the American flag upside down in protest of the Vietnam War. All across the nation students were protesting, and they weren't just the black students. They were of all colors and races.

I felt that my university should provide many of the same services and programs that some of the articles were talking about, some of the very things that college students across the country were demanding. But in the schools that were considered as campuses in turmoil, overrun by militants, were black students just like me. Was I a militant, an inconsiderate troublemaker? I never considered myself as such.

The last headline that I read that Friday night said something about how protesters deserved to be tarred and feathered. I kind of laughed to myself even though I really didn't think there was anything funny in the article. I guess I was thinking about how my mother went up to my elementary school and demanded that the librarian remove the second book in the Uncle Remus stories, which had been published in 1881 and which used the name of the fictional character Tar Baby, from the school shelves. My mother said that the phrase *tar baby* was another name for *nigger* and was used by ignorant, bigoted people. She just didn't see any place for it on the library shelves of our elementary school, or any school for that manner. Boy, was she mad, and she didn't hesitate to let them know that the book was offensive. I don't exactly know what happened, but I do know that the next time I looked for the book in the library stacks it wasn't there.

I grew up in a house where we were encouraged to question most things, and I was always taught to stand up for myself and if possible to be a voice for the voiceless. That was my role and responsibility: to stand up for others. I knew that could be difficult, but it was always my purpose.

After the Miss Nebraska contest I was more involved than ever in the affairs of my university. I was committed to every child receiving a good education, not just in K–12, but a good college education that would lead to our ability to successfully contribute to our families and our race.

That night on the way to the meeting at the Wesley House Community Center my thoughts were absorbed by what I had read earlier in the paper, but as Frank pulled into the parking lot I refocused my attention. "Oh, I'm sorry Frank, were you saying something?"

He kind of laughed and shook his head. "No I didn't say a thing, and neither did you. I can tell that you're in very deep thought as usual. You know I keep telling you not to think too hard, that your brains might snap." Picturing what that would look like, we both laughed. I had been extremely quiet and not very social on the ride to our meeting. These days I always had a lot on my mind, and it was very evident to most of the people who knew me.

It just so happened that the discussion that evening was of the growing unrest at the universities around the country.

There were organizations and groups springing up in major cities across the country, and the heartland was no different. I was beginning to experience this unrest in Omaha and specifically at UNO. UNO would soon make vital contributions to the awakening of the consciousness of the entire country. I was destined to be a part of that history. As Uncle Booker, my mother's brother-in-law, often said, I found myself right in the middle of it all.

I was still going to my classes. School was a cherished part of my routine. It was about seven months after I'd won the title of Miss Omaha and five months after I did not win the title of Miss Nebraska. In the evenings and on weekends, I happily fulfilled my duties as Miss Omaha, appearing on television and in special ribbon-cutting ceremonies, and making speeches before large and small groups. I also still spent a great deal of my time cooking, cleaning, and taking my mother to her medical appointments, which were becoming more frequent. She had suffered from a number of strokes, and my father was becoming more concerned with each passing day. When you looked at him you could see the worry on his face and the puffiness under his eyes that showed that he wasn't getting much sleep. Even though he had little money, he tried to take her to expensive doctors that he thought could help her. However, my mother refused to go to any of the new doctors that he found. She felt safer in the hands of a doctor that she had known for years. Even though I was very concerned about my mother's deteriorating health, I never missed work at Uta Halee Home for Girls, where I taught etiquette, or the Eastern Nebraska Council of Mental Retardation, realizing what my income meant to the sustainability of our household.

Most of my life my family was either directly involved in civil-rights activities, working for the NAACP, Urban League, and other organizations, or supported them by contributing money or their time delivering newsletters and making phone calls. I found myself in protest groups, marching beside community leaders with my mom and even being forced off of stools as a little girl while trying to eat a hot dog at a Woolworth lunch counter. What I thought about all of this at the time is very hard to tell, because when you're in the middle of it you have a hard time analyzing your involvement.

Since being admitted to UNO I had struggled with the same things that most of the socially aware black students in a university found themselves struggling with, and that was finding out who I was. It seemed easy at first, but it really wasn't. So here I was, along with so many others trying through a college education to make sense of it all. During my second year of school at UNO there really weren't any classes that I could take that would make me feel better about myself, more self-assured. Through friends that I socialized with in the student union I learned about an organization that had been formed several years before I enrolled at the university. The organization SCOPE, "the mouthwash club," was formed by a young man, Rudy Smith. The name was an acronym for Student Connection to Organize Public Effort. There were several times when I had an opportunity to cross paths with Mr. Smith. He was a handsome black man with piercing, intelligent eyes.

Mr. Smith intended for the group to be a little more radical—"moderate radicals." They knew what they wanted, when they wanted it, and basically how to go about getting it. According to the members of the organization, SCOPE was the first organization of its kind, not only for blacks but for any student who grasped for the taste of the new liberation or for change.

There were only a few members in the club, so the group decided to form another organization that would operate outside of the mainstream. In 1968, during my freshman year, I became an active member of Black Liberators for Action on Campus (BLAC). The students in this new group were more militant, and I was one of those students. In Rudy Smith's view, the actions of BLAC were initially orchestrated by SCOPE, but it soon evolved into an organization of its own with less and less control by SCOPE. He felt that the takeover was the culmination of three things: the times, little or no representation in campus affairs, and racism and discrimination. Many of the students felt housing for black athletes was poorer than that provided for whites and that the UNO housing program was aware of this but did nothing to correct the problem. There were many other issues that arose from time to time on campus, and black and white supporters and sympathizers reached a point of intolerance for each other. I knew that something more needed to be done to awaken the consciousness of the leaders of the university. The ultimate result of our frustration and anger was the takeover. This became the logical consequence, a means to voice grievances with the administration. I was concerned about the same issues. However I was even more concerned about a strongly functioning black student union, where students could go and seek help on a number of levels, like an offering of a degree in black studies, representation at the cabinet level, study groups offered to students at all levels within all departments, student aides, and a health office that concerned itself with not only the medical needs, but also the emotional concerns of black males and females, such as support while away from home. I also wanted to see more black professors in various fields, not just sports. I wanted students to have connections through the university to a church of their affiliation.

The student newspaper, *The Gateway,* included articles that expressed our views. Several of the articles were sympathetic to our causes and even published accurate quotations. The president of BLAC, Robert "Jericho" Honore, a Vietnam veteran and reserve army officer participating in UBO's Bootstrapper Program, which offered tuition support to WWII vets, was allowed to publish articles in *The Gateway* that were viewed as radical by some people in the school.

Some people called us a core of angry black radicals. Of course I was extremely surprised at that because I saw myself and the others in my group as concerned citizens trying to make a difference, trying to improve on and enhance the learning experience for young men and women transitioning from their youth into adulthood. I couldn't figure any other way to make that happen, especially within a system that refused to change.

For weeks I had worked with a small group of students, spending hours and hours developing a plan to address the needs and concerns of the majority of our black student population at the university. On several occasions I had gone to the heads of the student union to ask them for our money back for the poorly organized dance on October 31. There wasn't even a response to my request for a meeting with them. I was so frustrated and irritated with the administration that I called up several people in our group, BLAC, and asked to meet with them. When we met, Honore told us that he had been trying for days to set up a meeting with the university administration but was told that because of everything going on, we would have to wait.

"What else is going on that is so important that we can't even get on the calendar? I really don't understand. What I do understand is that all of us need to meet and plan our next move." We met a few more times. I was growing excited in a frightened kind of way. Once I even asked Honore what he thought could happen to us. "Is it possible to take things too far? I mean, I'm not planning to back out," I told the group. "I just want to know if you have a backup plan in case things don't turn out exactly the way we plan. What I mean is what are we are going to do if the school doesn't go along with our demands? You must be aware that is a strong possibility." I quietly waited to hear some reassuring remark from the group. As I recall we were at a café, maybe the Fair Deal Café on Twenty-Fourth Street in North Omaha. We ordered something—soup, sandwiches, something. I really wanted something else to eat, but it was cold outside and soup was really a good choice. On this particular evening the place was full of people, mostly men whom I felt didn't want to go home to an empty house and cook. But there were several women seated in the back at a small booth. I noticed that they were watching us.

"Robert, do you know any of the women sitting at that back booth?"

He was so involved writing up our notes and quickly scarfing down the large bowl of soup before it cooled off that he didn't hear my question. I was annoyed at him, but more importantly I was annoyed at myself for even being concerned about the women behind us. I'm sure that they didn't know who I was or why we were there.

The ladies could have said "boo," and I would have jumped right out of my boots. I was always being followed around by the FBI. Some of my friends said that I was paranoid and that there was no substantiated reason to believe that they would ever be interested in someone like me. However, I knew that the friendships that I maintained throughout the years made me a target.

Friends from elementary, junior high, and high school who later got involved in the civil-rights movement were friends that the FBI took a strong interest in, and because I was involved in the movement and financially supported the Urban League and NAACP, I was a target, like thousands of others across the country.

My parents were questioned by the FBI in the twenties and thirties because they accepted money and food from friends who were suspected of having Communist sympathies. Their friends had gone to Communist Party meetings in Omaha and were given jobs—jobs that got them through the depression. In turn they shared what they had with those living around them. But that was long ago, and it really shouldn't have had anything to do with why they were following me now. My parents told me that the FBI were probably following me to keep me safe since there had been so many threats against my life. I couldn't tell if they were acting as good guys in my behalf or if they were afraid that I was a Black Panther or sympathizer.

Honore ignored me and went right back to how, when, and where we would address the president of the university. I was a little confused at that, since the group had already made many of those decisions several days before. I was concerned about the events that were planned by BLAC. I had decided that before we left the café I was going to discuss my concerns with Honore. I needed to be very clear on what was going to happen at school. If I had to, I would tell the rest of the group how I felt, but I needed to run my concerns by Honore first.

"You know, Honore, I need to know what's going to happen at school. How are we going to get the president and the regents of the university to agree with our demands?"

His response came quickly. "Cathy, there aren't any guarantees. We just have to see how he responds to us and then go on from there." He was starting to get loud, but that didn't prevent me from continuing. That answer just wasn't good enough for me.

"We'll go on—go on where?" I asked in an agitated voice. "I'm still Miss Omaha, and I have more to consider than BLAC." I didn't realize it, but I was also getting louder.

"Cathy, quiet down. Slow up—you're drawing attention to us, and you know I'm not into that."

"Neither am I. Anyway I'm committed to what we're doing, you know that."

"Well, you had me concerned for a minute. I just want us to be able to talk about this calmly."

"And I'm not—not calm, I mean?"

"I can't tell, are you?"

We knew each other, but really we didn't know each other well. I liked him, and I just went off of that when it came to forming my opinions about him. He was average height for a guy. He had curly, dark hair and wore a beard and a mustache. His glasses were thick and round, and he usually wore a military-looking jacket and a thick, wide band around his head with a large hanging tie in the back. I know he had confidence in who and what he was, because he was the first military kind of guy I'd ever seen who carried a bag. He was always so dramatic, so secretive and evasive. Some of the other students in the group didn't trust him. Several older members of our group said that he had been planted into our organization by the FBI. That wasn't uncommon on university campuses in the sixties and seventies during times of student protest, unrest, and rioting. We were also in the midst of the Vietnam War, and many students sorely disapproved of the draft. Some young men that I knew chose the path of refusing to go to Vietnam, opting to become a conscientious objector or even leaving the country. Protest and civil disobedience were the civic lessons in most college classrooms in America.

"I'm sorry," I said. "I am committed, but I always have to know where things are going."

"Then you're on the wrong planet. Life is not like that. It's a crapshoot. Listen, if you feel this is going to damage your image or mess things up for you and yours, then you'd probably better back out now."

"I'm not saying that I want to back out. I just know that we need a tight plan for things to work out the way we think that it should."

"Maybe you should just back out. We can get someone else to help keep our records and act in a leadership role. Our secretary can keep up with what happens during and after the meetings." His words were quiet now, and obviously filled with what I would consider disappointment in me.

"I can tell that you're now thinking that I might be too young to handle all of this, too young and too immature to handle this cause, but I'm not. We need to stay on topic, and I guess I haven't explained myself very well, so give me an opportunity to. This will probably be our last chance to make a significant change in the policies and culture at our school. This is not just about a dance. It's about the curriculum, the lack of diversity in the teaching and support staff, the low number of black students being admitted to the university, and flunking out or transferring when do they get here because of the lack of support culturally and socially.

"The school has no direct ties to the community that would create a direct line from elementary, middle, and high school as a pathway to college. It's personal for me. You're not from here, but most of the kids where I come from—the projects, the North, and even the South side—haven't even toured the universities in this town, let alone had an opportunity or will ever be given an opportunity to attend." I could have gone on, but I was out of breath.

"Okay, I understand, I hear you."

"Do you? Can you? You can go anywhere in this country when you leave here. Even if I leave, most of my family probably will remain: my children, if I have any, and my nieces, nephews, maybe even grandchildren. I'm sure to some I might sound a little theatrical, but I believe—no, I know—that this has to be done right the first time."

"We're going to change things, Cathy."

I wasn't quite sure of what he meant. The FBI were always around our campus and students and peering especially over my shoulder. All across the country on college campuses they were making their presence known, and my school was no different. I was used to agents following me around ever since it had become known that I was participating in a local Miss America Pageant. And, in fact, there were those individuals in our group and around the school that made it known that they felt Robert Honore was one of them and not one of us. I never really thought that, but as a person who always researched everything, I kept an open mind. He wasn't what I imagined a G-man would look like. I began to chuckle a little at the thought.

"What's up, hmm? You're laughing."

"No, I'm not. Anyway, of course I'm with BLAC. I'll go along with what you say during the meeting as long as it doesn't compromise any of my expectations or beliefs. You might not see it, but I am putting my reputation on the line." I was getting cold, and the Fair Deal wasn't noted for good insulation, so I suggested that we call it a day and go home.

On Friday, November 7, at 1:30 p.m., BLAC held a news conference in the Milo Bail Student Center. Robert Honore read to the assembled newsmen a list of six demands. Thirty minutes later, Honore, I, and about fifty others marched over to UNO President Dr. Kirk E. Naylor's office, to present the list of demands to the president in person.

Several days before, BLAC had met to finalize our demands. We thought we should be selective and present those items the administration could respond to and address right away. We were focused on the conditions for black students on campus, along with our education and overall race relations.

One of our major demands was the addition of a black studies program on campus. Why did we even have to ask for that? We demanded an equal voice and a fair way to address our concerns without waiting or not being heard at all. We wanted to have a seat at the table to serve our interests in the university. There were those in our organization who thought our demands were too weak and did not fully address the needs of the majority of the black students on campus. However, they were patient and willing to wait and see what the school would do with the written statement that we would soon present. Many of the organizations and students, whites, blacks, and others, were sympathetic and supportive of our cause.

Our demands were prefaced with the claim that Negro students at UNO were "appalled by the contemptible attitude exhibited by key administrative personnel towards them," comprising blatant racial discrimination that left them "both personally and as a group, in considerable anguish" and unable "to function within the University system."

We demanded the following:

1. Student control of the student center and its employees
2. The resignation of Frederick Ray, the director of student activities, along with the resignation of his assistant, Mrs. Thelma Engles
3. Benefits for athletes, including a training table, along with helping them with sports health concerns
4. A voice in finding and selecting black instructors and speakers, along with programming of the black studies curriculum
5. An explanation for the reduction in spending for black-oriented extracurricular activities
6. Reimbursement for the money we lost when a dance that we held in the student center October 31 had no music because the center management did not provide sound equipment

We also said that we felt both Ray and Engles were usually condescending to us whenever we approached them about our concerns, and that they had not given us control of our own activities in the center as they did with the white students.

We saw our demands as basic and minimal, and they were presented to Dr. Naylor for immediate action. Failure to act would be met with "a black student boycott of all University functions" and "a demand for the withholding of all federal and state funds until the University was investigated on grounds of both racial prejudice and financial mismanagement." The demands had been unanimously approved by our membership.

We made up our minds prior to this meeting that if our demands weren't met we would not only boycott all extracurricular activities, we would also seek to have state and federal money withheld from the university until after the school had agreed to investigate discriminatory hiring practices and closely review its description of what comprised a black studies program.

As I entered the Administration Building I thought, *How novel: I'm in a traditional building engaging in nontraditional activities and making demands of the university and its board of regents.* I considered myself a part of what represented the best of the new voices present in the Midwest. Then I thought about my hair. I didn't have much time to come up with a hairstyle, so at the last minute I took several large bobby pins and piled my hair awkwardly up on top of my head. I looked in my mirror and reapplied my lipstick. After that I thought that I looked okay. I wasn't enamored of myself, but I was Miss Omaha after all. The issues that I concerned myself with in all of this were paramount. I seriously wanted to create a fair and equitable world where gender, class, and of course race were not just tolerated but respected. I couldn't think of any better place to start than on my own campus.

When I got to Dr. Naylor's office, the room was packed. I was somewhat anxious and angry, and as I looked around for a seat I heard someone call my name. As I was directed to a seat at the front table I felt a warm flush of air pass over my body against my damp flesh. The last thing that I expected or wanted to feel was clammy and hot, but I did. I got to my seat, removed my coat, and placed it on the back of my chair. I removed my scarf from around my neck and placed it across my legs. I smiled, nodding to several of the students that were already sitting at the table. Students kept entering. They greeted each other with the black-power sign first demonstrated by Stokely Carmichael, some with arms bent and fists closed and others with arms extended and fists tightly closed. Still others were acknowledging each other by clasping hands, leaning toward each other, and then patting each other firmly on the back. They were surrounding the table where

I sat. They tightly positioned themselves between the newsmen and TV reporters that were setting up their equipment. Various sounds could be heard throughout the room: murmuring, talking, arguing, even at times laughing and joking among the students. I nervously opened my notebook, took out a large notepad, pens, and a small tape recorder, and placed them on the table in front of me.

Inside the president's office were quite a few BLAC members wearing large, pristine, well-shaped Afros. Some of them proudly wore picks, or wooden combs, in their hair. It was rumored that the meeting wouldn't take long because President Naylor had received the demands ahead of time. This was an opportunity for him to address our organization; if the response was met with dissatisfaction on our part, he would respectfully listen to us and then take some questions. It was a way to begin a fair and equitable dialogue. This meeting would set the tone and a beginning structure for the university and students of color, predominantly black students, to formally and at times informally come together to discuss issues and concerns. I saw it as a possible model for years to come. I was of the mind that our organization needed to at least create the possibilities and the school needed to embrace us on this journey. I felt excited as everyone in the room turned in acknowledgment of Dr. Naylor as he entered the room. The press lights turned on him first, then on me, and next spanned the room and returned to Naylor. I stopped talking along with everyone else and the room became quiet. When I was sure that the meeting was starting I pushed the record button on my tape recorder, looked up with pen in hand, and waited. I would let the recorder imprint his actual words and I would orient my body toward Dr. Naylor, write down what he was saying, and focus my thoughts on reading through the lines and trying to understand his intentions. Later on I wanted to be able to discuss with the group the pros and cons of his statements to us.

President Naylor held our demands in his hands and then placed them face down on his desk. He looked worried. His face expressed disbelief that we would have the audacity to come onto the campus, let alone into his office, making demands of the university. I could tell from his expression and how he clumsily began that he wished he had given this situation more thought, even conferred with a few of his colleagues from the academic world as well as leaders within the black community. But it was obvious by the tremor in his voice and the way he fiddled with the one-page paper in his hand that he hadn't. He kept shifting his weight, looking up and looking down, avoiding looking into our eyes. Beads of sweat began accumulating on his forehead. He began addressing us by first describing his role in the school and how that impacted all of us. I seldom looked up at him after that. I could tell the excuses were coming, and they did. I wanted him to focus less on the excuses and more on our concerns and his remedies. When he finished speaking, we wanted to ask questions but were told that wouldn't be possible. I believed that he wanted to take more time to investigate our concerns. The newsmen asked a few questions, but these were glossed over and again I felt like he needed more time before he got the university into any more trouble, not only with our organization, but also with the Student Senate, who were closely watching all of the events as they unfolded. They were looking into our complaints because it was their responsibility to support all students and negotiate conflicts between students and the university to the best of their ability.

Honore asked President Naylor to meet with our organization on Monday, November 10, to answer our demands. I must admit that I was surprised, but Naylor agreed to meet with us on Monday morning at 11:30. However, before he left the meeting he said, "But I'll not be put in a position to be handed demands and then be asked to react to them." While he was in front of us, he didn't read any of the demands presented to him. I suppose that was his way of maintaining control of the situation. He let us know that he wouldn't comment on any of our demands until he'd had an opportunity to study them. He looked squarely at us, picked up the papers, and left.

We were not satisfied with the outcome of the meeting, and we made it known as President Naylor hurriedly left the room. He looked irritated and mad, but along with that he appeared extremely concerned and frightened. Some members said he was scared. I turned off my recorder and put my other things into my book bag. As we left the room, we all began talking at once, not giving anyone a chance to be heard. I could tell that most of us in the group were more than upset—we were angry. We felt disrespected and then dismissed. I couldn't believe what had just happened, but I would listen to the tape and read through my notes again and again over the weekend, looking for his intentions.

Honore said that the meeting in the president's office and the march in the student center as a large group was a show of solidarity, "to bring black students into the main tide of social events on campus." He also said that he hoped to "gain significant white student support for our demands."

Over the weekend, President Naylor deliberated with Emmett Cribbs, the BLAC faculty advisor and also a member of the university's Human Relations Committee. Cribbs seemed to be ignorant of the BLAC movement on campus prior to our news conference. Dr. Naylor also met with his University Executive Council, Dean Carter, Fred Ray, Thelma Engle, and Ron Pullen. He made no effort to meet informally with Robert Honore. Instead, both sides, BLAC and Dr. Naylor, girded themselves for the Monday-morning confrontation with very little other preparation, although several of the BLAC members met with leaders of the Student Senate to explore ways to come together in schoolwide support of meeting the needs of all of the various groups on campus.

I spent time with several leaders in my community, seeking advice on how to communicate with the school, as well as how to encourage President Naylor to engage in a two-way dialogue with us. I knew that structure would have to be created, and I was willing to participate on a committee that was devoted to positive constructive exchanges. The rest of my time I spend grocery shopping with my mother and helping her clean the house. Housekeeping was always a way for me to calm myself down by doing something other than gossiping on the phone like girls my age at times had a habit of doing. The Sunday before the meeting, I had a difficult time sleeping. I had a lot on my mind. I kept thinking about the school's response to our demands and what our reaction would be if they continued to dismiss us. I tossed and turned in my bed most of the night.

The police escort us from President Naylor's office.

26

The Demonstration

"There was no violence. They did not sit in my chair or in the secretary's chair and keep us from carrying on our activities. The disruption, of course, came by virtue of the fact that there were so many people in such a small space. It was a regrettable thing to have happen on campus, but I am happy that there was no physical violence, and that the students went peaceably when the police come to remove them from the Regent's Room."
—*University President Kirk E. Naylor*
November 11, 1969

Under normal circumstances, I would disengage or intentionally have an out-of-body experience when I was utterly uncomfortable. Today, however, wasn't an ordinary day. Today was Monday, November 10, 1969, and being uncomfortable was unwarranted. People, especially President Naylor, understood our student demands. I was determined to be positive about this day. For years, especially over the past two years 1968 and 1969, life for me had been extremely unsettling and confusing, and I was determined to see to it that today would be different. It just had to be, because it was time for a change.

This morning I was awakened by the sun streaming in through the window. Opening my eyes was difficult because there was a glare from the sunlight striking the snow. The light bounced from the snow into my window as if it were already noon. It was difficult moving out from under the covers so I could get out of bed, but I quickly did just that, shivering the whole time. My rug was not in its usual spot right beside my bed on the cold, worn red-and-gray linoleum floor, so I quickly flung my legs over the side of the bed and dangled them to let my toes gingerly touch the floor to test whether or not I would get a chill. I stopped procrastinating; both feet hit the floor, and I grabbed my robe and ran into the bathroom. Looking into the mirror, I scarcely recognized the face looking back at me. It was obvious to me that the Noxzema and other face creams I had generously applied the night before didn't seem to be working. I really don't know just what I expected the elixirs to accomplish, but from my observation they had done very little. I wasn't at all satisfied with the results. My mother always said, "Cathy, you are your biggest critic. Why are you so hard on yourself? You know you could have saved that contest a lot of time and money, because you were quite capable of participating and judging the contestants all by yourself."

It was obvious why I looked the way I did, with bags under my drooping eyes, lines on my face, and marks from the wrinkled pillowcase that I always clutched tightly under my head. I could barely sleep the night before. I tossed and turned, first, from front to back and then the reverse. I just couldn't get comfortable. Relaxing just wasn't in the cards.

It was obvious that I hadn't foreseen the vast magnitude of the decision I'd made, to be an active participant in the BLAC meeting with President Naylor. I really didn't realize all that I was in for until—well, until I was in the thick of it.

The days before the response to our student demands from President Naylor were extremely taxing. I spent several evenings worrying about a well-planned meeting, wondering if that could turn into a confrontation or riot if not handled correctly. Tempers could flare, anything could happen, and I had very little control over any of it.

Most of the students participating were putting their academic careers and scholarships on the line. Many of the students were only able to attend this school through academic, military, or federal grants and student loans, all of which could be snatched away based on their decision to stand up for what they considered to be their civil rights. They were in jeopardy of losing everything they had worked for years to achieve.

I knew that my participation would put the demands of our organization in the headlines, so I didn't have any misgivings surrounding my role in the ongoing events. There was a lot of responsibility resting on my shoulders. I wondered sometimes what would happen if I withdrew my support and participation from our cause. As I continued preparing for the discussion many thoughts swirled around in my head.

I remember that Monday, as I was coming down the stairs from my bedroom, my father saying, "Damn it, Juanita, you know Cathy probably won't eat anything before she leaves for school. You know how troubled she's been over that contest." It was very obvious that Dad did not agree with most of my logic. I was still waiting to receive my prizes from the first contest, first runner-up, Miss Omaha 1968, now Miss Omaha 1969. Wow! I was focused on the meeting soon to take place at the university, and yet they thought my mind was on the beauty pageant. Neither one of them was really aware of the upcoming meeting with the school president.

Each and every morning they would ask if I was going to eat anything; my mother was a stickler for eating breakfast. "It's the best meal of the day," she would always say. Regardless of my response, she was always soft-spoken, even when I was short with her. I couldn't, however, mistake her kindness for weakness. Somehow, later on Mom would find a way to correct what she considered to be disrespectful behavior. Most of my mother's reaction to the morning had been positive, and it was my father who showed a low tolerance for my behavior in the kitchen that morning. In my mind I was pleading for both of them to just leave me alone. Knowing that they were also disappointed with the way things had turned out, I corrected my posture and my tone. "I think I'll eat something at school" was my response. I planned to meet several of my friends at school for a quick bite of food in the Milo Bail Student Center. Sitting down to breakfast and trying to carry on a conversation was a small part of my troublesome day; even though I was stressed out, I couldn't ignore what was happening around me—my parents' conversation at breakfast, my household chores, my day-to-day life—because these events were the things that kept me sane.

How could my parents be tolerant of my disrespectful behavior when they had no context for my actions? I hardly ever made excuses for my behavior, and I wasn't about to now. They could tell by my sad eyes and my lack of words that I was extremely troubled. I guess it was obvious that I had a lot on my mind—a lot more than a twenty-year-old should.

Over and over again I tried to think of ways to handle the situation.

Many people, in both the black and the white community, felt that the contest was racist and therefore the results were rigged. They heard many things about what went on during the pageant, but I just wasn't sure that I was up to all of the scrutiny. I knew that it would only awaken anger and distrust on both sides, white as well as black. Several people suggested that we have the NAACP or the Urban League ask for the City of Omaha to conduct a formal investigation into the contest and the results. In my mind I felt that it was very clear to me that nothing speaks with more resolve than the truth. For me nothing is more precious or more lifesaving than the ability to stand up for yourself and tell those involved how you feel and what you want them to do. I was still waiting for the sponsors of the Miss Omaha Pageant to live up to their commitments to me.

Even to receive some of my prizes, like a car for the year or a wardrobe, would speak volumes not only to me but to those around me. All of our friends and neighbors were eager to see my gifts, especially the car that I told them I would have for my personal use during my reign as Miss Omaha. I was looking forward to all kinds of contracts for modeling and acting. I did accept several small modeling and acting contracts in the city, but I thought there would be a small scholarship or at least something for books. I don't know exactly what happened, but I have my ideas. Anyway, somehow I found myself forgetting to care about it. Besides, I had every intention of completing school, with or without the help of the Miss Omaha organization.

I didn't say anything, but I also thought there would be a trip. Then I could take my mom and dad somewhere special. It didn't have to be far, just somewhere they had never been before. They wouldn't even have to take me—it could be just the two of them. Neither one of them complained about not going anywhere together. It was just my idea, something special that I wanted to do.

"When something happens to you, it doesn't just happen to you, it happens to those closest to you and to those around you, especially to those who worked so hard in your behalf." My dad had strong opinions, and he expressed them. There was now sternness in his voice. I looked directly at him and saw his lips quivering as he looked back at me, not blinking or turning away.

Our breakfast was a time for us to talk and express our varied views on almost anything, and my mother had no problem doing that. "Bud, you should be telling the girl something else, something more suitable."

"Cathy, listen to me. We care about how you're feeling. We know that you're hurting. Look at you: your eyes are swollen from not getting enough sleep. You're probably worrying yourself to death. Just give yourself time to heal."

I was listening and staring right through the both of them. I looked at my mother's face and knew that her reflection would probably mirror mine in about forty years. "Cathy, listen to me. I'm trying to tell you that caring has no boundaries, although we would like to at times create some. I guess our hearts stand in the way."

"Mom, I understand you, but I also know that it's not appropriate to put your feelings out there for everyone to pick at. It all just seems to be weighing me down, and there's nothing I can do about it."

I could never understand why anyone would think that I could just get over such life-altering circumstances as I felt as a result of losing the Miss Nebraska contest without experiencing so much pain. Most people expected me to hide my feelings and not disrupt their days. I told my dad, "I don't know why that continues to get in my craw, excuse the expression." My mom laughed as she continued preparing breakfast. "I should never have expected the Miss Omaha Pageant organizers to behave with honor and live up to the commitments that they made to me." But I was still very young, idealistic, and hopeful, and somewhere in the back of my mind I thought they would honor their commitments just because they said so. However, today would change things, and I had no idea if it would be for the better or worse.

"The coffee's ready." Mom had a tendency to shift from uncomfortable and testy exchanges with the mention of foods or their smells. The coffee was brewing on the stove in an old metal percolator with a wobbly black handle. I'd always thought the thing was dangerous, and over the years I tried to throw it away. As a child I use to hide things when I no longer wanted them around. Growing older I realized that hiding unwanted items was a complete waste of time. My parents would look until they found them, and the lecture was far more unwanted that even the item itself. Inevitably it would wind up either back in the same spot or, to my dismay, in an even more pronounced location. I'm sure they did these things, like always placing their things in the same place or putting things away in an undisclosed location as if anyone would want it.

I looked out the window, pretending not to be at all concerned about the conversation taking place. You could tell that the weather today was just as cold as it was the night before. People were hurrying down the walkway with their heads turned slightly to the side and tucked down into their turned-up collars in order to break the wind. Most men were wearing hats, which they held onto tightly. Women were wearing furry hats, most of which flopped down in their faces covering their eyes, and others had scarves tied securely under their chins. Children were wearing brightly colored wool coats that were too long, with oversized sleeves and collars.

"Cathy, if you leave it alone it won't hurt you"—whatever that was supposed to mean. Anyway, I understood their thinking. Don't act as if you care so much about things; most things in this life are temporary, and if you hold on too tight you can get hurt. Both of them grew up in a time when material things, things that they considered valuable and important, were hard to come by. They had to scrape and scratch for every single thing in life, and even then, it sometimes was taken away from them. That didn't just go for material things; it also went for loved ones.

The day was a very chilly one, and although I had no intention of eating the oatmeal casually placed in front of me, I did think that I needed to drink a small cup of coffee. I let my mom know.

"Good," she said, as usual. "I think you will need something in your stomach—even if it's only a strong cup of coffee." The way she said it, with a motherly knowing, it was almost as if she knew more about the day that was ahead of me than I did. You know how parents can get a funny feeling. Like most people, it was not what she said but how she said it. Things were always said with such honesty and knowing. The cup that I always drank from was made of something called Melmac, a painted, hard-plastic dishware that appeared after World War II. I liked a special cup that had faded baby roses across the rough, worn top where I placed my lips to gently blow and sip. It was awfully thin and not very smooth to the touch. I supposed it had been used by some other family before us. My mom was used to shopping at secondhand stores or receiving used items as gifts from affluent families she worked for. As a child, I didn't notice the difference between what was old or new, cheap or expensive; our focus was on education, accomplishments, our personal responsibility toward others, and our contributions. We were expected to find ways to contribute to others, not take away from others in this world. As I grew, it seemed small and unkind of me to say anything negative about what we had. The dishes, pots and pans, and even the silverware might have been very old, scratched, and tarnished, but the meals that came from those items were tremendous, even superior. My mom began preparing meals for herself and for others when she was only ten.

When I lifted the cup up to my mouth, it burned my fingertips, just more proof of my spontaneity and willingness to act in the moment. I spilled some of my coffee on the floor. "Are you still thinking about that beauty contest?" That was how Dad commonly referred to the pageant. I called it a scholarship contest, a description that kept me focused on the fact that I was yet to receive the many prizes promised to me. "You know that I just wanted to forget about it. Not the good things about it, but things like the promises." He stayed up late nights and I would hear him walking the floors, back and forth, back and forth. The hollow path on the carpet that looked as if it had been vacuumed over and over again was an obvious giveaway. This last contest had made him overly worried and frustrated, because he couldn't do anything to reverse the situations in the present that stemmed from the past. He chewed on his pipe, a habit of his whenever he was in deep thought. In this instance he was openly worried about the way that I'd lost the Miss Nebraska contest. When he looked into my eyes, he could see that some of those events made me sad and at times even mad. The judges asked questions of me that made me nervous and even frightened to remain in the contest. They openly asked me how I felt about Stokely Carmichael and H. Rap Brown and what I thought about the violence in the streets, while the other girls' questions revolved around housekeeping, women in the workplace, and world peace. Even I had thought that the judges were being unfair, but I was determined to stay in the contest.

While I was preparing for the contest, both my mother and my father would be up and dressed, even before me, whenever I had to make an appearance somewhere. I could hear the extent of their enthusiasm when they were outside leaning over the front porch talking to the neighbors. "Why yes, she's ready, and she's been practicing all along. I know her chances are slim, but why shouldn't she win? She's as talented and as beautiful as any of them and just as smart. Anyway, only God knows for sure, don't you agree?"

Mom always spoke with authority and resolve whenever she took time out to speak to the community. There was no doubt in my mind that what I did at the time was correct and that my parents cared about how the contest affected me, and cared a great deal. It became clear to me why I just had to remain in the contest.

And now that loss was haunting me. I couldn't believe that losing this contest could cause so much trouble. Strange people were still following me and my folks around. Some would say disgusting things to us as they passed, like "Nigger, you didn't think that you could win in a white contest, did you? You're a token and nothing more. Nobody wants to see a nappy-headed nigger win an all-white beauty contest. You'd better get somewhere and hide. Why, things are bad enough for your people. You and your family had just better watch your backs. It wouldn't take much for a dark pickaninny to come up missing in the dark. Why, it just wouldn't take much at all." I couldn't shake it loose. All of my memories about it were making me second-guess myself. Now my family was involved in my day-to-day unrest. Little by little, despite the fact that we spent a great deal of our time in our own home we would catch each other hesitating before answering the telephone, picking it up slowly, waiting for the person on the other end to speak first, and then responding slowly, all the while diminishing the volume of our shaky voice. Most of the time, discovering who it was, we'd sigh, smile, and speak to the person on the other end happily. My mother would walk into the living room when she heard the doorbell ring and peek through the heavy drapes, which were kept closed, in order to be able see who it was on the other side before proceeding to open the door. What was startling was the fact that before, she'd hardly ever kept those drapes closed, especially in the daytime. But now she did. She made it her business to keep them closed tight most of the time, along with securing the locks, now three on the door. It was obvious that even though they never said they were afraid, they were. My father was afraid for me and our family, and my mother was afraid—well, she was afraid for me and our community.

I just didn't want to bring anything else on my parents or my family or friends. My family, friends, and neighbors had been accosted by the FBI. My mother's friend Mrs. McIntosh came over one evening. I overheard her talking with my dad in the living room. I was curious about their conversation; I knew it must be important because my mother wasn't home, and Mrs. McIntosh hardly ever spoke to my dad out of my mother's presence. So I listened quietly and intensely from the kitchen. "It's all happening again," she said. I couldn't see her face at the time, but by the tone of her voice, she was not just concerned—she was frightened.

"Now calm down, Iola, just tell me whatever it is that you're talking about, and take your time. Do you want to wait until Juanita gets home?"

"Oh no," she said raising her voice. "I came over, caught a cab as a matter of fact, because I knew that Juanita wasn't home. I came to tell you that the FBI came to my house."

"Well, did you tell your kids?"

"No, Bud, you don't understand. They weren't asking me questions about my family, they were questioning me about you and your family. They were asking all kinds of questions," she responded in one quick breath.

"Well, don't just stand there, sit down and tell me what they asked."

"Well it's difficult for me to remember everything, I was so nervous, and they did catch me off balance—I mean it's not every day that the FBI shows up at your door. I still can't believe it. It was just like in the forties and fifties when they use to come around asking questions about our neighbors and friends. Remember all that McCarthy stuff, Bud?" She was just rambling and talking fast. "Well do you—do you remember?"

"Of course I do, Iola, but what does all that have to do with what happened today? Why were they at your home today?"

"This time it was Cathy that they wanted to know about. It was true, all of the rumors about the FBI asking questions about her during the Miss Nebraska Pageant. They even went so far as to question several of the girls in the contest about her civil-rights activities. They wouldn't tell me much, besides they made it clear that they were asking the questions and I had to answer them. They asked me about her involvement in an organization on campus. I think they called it BLAC, but I'm not sure. Little by little they were digging deeper and deeper into y'all's business, and I really didn't know what to say and what to think. They were both dressed in well-tailored black suits, bulged on the side of their right pockets. They proudly wore black ties and crisp white shirts. Their hair was freshly cut and lined meticulously around the ears and neck. I just keep thinking, 'What has that girl done now?' You know, Bud, what you always used to say, 'Little girls, little trouble—big girls, big trouble,' and Cathy—well, who knows?"

I was steaming and couldn't say a thing. I put my arm on the kitchen table and knocked over the sugar jar.

"What's that, Bud? Is someone here?" Mrs. McIntosh stopped talking, and all I could hear were her footsteps as she walked across the room, opening the front door. I heard the door slam, and she was gone. She left without another word. When I came out of the kitchen all I could say was, "What's new"?

I can remember most of these events because I began to keep a diary, as I did when I was a little girl. As a child, I wrote about the things that happened to my friends and family and even used some of the juicy stuff in the newspaper that Terese and I distributed to our neighbors in the projects. I even wrote poetry. My diary is where I got the idea for the recitation that I used in the contest, "I Have Looked over the World." Now and then I would write about my personal life—who I liked and who I didn't. Sometimes I would write about things that happened to me and how I felt about those things. I wrote about my mother's sadness, which I later came to realize was depression.

At times I would even write about my family's reaction to her sadness. One entry ran, "Dear Diary, my sixteen-year-old sister Rose Mary is in an oratory contest. We are all going and I hope I get a new dress to wear. Special occasions like this one always call for something new; I'll keep my fingers crossed." Several weeks later I briefly wrote, "Dear Diary, the contest was held in the church basement this past Friday night at our church. Something was wrong with Momma. Dad isn't really interested in going and he only goes because Momma makes him, besides he's tired from working so hard this past week so we can't go. Some of my sister's friends came and got her." I was fortunate enough on that occasion, however, to listen to my sister practice her speech. I can remember how proud our mom was practicing with her in the evening to prepare her for the speech competition:

> *As the Negro rides forth out of the Land of Darkness and Despair, he comes not as a conqueror nor as a thief to his prey, but rides forth out of the darkness like the gallant knights of old, although he wears no armor but of silver or of gold.*

Wow, I could see how proud my mother was of her, and I was determined to see that same expression on her face when it came to me. Rose Mary won the competition at our church and later went on to give the same speech at the Baptist Convention, which was also held in Omaha, and she even won that contest. My sister went on to participate in the national contest, which was held in New York City, and placed third. All of us in the family as well as our church family were very proud of her. I later discovered that my mom helped her write her speech. This didn't at all surprise me; mom was such a great writer.

It always made me feel better when I could remember what was happening around me at any given time. Not by someone else's perspective— oh, that information was always available through the media, gossip, and even though friends and foes. I just wanted to remember how I felt about things happening around me at the time. It was always comforting to me to express myself, even if there was no one there to hear or listen but me. I learned that from my mom.

As long as I could remember she would always write about things of interest to her or write things down about her community. She would write letters to companies when she was pleased or displeased with a product. She would write to her friends. She wrote Christmas letters, poems, plays, books, and original recipes. On several occasions she even wrote the president of the United States of America. I sometimes laugh to myself that if she would have kept him abreast of the pageant I probably would have won the whole thing!

My dad was always quick-tempered, and he was known for his short fuse, especially when he was a young man. I noticed that most black men where I grew up showed few emotions outside of anger, and they had very little time for any foolishness. There were times, however, when the laughter that filled the air was hardy and robust, not because of any alcohol that colored their thinking, but because they were able to provide for their families, or a child received good grades on a report card, or the rent was paid on time.

I blew on the coffee to cool it off so I could drink it and leave the house without an inquisition or any further disruption to my mother's day. I usually liked my coffee as hot as I could possibly stand it, especially on cold days like today. But today, inside my body I was all twisted and for some reason I was developing a slight headache. Before I knew it I was experiencing a strong urge to go to the bathroom, and I did. I barely made it. I don't know why I was having diarrhea. It was so unusual— almost unnatural for me so early in the morning. It was clear that I was experiencing a lot of things: anxiety and frustration, and I was just plain scared. You might as well say I was a basket case, and the coffee that usually seemed to help for most things just didn't seem to be doing an adequate job today. Nevertheless, for some reason I felt today would be the day I finally made my parents proud. Today I would represent my people, my family, and myself in a way that I could not do in the Miss America Pageant. That experience had overwhelmed me, and it made even the white people who supported me feel as if I'd let my people down, or so I thought.

It was time for me to leave for school so I quickly finished my coffee, roughly scraped the now-hard oatmeal from my bowl, and prepared to excuse myself from the room. I was slightly thrown off by seeing my father sit so long at the kitchen table. I put on my weathered black-leather coat, cradled several books in my arms, and walked out onto the porch, cautiously looking around. I made it a practice to be aware of my surroundings after the cowardly hanging of the noose in the tree outside of our home.

I admit that I was frightened by it, but more importantly I was concerned about the intentionality of the act. As my thoughts drifted back to that frightening time, I was brought into the present by the wind blowing through the trees that lined the street. The concrete stairs were pitted by the salt thrown onto them to melt ice during the winter, but they remained slippery—especially slippery today—and when my thin-soled, black-leather shoes made contact with the worn, irregular first set of steps, I instinctively grabbed for the narrow iron rail and slowly made my way down. The second landing was even more dangerous, because the rail was barely hanging on to the old concrete. I turned left onto the sidewalk and slowly walked past the alley to the left of my house. Alleys were common, and local traffic had a habit of driving down them to take shortcuts, leave their garages, and even dump unwanted items (especially if they lived on a different street). When I reached the corner, I crossed and continued to the next street. I then crossed again, turned left, and continued toward the major intersection at Thirtieth and Hamilton to wait for the bus. It was still early, and I planned to go to my classes before going to the student center, where I was to assemble with many of the students.

I stood on this particular bus stop for many years to go to the library, downtown with my mother, or to our doctor at the city medical center. The building across the street was a home for retired and elderly Catholic nuns that was enshrouded by overgrown bushes and broken thistles that lay dying against the fence. It was a place where beautiful plants and flowers had once grown, but now dead grass covered the ground inside and outside of the property line. Vague memories of a grand monastery occupied my mind. As a kid, I would push aside the tall, full, beautiful bushes; walk through thick, lush grass unlike any I could see in my neighborhood; and go right up to the gates with my friends. We would press our faces between the large, majestically sculptured iron bars that seemed to stretch to the sun to see what we could glimpse beyond.

Everything seemed large in those days. I was so small that on several occasions during my early years on Thirty-First Street kids would have fun leaving half-and-half or cream on my door step as an indicator of my need to fatten up. I was awfully skinny in those days; some would say sickly or kind of homely, with thick, long, kinky hair—not at all a girl who would or should be chosen a future first-place winner in a beauty contest.

I always thought the large Gothic building across from the bus stop was a cathedral—placed serendipitously in our community to make us continually aware of the fact that each of us is merely a microcosm of a greater being. There were many buildings in our neighborhood of such grandeur. Their distinctive characteristics were always overlooked. But on a day like today no such thing could or would occur, at least by me. Local influences would always add flair and a sense of style to their magnificence and the everlasting testament to the glory that was. They would appear as the background of my day-to-day life.

The bus that I took, when I didn't have access to my father's car, crossed through the inner city to the more affluent part of town where the University of Nebraska was. I stood waiting anxiously on the corner with several other people I was used to seeing when I left for school on Mondays. Students were listening to their transistor radios. Two people were talking about their jobs at the hospital. Many of them were employed in the housekeeping or dietary departments at Saint Joseph Hospital. As I waited for the bus, and later after I had boarded it, I could hear others discussing the events and activities surrounding all of the riots and unrest that had been going on for several years in the city. I recognized several people from school. Some of the people I only knew from the long bus rides back and forth to school. You can get to know some people very well when you spend so much time on the bus—at least you can if you really want to. I wondered if any of the UNO students on the bus were aware of the events planned for today. I recognized Sandra. She was a white student who went with one of the black students from Creighton University. Sandra wanted to attend Creighton University along with her boyfriend Frank but couldn't afford it and Frank was on a local athletic scholarship, which meant that he was happily stuck. Both were sympathetic with what was going on at UNO and wanted to further the cause of the black students there, knowing that inevitably it would improve their own situation. Students from other schools around the city were in support of our cause and were diligently watching and waiting to see how UNO would respond to our demands.

The bus was on time today. I dropped my coins into the large receptacle and smiled at the driver. "Watch your step and quickly find a seat," was his reply. It was better than in the past, when the drivers would say, "Move to the back of the bus." That would only cause some of the older riders to frown or raise their eyebrows. Now they just quickly found their seats. I reflected on how words make all the difference in the world, especially to those affected by them. I quickly sat down close to the window, holding my coat and books so as not to be in the way of anyone wanting to sit next to me. Looking out the window, my mind drifted to my meeting later that day in the student union.

I was lost in thought when I heard "Is this seat taken?" I shook my head. "Well, do you mind if I sit next to you? The bus appears to be a little crowded today. Thanks," a woman said in a quiet voice. "Dear, you dropped your purse on the floor, and it's open. You'd better pick it up." I reached toward my tattered purse and picked it up.

"What's that?" she asked as I was closing it, frustrated by her unwelcome intrusion into my morning commute. I was not in the mood to carry on a casual conversation.

"What's what?" I sighed.

"Sorry ... but ... that book, the books that you're reading."

"Oh, these are my textbooks. I'm in school."

We slowly eased into conversation, while most of the other passengers sat quietly next to strangers. It was not unusual for me to remember conversations like this one because I had very few exchanges with people I didn't know, especially since my experiences during and after the pageant.

"Today I have a history and an English class. That must sound boring to you."

"No not at all," she responded. She was white, but she reminded me of my mother, the way she politely asked so many intrusive questions. She wanted to know why I had decided to go to college, how much it cost me, and how was I paying for it. That last question was really a surprise. She looked to be in her sixties, with a face rough with memories and aged with wisdom, but her eyes shone like a much younger woman's, especially when she smiled. I turned away, but she continued talking as I looked ponderously out the window. "You must really have to be smart to go to a university; especially one as grand as that big school on Dodge Street."

"Well, I'd like to think that I'm smart; I know I try hard, at least when my mind isn't distracted on other things. Otherwise school's not so difficult, especially if you like the classes—I mean the subjects. As far as the tuition, I work several jobs, and I have several small grants and scholarships. I'm trying my best to stay away from loans." I didn't know why I was talking so much now. It wasn't like me to just carry on. Maybe Miss Whoever was a welcomed distraction to my otherwise stressful day. "I'm sorry, my name's Catherine, Catherine Pope. And you?"

"I'm Sarah," she quietly responded.

All morning I'd felt like I was coming down with an upset stomach, but now for some reason my stomach was feeling better—queasy, but better.

"I never finished high school, although I always wanted to. My family didn't have enough money to send any of us to school—I mean my brothers and sisters. Of course if they did, they probably would have sent one of my brothers, because the boys always came first whenever it came to thinking about bettering the family. Besides, being the oldest, it was my responsibility to care for my younger brothers and sisters, you can understand can't you? I even thought about going back. I wanted to learn about faraway places. I grew up on a farm in Nebraska, and somehow I never made it off of our family farm until I got married. I was always curious about the places that my family came from besides our farm."

I was now beginning to pay a little attention to her. "I'm sure that you would enjoy learning about your family in school, but of course if you can't talk to the oldest member of your extended family, if someone else in your family is still living you could find out a lot of interesting things about yourself," I nicely encouraged.

"I think that formal schooling—I mean finishing high school—would make me want to go even further in school, even college," Sarah added.

In an encouraging way, I let her know that it was never too late. "Oh I haven't given up. I'm investing in my children and grandchildren, and I won't make a difference between the boys and the girls. Each and every one of them will have a chance to go to college if I have anything to say about it." A sad feeling came over me, warming my whole body as if I were getting a fever. While this woman was talking I couldn't help but think about my mother, who only went to the eleventh grade before she had to drop out. I preferred not to extend our conversation, so again I turned my face toward the window, hoping she would understand that I was no longer interested in carrying on a conversation.

I became irritated, just as I was from time to time with my mother. I had just finished arguing with my parents about things that we had hashed and rehashed time and time again. We could never resolve anything, and our talks and discussions only left me tired and frustrated. Sometimes I didn't want to answer the phone or even come out of the house because I didn't want to hear about the first pageant, let alone the second one. "Cathy, maybe if you would have sung a little slower. You know I told you not to give a recitation along with your song 'Exodus.' Besides, most people might have thought it was a little too controversial, and of course there are always those who would think your song supported the Jewish religion. Of course you probably didn't realize it, but the town York is primarily made up of Christians. And the callers who were too cowardly, hiding behind a fake-sounding voice, would say you were just being used by the whites, a token."

Today I just didn't feel like I had the time or the space to listen to the woman who was sitting beside me. I just had too much on my mind. I felt that I didn't know this lady, so I didn't want to involve her in what I had planned that day. She had the ability to make me want to talk, and she was the very type of person who could make you talk a whole lot, especially about things you weren't quite sure you wanted to talk about. Looking out the window I realized that the stranger sitting next to me was only validating my intentions for the day. I was about to speak to the president of my university about changing the widespread racism on the campus, and now I was more sure of my intentions than ever. A total stranger, an old white woman on the city bus, had helped me to realize that I was doing the right thing. Kids needed to learn more about each other in school so when they grew up they wouldn't feel so distant, and it was not the responsibility of others but my responsibility to make it happen. This bus ride, with someone I'd just met, made me realize how out of touch the races living in Omaha really were with each other. Not only did it become very clear to me the importance of learning about myself through black-history classes, but it also became very clear to me that whites needed to sit in the same classes and learn about blacks.

"Ma'am, I noticed you got on the bus right after I did. Do you live around this area? I've never seen you before, so I was just wondering...."

"I live near Cuming Street, not too far from you. I know who you are," she said. "You're the young lady who won the Miss Omaha beauty pageant."

I began fooling with my hair and adjusting my coat. I had no I idea what I looked like really, but whenever anyone noticed me as Miss Omaha I felt somewhat less than that title was supposed to represent. I don't know why. It probably had something to do with the fact that I lost the Miss Nebraska contest. For some reason, when you lose the next contest the first contest is no longer important. I don't care what your title is; it just no longer counts.

Usually on my long ride to school I would pass the time by playing my own special game, which involved interpreting the meaning behind the pictures on the billboards, especially if my homework was completed. On this day—especially on this day—I was instead consumed by thoughts about all the things that divided my community. Signs were always a distraction, a game, a way to pacify myself and distract myself from the realities of my surroundings. My mind was drifting as it usually did on the bus ride to school.

I always had a habit of looking at the billboards to pass the time on a bus. Most of the signs featured people smoking cigarettes and drinking alcohol. Some of them made you think about social causes, encouraging you to spend your money, not on the things you needed, but on your dreams. All of the places on the billboards and signs were usually exotic, with mansions in the background and beautiful white people in the foreground. A lot of the billboards tried to make you think that you could be just like them if you spent your money or wages with them.

One of the signs that usually made me laugh depicted a cowboy with a cigarette in his hand, wearing a large hat and riding a horse. The sign said something about smoking in "God's country." Of course the man was the picture of health, except for one thing: he was smoking a cigarette while riding a horse. The large billboard identified him as the Marlboro Man. So many things in the ghetto were represented by a paradox like that one. It was like Jefferson, who wrote the Declaration of Independence. The words said that all men are created equal. All the while he was writing this great document, his slaves were probably preparing his meals and keeping his house—and oh yes, let us not forget Sally Hemings, who bore him many children. He promised her they would be set free, but in the end it was recorded in his ledgers that they had left of their own accord.

Passing Cuming Street, I could see familiar billboards about banks, places to make investments, brokerage firms, and mortgage companies, which led to pictures of vacation homes and resorts. These signs let me know that I was now out of my league—oh, I mean district. Among the many beautiful buildings we passed were the insurance company Mutual of Omaha and Creighton University. "Oh well, they're just signs and buildings," I told myself.

After we had crossed Cuming Street, I thought about my high school,

Technical High, and Carl Palmquist, the principal. It seemed as if he had been there forever, just like that school and Kellom School. I even thought about the whites who lived in our neighborhood. Two of the white students I went to school with became good friends of mine. Kathy and Vicki were kids that I will always remember. They could do all kinds of dancing, but my mother always said that they were two of the best young tap dancers that she had ever seen, and my mother was a very good judge of talent, especially tap dancers. My mother's brother was one of the best dancers in the city. I believe that I picked up my ability to dance, especially tap dance, from him.

I felt a little insecure as we moved on, especially when we passed Dodge Street and turned toward the university, because as a kid I very seldom went into this area. My family and friends were always told that we really weren't wanted in West Omaha. As we continued on, things seemed to get bigger. In the winter months it looked barren, but in the summer months, it was greener here than anywhere else in the city.

The streets in West Omaha were wider and lined with large maple and oak trees. I could see white men bringing their newspapers and briefcases out the front door or backing their cars out of the garage. Sometimes you could even catch their wives and children waving goodbye to them as they left for work for the day. There were very few white people walking in these neighborhoods. Most of the adults had automobiles. The white people that you did see on the street were, more often than not, house workers. They were the nannies and butlers who managed the house, or they were the head housekeepers. But usually African Americans were the people that you saw out in the street, coming and going to work each day. You could always tell exactly who they were by their uniforms. They were the maids and dayworkers, headed for work in the morning and leaving before dark in the evening. They always seemed to know exactly where they were going and why they were going there. During the winter you could see black men shoveling the snow to clear their own walkways and driveways, but the streets were always cleared in the white neighborhoods before anywhere else. In the summer men were busy working, cutting the grass and manicuring the yards.

Riding through the streets, my mind drifted like the snow. I didn't want to think about what might happen today, I just couldn't. Just like so many times when I was a little girl trying to use my imagination in place of my legs, my thoughts continued to float to a different time and place so long ago.

Although it was 1969 and my mom was no longer doing daywork, I couldn't help but think and reminisce about the past. I remember as a small child both of us going to houses that looked like these grand homes and estates. The houses were not cookie cutter; they each looked different from one another. They were large brick homes that looked like they came out of a guidebook from England, France, or Italy. Most were adorned with domes, peaks, pergolas, and ornamental trellises with beautiful vines that bloomed in early spring and summer. Some of the houses had colorful plants in large pots lining the front walks. I went to these houses not as a guest but as my mother's little helper, as she would call me. I wasn't much help because I had difficulty climbing up and down the stairs, so my job was to sit quietly at the long dining-room table, cleaning the silver, wiping the knickknacks, and folding the beautifully embroidered doilies, napkins, and small tablecloths. I'd sit under chandeliers with hundreds of glass tears dangling from rows and rows of gold. When they moved and pinged, I heard music. Mom told me that each piece of glass had to be taken down one by one and cleaned. All I could think was that I was extremely glad that nobody ever considered me for the job. I sat there polishing, worrying if that big light would fall right on my head. I never got to see it lit because we weren't allowed to turn it on.

I was never allowed in the bedrooms, but whenever I would see girls or boys playing in the yard or in the back of the house I would wonder what it would be like to live like them or to even be them. Of course they weren't like the white kids that I was used to seeing or playing with. These kids were rich. Even their toys were special.

In one particular house one of the boys would play with his Lionel Train, set up in a special room just for his trains. I wasn't allowed in most of the rooms in the house for fear I might break something. But I think my mom really didn't want me to go into those rooms for fear that I might be accused of stealing something. She knew that if that happened she would lose her job.

The girls in these homes always had beautiful, ivory-colored dolls with painted faces. The dolls had long, flowing hair and eyes with long, dark lashes that opened and closed, and arms and legs that moved into almost any position. They usually were clothed in beautiful dresses with petticoats. Peeking under the petticoats you could see fine underwear that was made especially for them. They wore shoes with lace socks, the same kind that my mom always dressed me up in when we were going to church. I always seemed to notice the boxes the toys came in. They were barely used, not a broken piece of cardboard anywhere, not even the game boxes. I could tell that most of them had barely been used. I think I liked my doll better than any of the ones that I saw in the grand houses. My doll was old when I got her, and I only had one, but I knew she had been very important to someone. My doll was special because she had been loved by another little girl before me, and now I was entrusted to love and care for her even more.

There was one house that I remembered specifically. It was different from the other houses that I usually saw because it had a large gate supervised by a guard. He made my mom show her identification before he let us in. I know she saw the dumbfounded look I gave her, but she pretended not to. I couldn't believe it when the gates opened by themselves without the man even leaving the small building. They squeaked as we walked through them, and they squeaked even louder as they slowly closed behind us.

The top of the tall gates had large, Old-Testament-like letters scrolled into the center. When we got through the gates, a man picked us up in a funny-looking car with no doors. The wheels were large, and it also had several large blades attached to the back. I had never seen a riding lawn mower. The path leading up to the main house and the unattached garages formed a long, curving drive with towering evergreen Italian cypress trees lining both sides. It split into two different directions, one leading to the stables and the other to the circular drive in front of the house.

The house itself was bigger than any I'd ever seen, with large, expansive windows. It was difficult to see through the windows from the outside, because they were covered by draperies that ballooned down the front with valances across the top made of a light blue-gray taffeta. It was the most beautiful thing I had ever seen. In my dreams I couldn't have imagined such a wonderful place. There were six garages, and the maids and butlers lived above them in individual apartments. The stables housed three horses. I could see a small one looking directly at us as we approached the house.

It was a very quiet day on the estate in the city. My mother jokingly called the house Tara because of the oversized pillars in front of the grand porch. Most of the people living there were out, attending to whatever rich people attended to—I couldn't even begin to guess. My mother was helping her friend that day, and they were both washing linen and making beds; they were up and down the stairs, from the basement to the top floor. Not doing what I was told, which was to stay put, I began to wander around the house, and when they went to the basement, I ventured clumsily up the stairs. I walked through the first door that I saw and found myself in a large room, apparently connected to the children's wing of the house. The furniture was bigger than I'd ever seen. The bed was a full leap off the floor, with four tall posts. In one corner was a bookcase with all my favorite books crammed mercilessly on each and every shelf behind two large glass doors. On the wall opposite the bed was a cozy fireplace adorned with pictures precisely positioned on the mantel.

After I quickly went through that room I found myself in what had to be the girl's room. It had beautiful paint on three walls and paisley wallpaper behind the tufted wooden headboard. The carpet was so soft that even I could dance on it without falling down. I was drawn to the Mickey Mouse characters mounted on the walls. They were funny and adorable at the same time. But what I liked the best was the bed full of dolls. There were so many of them. Why would one little girl need so many dolls? I thought I heard someone coming so I quickly turned, opened the closet door and hid inside. The closet door opened as quickly as I'd closed it, and I could tell by the long, narrow shoes exposed under the bottom rack of clothes that it was my mom. She parted the clothes, and there I was, smiling from ear to ear. She shook her finger angrily at me.

"What are you doing upstairs? You know you're not to leave the dining room! I could lose my job if they ever found out you were in here! You didn't touch anything did you?"

As I was coming out hand-in-hand with my mother, unperturbed, I looked back excitedly at all the pretty dresses, skirts, and sweaters on satin hangers. I had never seen billowy hangers like that before. I continued to look back at the shiny shoes stacked neatly on racks as Mom dragged me back to my sad post in the dining room.

Coming out of my reverie, I gazed out the window of the bus at the downtown streets. They were anchored with large buildings guarded by beautiful lampposts. Most of the front doors had large gold plaques affixed securely to them announcing their occupants. The large shop windows had words etched on them, instead of the roughly painted words in awkward sizes on crooked lines I saw in our neighborhood. At Christmastime I would see people painting holiday scenes on the windows.

We had made it to the place where I changed buses. Several people got off the bus with me and quickly crossed the street. It didn't take long for my second bus to arrive. I anxiously awaited my turn, boarded the bus, and again found a seat next to a foggy window. As I was getting comfortable, I heard, to my surprise, "Would it be okay if I joined you again?" It was my newfound friend from the last bus ride. I laughed out loud as I pointed to the empty seat beside me.

"Sure," I said, "I don't mind at all."

The bus slowly pulled away from the stop. This ride was much smoother, with fewer bumps. The buses in this neighborhood were newer, with nicely padded seats. Workmen were busily repairing the cracked streets after several harsh winters. In my neighborhood, bus drivers knew how to cautiously maneuver around the pot holes and gashes in the streets. My dad said that he was so used to them that he considered them landmarks. No one complained, because they knew they'd never get results.

As the bus went farther up the street, I could see land cleared for new construction, hopefully a much-needed extension to our Nebraska Medical Center. One of the large hospitals, Saint Joseph, was run by Jesuit priests, with long-standing bonds and ties to the inner-city neighborhoods and the entire Omaha community.

I wanted the church community to help bring about the needed change to North Omaha. I knew that they had a great deal of influence in the greater Omaha community, and they could bring people together to find solutions to our social and political problems. They participated in the community and were dedicated activists and change agents. I wanted them in my community, and I wanted them to participate in our events. They reminded me of the VISTA workers, a domestic version of the Peace Corps. They were young, white college students who moved into our neighborhoods to make a difference, especially in child development and healthcare. They were also looking for ways to bring meaning to their own lives. Many of them no longer accepted the status quo. They were having problems understanding why we were in the Vietnam War, and they were also having difficulty accepting the poverty and the unjust behavior of the establishment. Some of them knew that their parents were a part of the system, and therefore they wanted nothing to do with it. They were always there, always involved in the change. I saw them as a part of the history and the future of our community and our schools.

Before I knew it, the had bus stopped in front of the UNO campus at the bottom of its rolling hills. People were all over the place, even though it was a very chilly day. Students were milling around, talking with friends or standing alone or in small groups, waiting patiently for something. I reached for the cord to ring the bell and let the driver know that I was ready to get off, but someone pulled it before me. I gathered up my books, my shabby black purse, awkwardly apologized for not being very social, and quickly stepped past Sarah. She briefly opened her eyes; she had dozed off while I was taking in the view of the streets. She smiled and proceeded to look at me with a strong sense of maternal obligation and admirable concern. My uncertainty was obvious.

"Cathy," she called out to me, "you have a nice day." I looked back at her, puzzled. I couldn't believe that this old white woman knew my name. I stumbled off the bus, almost tripping on the final step.

"Cathy, your scarf!" it had come off my neck as I rushed to exit. I turned. "It's a cold day, and you might need it," she said. I hurried back, and she handed me my scarf and briefly smiled at me. It felt good to have her smiling at me.

As she spoke to me I could hear my mother. "Wrap up tight, and don't let the wind slip in between the cracks. You might catch a cold."

Just as the double doors to the bus shut behind me, I turned my head and tried to ask her name. I saw her lips moving, but I couldn't hear her. I still wish I had thought to ask sooner.

When I got off the crowded bus I knew that I had to stand on my own and that any decisions that I made rested on my shoulders and mine alone. For the most part, most of my life, I had allowed my parents to make my decisions for me. Making them seem responsible somehow made it easy for me to blame them whenever I made a mistake; it was so convenient. It was almost comforting not to take responsibility for my thoughts and actions. I looked back at the bus and watched as the last passenger boarded and the large Omaha Transit bus pulled away. I felt my eyes watering. It was hard for me to understand how a bus ride could evoke such strong emotions from me, for an individual trying to find her way by seeking the truth. At that moment, because of one person, a stranger on a bus ride that I had taken many times before, I couldn't help but feel a little confused. I felt surrounded by kindness and empathy for my fellow man; I couldn't possibly tell anyone why.

Riding the bus gave me the time that I needed to discover and reflect on the things that challenged me. Today's ride had caused me to reflect on past events in my life that I honestly tried so very hard to hide from day to day. I stood by the bus stop for a while, looking around and enjoying the smells of the many fir trees that stretched across campus. The new snow had softly fallen and gracefully laid itself on top of the old, making the sidewalk an awkward space to navigate. I wondered if I had done enough preparation for the day. In our secretary's place, I had taken notes at BLAC meetings on several different occasions. I had made phone calls the night before instructing the students on my list to be on time. I even called students to be sure that they had car rides to school just in case the bus wasn't able to get down their streets, even though I had to ride the bus. I suddenly looked down at the torn pocket on my coat and began fidgeting with it, trying to tuck it in or straighten it out so that it wouldn't hang down in such an obvious way. I put my hand down in the side of my partially opened book bag in hopes of finding a safety pin, but I only retrieved some lint. All I could think was that the black-leather coat I was wearing should have been given away years ago. I wanted to look my best this morning. This would be my only opportunity to make a good impression before the president of the university and his staff, and I was blowing it.

Now I noticed the streets. They looked like a canvas washed in watercolors. The streets appeared like large, unstable strokes made by brushes in the snow. Some strokes needed very little paint; they looked like the stingy, unsure movements of a beginning artist dabbled onto the ground. It reminded me of a botched Thomas Kinkade painting, a scene of peace and prosperity in America.

Because of the size of our group, which included supportive white students and newsmen in addition to about seventy-five of us, Dr. Naylor moved the meeting to the Regents Room, a conference room adjacent to his office. Once we were settled, Honore asked all of the press to leave so that we could meet with the president in private. We were seated on chairs, on the floor, and standing around the room in Dr. Naylor's office as he read a point-by-point statement in reply to our original demands.

I couldn't help but wonder and ask myself why I was there. I felt as if I were having an out-of-body experience. I didn't hover low like a small bird with a wounded wing or like people in movies, moving slowly just above a well-orchestrated scene. I was soaring swiftly like a hawk focused above the president of the university, his secretary, the media, my friends, and the supporters and members of BLAC. My eyes moved quickly and intentionally from speaker to speaker. I listened intently while watching all of their moves and gestures as I wrote down Dr. Naylor's words. Most of the time his words did not seem to match his facial expressions. He was angry—that was quite obvious. There were times when he looked directly at me, and he made me wonder what he was thinking and more importantly what he was going to do. I reached in my purse and pulled out my compact. I shouldn't have, but I was interested in exactly what he was looking at. While looking in my mirror I pulled an old tissue from my pocket and nervously wiped my face; it was oily and covered with perspiration. In retrospect, I suppose he really didn't have the time to think that far ahead, but I also knew that a good leader always has his plans laid out well ahead of time.

I was becoming nauseous and dizzy; I hadn't eaten since breakfast and really didn't eat then. I'd only had some coffee. Trying to stay focused, I scanned the room and took stock of the fact that we—meaning all of us seated in that office—were making history in Omaha. Maybe that was why it was so hard for any of the administration to listen to us or to understand our commitment to our cause.

In response to our charges of racism being tolerated on campus, Naylor said that he was unaware that any racism existed but that he would immediately act on any documented incident of discrimination. He then stated that our concerns would be aired through normal university channels. Standing silently and listening attentively to President Naylor, I really had difficulty believing what I heard. Many in our group found Dr. Naylor's attitude to be patronizing, insincere, and unsympathetic.

After he had stopped speaking, Robert Honore asked President Naylor if there was anything else he wanted to say.

"No," he replied.

At that, Honore rose and said that Dr. Naylor's response to our demands was inadequate, and that members of our organization would occupy the president's offices until he capitulated.

At that time a number of us left the Regents Room and dispersed throughout the president's office and that of his secretary. We made sure that no black athletes were involved in the sit-in, as they would be liable to lose their scholarships. We didn't allow any white students to occupy the rooms to avoid their being seen as agitators; they needed to use their influence outside of the organization. We were very aware that there was a possibility that we could be suspended or expelled.

White as well as black students would bear witness to all of the events, whether positive or negative. About 200 additional students, white and black, filled the hall outside the offices we were occupying. I really didn't know what was going to happen next. What I did know was that I couldn't compromise: I was committed! This was one of many times when I was faced with making a decision that could possibly have negative repercussions for me and my family. Agreeing to participate for the second time in the Miss Omaha pageant resulted in my life and my family's life being threatened; going through with the Miss Nebraska Pageant I had become aware that there were people in York, Nebraska, who would do anything to keep me from competing in the contest. There were times when I walked away, but on this day I was committed to seeing it through to the end.

Dr. Naylor went out of his office to confer with Dean Pflasterer. When he returned, he informed Mr. Honore that we had fifteen minutes to clear out of his office, and if we were not out by that time, he would authorize Dean Pflasterer to call the police. Honore replied that we had no intention of leaving. After fifteen minutes, Dean Pflasterer called the police.

About 200 onlookers, mostly young whites, lined the university's halls that Monday, and many showed their sympathy by singing "We Shall Overcome." Some of the onlookers raised clenched fists, the sign for black power or student power. We viewed the clenched fists as a way to signify our respect for ourselves. Others showed the two-fingered peace sign.

Within the hour the crowd grew to about 250, mostly white students. They again sang "We Shall Overcome." From inside President Naylor's office, I could hear the singing. They sounded like a choir to my ears. If I had any apprehensions about being there, all doubts vanished when I heard that music penetrating through to us. I was where I was supposed to be.

At 12:20 p.m., the class break time, a black student from Creighton University cleared the hall and stairway so that students could pass to their classes, my sister Rose Mary and many of my friends among them.

Black students from Creighton University were supportive of our cause and often attended our meetings and social events on and off the UNO campus. Several of us also made a habit of attending events at Creighton, especially basketball games and black-sponsored events held there. I was always comfortable attending events at Creighton since I had attended school there while finishing up my senior year in high school.

A little after 1:00, members of the Omaha Police Department arrived in the Administration Building. Several of us standing close to the window could see them coming, their numbers growing quickly. I could hear their tall boots pounding the ground in unison outside as they swiftly left their cars, wagons, and vans. Their large guns rattled as they got closer. As they came up the stairs they swiftly passed the students in the hallway, who stood their ground, still singing.

The police barged into Dr. Naylor's office. BLAC leaders shouted to the occupiers not to get in the way of the policemen. The singing became louder, with more conviction. More police officers began to arrive, wearing their riot gear. They stood there, several hundred strong, with their legs spread so they wouldn't lose their balance in case chaos set in. With feet firmly planted on the ground, I could see through a small crack from inside that they were swaying.

At 1:30, a black police inspector appealed to us to vacate the premises. It had been about an hour since the first request for us to clear the offices. After we again refused to leave the premises until our demands were met, fifteen more policemen entered Naylor's office. Not knowing the exact situation on the campus, the policemen arrived helmeted and armed with nightsticks. We were asked three times to leave peacefully, but nobody moved.

By now I was seated on the floor with many of my fellow students. I felt weak, as if my limbs might give way from under me, a feeling that was not foreign to my trembling body. My heart was beating like the water drums of my ancestors. The makeup that I had so meticulously applied that morning was now almost gone except for the black eyeliner applied to the outer edges of my eyes. My lipstick had entirely disappeared with no hint that it had ever been applied in the first place. I had unknowingly, in my nervous confusion. chewed most of it off before it even had a chance to dry, a nasty habit of mine.

"Miss Pope, would you like to leave? We're giving you an opportunity to exit the premises before anything happens. I can't make guarantee your safety or the safety of anyone in this room unless you begin exiting this building right now." The police officer appeared to be very concerned about my safety.

For one moment I started to steady myself and get up off of the hard floor. I looked up from my awkward position on the floor and saw a large hand reach for me. I believe it was Harry or Carl, although I can't be sure, but he helped me stand up and with a smile led me to the front of the group. The police began leading us away in groups of three to awaiting cars and paddy wagons. We walked out quietly, with arms linked, always one female between two males. I was in the first set of three, with Honore and another committed student that I didn't know by name. Students, waiting in line, extended their right arms straight up and out with their fists clinched and yelled, "Power to the people!" and "Black power!" I was warmed by the camaraderie. I closed my eyes, sighed, and looked straight ahead as I was led out the door.

Other students were placed into paddy wagons, but Honore and I were separated from the group and placed into a police car. As we left the parking lot and turned onto Dodge Street, I looked into the crowd that lined both sides of the wide, busy street. They were waving and yelling, "We are with you! We believe in your cause! We love you!" It took my breath away. We were silent as we rode to the police station. The streets were lined with all manner of people: whites and blacks; young and old; city officials and civil-rights leaders; Catholics, Protestants, and Jews. I recognized university professors, high-school teachers, and even elementary students. My eyes stopped when I saw my parents standing in the cold on the sidewalk. They looked as if they were praying.

As we rode through the streets, I was struck by the words of Thurgood Marshall, the first African American Associate Justice of the United States Supreme Court: "I agree with that old saying, *I love peace, but I adore a riot.*" I now understood what that meant. If something is worth anything at all, it has to be worth fighting for.

Along with Honore, I refused to be removed from the building but requested that BLAC be specifically charged. The newspaper report stated, "Among those arrested were Honore, Miss Cathy Pope, the reigning Miss Omaha, and 52 other black students." Once at the police station, we were booked under Nebraska's new antiriot statute by Assistant City Attorney Gary Bucchino. Nebraska Legislative Bill 1381 provides that "no person shall willfully refuse or fail to leave the property of . . . any educational institution upon being requested to do so by the chief administrative officer . . . or his designee charged with maintaining order on the campus."

Members of various community civil-rights groups had attorneys on hand to negotiate our bonds. The judge set each individual bond at $25.

Our bonds were posted by Jack Clayter, executive director of the Nebraska Urban League, who said the money was put up by his organization and John Butler, president, Central Omaha Chapter, NAACP; Bennie Johnson, Omaha Star Newspaper; Rodney Wead, director, Wesley House; and Ozzie Wilson, human relations director for the City of Omaha.

At 3:30 p.m., Dr. Naylor held a news conference during which he claimed we "had not learned to live gracefully with democracy." He further explained that the university had the proper channels for correcting the grievances we presented. He said he didn't want to establish the president's office "as the one and only source for the adjudication of concerns." At a later press conference, Dr. Naylor said students should learn "to live gracefully" with democracy, which he conceded sometimes seems "inefficient and cumbersome."

Both sides set about getting their actions on Monday endorsed by as many groups and individuals as possible. On Tuesday morning, Naylor met with Honore to talk over the demands and the events that led to them. That same morning, we held a press conference and attached a seventh demand to the earlier ones. This demand was that "All charges are dropped against all of us by the state with the blessings of the administrative personnel at UNO."

For the most part, all of us stuck to our original written positions. Honore said that student control of the student center was the most important of all our demands. But I didn't agree. Yes, Fred Ray needed to be removed from his position, but I wouldn't be satisfied with revisiting the outcome of the events leading up to BLAC's dance. I made it clear to Honore that I would only continue to participate in the meetings if we kept to our demands or even added to them. I was definitely opposed to dropping the vast majority of them to placate the university. He then added that the proposed Student Center Policy Board would be another red-tape committee and that nothing would change until Fred Ray was removed.

On the following day, Wednesday, November 12, President Naylor was described in the newspaper as firm and cool in his handling of us. Of course, if you had an opportunity to look at his face in many of the newspapers throughout the week, and I did, it was very obvious from his worried expression that he was anything but cool. In effect we were told that we had no business pressing demands on him, especially as we had not, according to him, explored avenues for redress below the presidential level. That being said, it was obvious to me that he really didn't listen to us or read our demands or he would have known that we had been trying for not weeks, but months to find someone employed by the student union or school or cabinet to listen to our dissatisfaction with the procedures, function, and educational decisions of the staff and faculty of the school.

Now the ball was in his court, and Dr. Naylor and his colleagues had to decide how they were going to discipline us—not only me, one of the leaders, but all of the students who took part in the sit-in. Their actions would not only be about us. As in any bureaucracy they were focused on and concerned with how they would respond to any future disruption on their campuses. Again and again the newspaper stated that Dr. Naylor and his staff would have the support of the vast majority of the university's public constituency.

However, many people throughout the city realized that there was a breakdown in communications between the university and the black students. Even President Naylor, despite his rhetoric, had to be aware of the ongoing mistrust and dissatisfaction. It was like a keg of dynamite that was lit by the poorly handled party held in the student union.

On Wednesday, the Student Senate got involved with its own news conference. The Student Senate president, Kent Wild, and his vice president, Mike Nolan, issued a scathing indictment of the administration's use of police and Dr. Naylor's refusal to back the Student Senate and acknowledge that they were the most legal and obvious means of addressing student grievances.

"If President Naylor had asked me to act as an intermediate, he might have made progress," Wild said. He listed himself among the friends of Robert Honore, "and I would have talked to him," he stated. Wild, a student leader on campus, felt that it was wrong for university officials to call the police.

Wild said that the incident demonstrated how much the administration was acting like an authoritarian government. He said that we wanted a say in the university's operations and that we were frustrated. "Every major organization on campus feels the same way as BLAC," he said. Wild said we had presented the administration with a policy statement weeks before the demonstration in an effort to improve communications. He closed by calling for representatives of the students, the faculty, and the administration to discuss ways of improving the communication between the students and the university. He, like so many of us, wanted to bring all sides together to improve racial relations in our school. Many people reported on and responded to the actions taken by BLAC, President Naylor, and the City of Omaha.

The Student Senate was also critical of some of BLAC's statements and demands. Its analysis of the meeting tended to slant the facts in support of the university. Leaders of the UNO Young Democrats present at the press conference supported BLAC's actions. Student Senate President Wild offered his services as a mediator.

That same morning, Dr. Naylor called in the Human Relations Committee at the university to arbitrate the dispute between his administration and our group, BLAC. The meeting was held in the Regents Room with all of us involved in the disagreement that brought our arrest on Monday; Frederick Ray, director of student activities, and his assistant Thelma Engle; Eugene H. Freud, assistant professor of education; M. N. Reddy, associate professor of engineering; Pauline Campbell, an employee in the student placement office; students Jacqueline Hammer, Cathy Burgess, and Susan Dickerson; and student alternate Romeo Stockett. Naylor sat in on part of the meeting.

During the meeting, Honore said that the Human Relations Committee had the potential to mediate the differences, if charges were dropped against those who had been arrested. He said that the charges were the main thing standing in the way of a settlement. He also said that we intended to go ahead with plans for an "all student speak-out" at noon that day on the UNO campus. When I spoke with Robert during the meeting I let him know that I was still suspicious of their intentions. I felt that they had thrown this group together only to appease us. Besides, where were they when we wanted to talk in the first place? As I was quietly speaking with him in the corner of the room I could tell that he was squarely focused on the expressions of all of the players on the Human Relations Committee. As for me, I was wary and unsure of the formation of the committee in the first place. The term *human relations* just wasn't sitting well with me. One of the students in our group had likened the committee's name to the phrase *certain humans and their relations,* and that became an inside joke. I saw us as being in the wrong room. The room we should have been in was the Race–Human Relations room. Oh well, the university didn't have a room by that name, and that surely told me something about how far that they needed to go forward. I was hopeful that the look on my face was an expression of hope, because I didn't want to expose my attitude, thoughts, or anything else to the committee. When I did have an opportunity to speak, however, I made it very clear that the charges were standing in the way of any settlement. We knew that it was all or nothing for all of us. My heart was beating like the sound of a distant drum calling to rally any and all supporters. We were focused on our education as black students and the race relations on our campus. The time was swiftly approaching for us to receive answers to our main question now. Would the charges be dropped?

"We came to a limited understanding," interim chairman Emmett Cribbs said after the two-hour meeting. "Hopefully, we can work it out." But he said the session had not produced any agreements or recommendations by the committee. "We realize there is a communications gap between students and faculty. We're going to work hard to cement understanding," he added. Cribbs said UNO must find better ways of communicating before an injured party "feels frustrated" and takes action. Cribbs, a Negro, also noted that Campbell, Dickerson, and Stockett were black, and that Burgess had been named the permanent chairman. The committee was to have several meetings over the next two weeks and that any proposals the committee prepared would be discussed first with Naylor and then submitted to the Student Senate, indicating that was the proper channel for committee actions.

University officials said that the school had received about 200 telephone calls locally and from various parts of the nation since the sit-in was publicized on Monday and that nearly all the calls had supported the school for breaking up the sit-in.

The following articles appeared in the *Omaha World-Herald*:

> *Date:* Thursday, November 13, 1969
> **Naylor Says UN-O Students Play Very Significant Role**
> **By Robert Dorr**
>
> *Students play a "very significant" role in formulating policies at the University of Nebraska at Omaha, UN-O President Kirk Naylor said Wednesday.*
>
> *He said the charge in a Student Senate statement that UN-O students are treated as "third-class citizens" with no voice in how the University is operated is "not true at all."*
>
> *Students now are voting members of many university committees, he said. "Students are not going to operate the university, but all segments of the University should have some participation," Dr. Naylor said.*
>
> *The UN-O head said many student positions on committees go begging because not enough students are interested.*
>
> *Dr. Naylor commented on a case in which the Student Senate was critical of the university administration. The student statement said the university book store was expanded last August into "an already congested and much-utilized food and recreation area of the Student Center.*

Policy Board

This work, done with student funds, was done without the knowledge of the Student Senate, according to the student statement.

Dr. Naylor said, "The students were absolutely correct in being upset about this." As a result, he said, a Student Center Policy Board, made up of four students, two faculty or staff members, one alumnus and the student center director, was formed.

Asked what would happen if the four students took one position and the four adults took another on a given issue, Dr. Naylor said the group probably would have to keep discussing the issue until an acceptable compromise was worked out.

The Student Senate statement sympathized with the 54 Negro students who took part in the Monday sit-in at the Regents Room near Dr. Naylor's Office.

It said:

"The Student Senate feels that the action of the Black Liberators for Action on Campus was wrong; however, the question the Student Senate asks is that if student government is really a viable, integral part of the university, as the president has stated, would this action have stopped?"

Charges

Student Senate President Steve Wild said Dr. Naylor should have taken a "more sympathetic attitude" toward the Negro students.

The 54 students arrested as a result of the sit-in were charged Wednesday with two counts of "obstructing educational facilities," a part of the riot control act passed by the 1969 Legislature.

They are free on $25 bond each and are to appear Nov 24 for arraignment in Municipal Court.

The charges allege that the students obstructed or denied freedom of movement and the use of the school's facilities and that they refused to leave at Dr. Naylor's request.

At a "speak-out" south of the Eppley Conference Center attended by several hundred students Wednesday noon, BLAC president Robert Honore indicated that a protest will be held at the football game between UN-O and South Dakota State here Saturday afternoon.

The university has 12,120 full and part-time trained including 4,392 who attend in the evening, and 5,143 who attend in the day.

———

Date: *Thursday, November 13, 1969*
Sit-in May Endanger UN-O Student Grants
By Larry Parrott

Some Negro students could lose federal grants and loans as a result of the sit-in Monday at the University of Nebraska at Omaha.

The Higher Education Act amendments of 1968 empower schools to cut off four sources of funds for students who disrupt educational activities.

UN-O officials Thursday declined to say how many of the 54 students who were in the sit-in and were later arrested were getting federal help to go to school. They said the federal programs carry a restriction against making public the names of recipients.

Probably Some

But it is believed that some are in at least one of the four programs covered by the 1968 amendments.

UN-O, like all schools that participate in the federal programs, signs an agreement with the Department of Health, Education and Welfare, to take such steps as necessary to keep order on camps.

The agreement authorized schools to declare students ineligible for National Defense Student Loans, work-study grants, educational opportunities, grants and the federally insured cooperative loan program between schools and banks for up to two years.

A school can declare as ineligible any student who, in the opinion of the school administration, "willfully refused to obey an order of a serious nature" or caused a "substantial disruption of the institution."

School Decides

The agreement allows the school to decide if the student is to be dropped from the assistance roll. It does not require that the student be convicted in a court of law.

The students at UN-O were arrested after they refused UN-O president Kirk E. Naylor's order to break up a two-hour sit-in in the Regents Room.

UN-O officials have not decided what, if any, disciplinary action they will take against the students.

The National Defense Student Loan program enables a student to borrow up to $1,000 in federal funds each academic year to a maximum of $5,000. No interest is charged until nine months after the student leaves the school. Then it becomes three per cent a year.

The federally insured loan program is similar except that students must borrow from a bank.

Under a work-study grant, a student may work up to 15 hours a week and earn between $450 and $810 a year at a job arranged by the school.

Educational opportunities, grants are outright awards of $200 to $800 a year.

Liberators to Hold UN-O Meet Sunday

The Black Liberators for Action on Campus announced plans Thursday for a meeting Sunday on the situation at the University of Nebraska at Omaha.

> *Marla West, secretary of BLAC, said it will start at 3 p.m. at St. John's AME Church, Twenty-second and Willis Streets, and will be for all interested persons in the community.*

On November 14, 1969, the University Senate declared its support of President Naylor and his actions in the handling of the student protest on the campus. The senate presented a resolution that proclaimed: "The University Senate firmly supports the actions of President Naylor on November 10, 1969, and urges all persons concerned to provide additional channels of communication; specifically, the senate directs its president to appoint an ad hoc committee to consider the demands and complaints of students and to report to the University Senate its findings and recommendations with all possible speed." (This resolution was the end product of a meeting more divided than the 18–3 vote indicated.)

Dr. Paul Stageman, professor of chemistry in the College of Arts and Sciences and president of the University Senate said, "The purpose of our resolution is twofold. The first is to demonstrate that we are firmly behind the president and strongly support his actions in the handling of the occupation of his office and its implied threat to the university. The second is to see that every avenue of communication between all segments of the university community—the student body, faculty, and administration—is free and clear and in use."

Newsmen were quick to point out that Dr. Naylor had received dozens of supportive phone calls and telegrams and cited early reports of at least two University of Nebraska regents condoning the president's use of police. The paper also said that some students countered that this show of support was coming from throughout the campus and on the basis of early news reports referring to the confrontation as a "takeover," rather than a sit-in.

Early efforts to get President Naylor to drop the legal charges against us met with no result. He claimed that the legal issues were now out of his hands, but that he would press charges even if he didn't have to, as we had knowingly broken the law, even though the protesters were orderly and he and his staff were free to come and go while the short demonstration lasted.

The charge, a misdemeanor, carried a maximum penalty of a $500 fine or six months in jail, or both. Our attorney, Martin Cannon, made a motion to quash the charges, which was immediately overruled. Cannon cited Supreme Court rulings on freedom of assembly and sought our dismissal by precedent. The judge ruled that precedent did not include interfering in the stated use of a building. Because the building was never intended to be occupied by a group of black students peacefully protesting, our acts of "defiance" were illegal.

Our attorney tried very hard to get the execution of the sentences suspended. He then offered two students for charges if the rest could be dropped. That request was granted. Honore and one other student were selected at random. All of the rest of us had to wait until July 1, pending a presentencing investigation by a probation officer. It appeared that my title as the reigning Miss Omaha was a major factor in their selection of two other students to bear the brunt of our protest. They would be the ones to be finally charged. But that didn't mean that the rest of us were off the hook.

Dr. Naylor said UNO would wait until "the matter has cleared the city prosecutor's office" before any disciplinary action was taken against us. Officials gave us permission to attend classes.

Later in the month Omaha Urban league director Jack Clayter asked Municipal Court Judge Paul J. Hickman to lower our bonds to $10 each. Judge Hickman declined the request, saying, that the bond was already too low. He also said that it wasn't excessive. All of us had to post a bond, and we finally were placed on six months' probation. I believed that all of us had a right to protest and that we made our communities proud. We were supported that day and many of the days to follow by white as well as black students. We were supported by the faculty, staff, and student body of UNO on that day. Many offered their support in silence while others sang "We Shall Overcome," linked arms, and showed the peace sign and the black-power sign. The community looked on from a distance.

The following article appeared in the school newspaper, *The Gateway*:

> *Date:* Friday, November 14, 1969
> **BLAC Defends Position**
>
> *Fellow Students:*
>
> *We, the members of the BLAC, know that discrimination and bigotry exist on the campus of the University of Nebraska at Omaha. We also know that it is the administration of this school and a certain number of its employees who are actively or passively maintaining this situation.*

We do not make these charges lightly. We realize the seriousness, however, we would be untrue to ourselves and to you if we pretended they were made without sufficient cause.

The black student sit-in at President Kirk Naylor's office Monday was our attempt to trigger a meaningful dialogue with the president. We had hoped, when we entered President Naylor's office, there would be an honest discussion of black and white student grievances. When we entered that meeting, we hoped President Naylor would at least offer us hope that substantial steps would be initiated on his behalf to deal with what BLAC's members and black and white supporters still know to be just demands.

Our expectations were destroyed during that meeting. They were drowned in floods of evasion, homilies, and vague denials that discrimination existed at UN-O. This rhetorical meandering was President Naylor's response to legitimate manner and to the top university official.

President Naylor said to the black students in his chamber that he had served as an officer with a black squadron during the Korean War.

He said that he built a "nice home" across the street from "Negroes."

In the face of the black student's situation at UN-O, we could not fully appreciate. President Naylor's autobiographical account of his love for the black man. The black students were at that meeting to talk about the issues. We are not ashamed of it or to admit it.

BLAC's members were prepared to remain in President Naylor's office until he would make a concrete statement regarding our demands. The events which led to their creation stemmed from the discontent with the status quo. Because the president and other officials of this university have shown an unwillingness to seriously consider our demands, they chose the authoritarian police approach; therefore, we have no other alternative but to unite all students for this common cause.

We, Black Liberators for Action on Campus believe:

1. President Naylor's position acts to condone discrimination on campus.
2. All students and faculty at UN-O can help black students by supporting our demands.
3. All charges against black students arrested Monday be dropped and amnesty granted.
4. Students at UN-O should and can have a greater say in the operation of the university.
5. Black students should have a voice in determining policies that affect them.
6. All black student demands should be met in fair arbitration.

Concerned Black Students

Now I had a police record along with many other students, including my best friend from childhood, but knowing this did not make it any easier for me when I opened up the *Omaha World-Herald* on the evening of November 11. I had appeared in the newspaper a lot over the past three years; more than I ever expected or even wanted, but never in this context:

Persons arrested, according to police records, were [first names only are reprinted here]:

Preston, 18; Johnny, 20; Marvin, 19; Barbara, 20; Thomas, 19; and Garey, 18.

Terry, 19; Douglas, 20; Geraldine, 18; Johnnie, 21; Vincent, 19; Ronald, 19; Vicky, 18; Wilbur, 20; and Jesse, 19.

Harry, 20; Daniel, 19; Aaron, 19; Warren, 23; Michael, 18; William, 24; Carl, 21; William, 24; and Rodger, 21.

Carl, 20; Thomas, 21; Joseph, 19; Terese, 20; Karen, 19; James, 21; and Lobeta, 20.

Simon, 25; Jesse, 19; Jennifer, 20; Richard, 22,; Palmer, 20; Ronald, 19; Haidee, 20; Michael, 18; Catherine Pope, 20; Howard, 18; LaVell, 18; and Clarence, 20.

Michael, 21; Maryl, 20; Wanda, 20; Gary, 20; Robert, 28; Paul, 22; Maria, 20; Constance, 18; Grant, 28; and Howard, 20.

———

Date: *Friday, November 14, 1969.*
12 at Sit-in Have Private Scholarships

Eight of the 54 Negro students who were arrested after a sit-in Monday at the University of Nebraska at Omaha have privately financed scholarships worth from $50 to $500 a year according to UN-O records.

UN-O has about 425 students this semester who are receiving scholarships for all or part of their tuition. It also has several hundred students who have federally financed grants or loans. The university has declined to give names of students with federal grants or loans.

———

Date: *Sunday, November 16, 1969*
UN-O Situation Stilted
Naylor Sympathetic to BLAC Problems

Dr. Kirk E. Naylor, president of the University of Nebraska at Omaha, said Saturday that his formal statement to 54 students who occupied his offices Monday "may not have conveyed my true feeling of concern for their problems."

Speaking at a Parents' Day luncheon, Dr. Naylor said: "My personal comments would have been more sympathetic. But I was not given an opportunity to make them."

Naylor said a "communication breakdown" occurred at the meeting because formal statements "must be couched in formal and precise language." He said he planned to speak more openly as an "individual and not just an official" after his formal comments to the group.

The 54, most of whom were members of Black Liberators for Action on Campus, refused to leave the president's suite of offices after he told them they should carry their grievances through the proper channels. In his formal statement, Dr. Naylor told them he didn't want to establish the president's office "as the one and only source for the adjudication of concerns."

The students were arrested and face the charge of obstructing educational facilities. They are free on $25 bond each.

Dr. Naylor also told the Parents' Day gathering that many of the letters he has received endorsing his action has been "completely anti-student."

"It is false to say that all students do things that are wrong," Naylor said. "They should not be categorized as all bad," he added.

More than 100 students, parents, and facility members attended the luncheon held at the Student Center.

Among the guests were Mr. and Mrs. Maurice Hall, 6612 Spencer Street, who reigned as "Parents of the Day." Their son, Michael, a UN-O junior, also a guest, nominated them earlier in the week.

Date: Monday, November 17, 1969.
Regents Back Naylor Move

The University of Nebraska Regents extended regulations covering campus disorders to the University of Nebraska at Omaha campus Monday.

At a meeting on the UN-O campus, regents approved the policy on disorders which they had adopted to cover the campus at Lincoln.

> Regents also issued a formal statement backing the action of UN-O President Kirk Naylor in handling the demonstrations by the Black Liberators for Action on Campus (BLAC) Nov. 10.
>
> The statement said:
>
> "It was indeed unfortunate that the student members of BLAC at the University of Nebraska at Omaha chose to occupy and disrupt operations of the president's office last week.
>
> "President Kirk Naylor acted responsibly and he has the complete confidence of the Board of Regents in actions taken."
>
> The policy on campus disorders covers student conduct during demonstrations. It states that students are entitled to express their views and support them as long as this expression does not infringe on the rights of others.

The following Sunday, November 17, 1969, more than 150 persons attended a rally in support of us, the "Omaha 54." The mass meeting was for "all interested persons in the community," according to leaders of BLAC. They filled all the chairs and stood in the rear of the St. John's AME Church basement classroom to hear and applaud brief speeches by some of the students and members of the Negro community. A number of us involved in the protest sat on the speaker's platform. We received a standing ovation when we were introduced.

Marla, our secretary, said that the arrests had "only made our cause more just. Black students have too long been ignored and pushed aside in the university community. This ended on Monday," she said. Robert Honore said the demonstration was not over racial matters. "This involves both black and white students, but the black students have taken the lead. Although we understand discrimination exists at UNO, our demands are not along racial lines," he said.

I did not speak that evening; I was determined to sit quietly in the back of the room so I wouldn't distract from the meeting. My voice would later be heard through political actions that I would take along with other community activists both young and old. I now had a public forum, and I planned to use my notoriety wisely to further my agenda. I was now an active member of the Young Democrats, the McGovern Committee, and an ongoing member of the Urban League, the NAACP, 4CL, and a supporter and face for many charities and organizations.

In the newspaper they always identified me as Catherine Pope, winner of the 1969 Miss Omaha contest and one of the 54 arrested. When I was asked about the demonstration, I said that both black and white students gained from the sit-in and arrests.

Some of the speakers praised our action as a nonviolent exercise of black power rather than student power. David Rice, head of the United Front Against Fascism, said the sit-in would have been more effective if the students had forced the police to carry them from the building. At the end of the rally, a collection was taken up to help support our organization.

A week later, the *Omaha World-Herald* ran a follow-up story:

> **Date:** *Tuesday, November 25, 1969*
> ***Naylor Opens a Direct Line for Students***
>
> *Recommendations of the student senate at the University of Nebraska at Omaha can now be submitted directly to President Kirk E. Naylor, a senate member said Monday.*
>
> *The senate member, Galen G. McClusky, said Dr. Naylor told him and another student senator, J. Patrick Anderson, that the school policy would be changed to permit direct communication between the student senate and his office.*
>
> *McClusky said the student senate's recommendations formerly were routed through the university senate, Dr. Naylor's highest advisory group. A direct line to the president's office has been one of the student senate's main objectives in recent weeks.*
>
> *McClusky said he and Anderson gave Dr. Naylor a petition Monday signed by 1,000 students who supported the president's handling of a sit-in by 54 Negro students Nov.10.*
>
> *Dr. Naylor called police to break up the sit-in after the students refused to leave his office and the Regents Room.*
>
> *McClusky and Anderson opposed a student senate resolution which blamed the incident on poor communications by the administration.*

> McCluskey said Dr. Naylor also told him the student senate will be permitted to select the students who sit on committees of the university senate.
>
> Until now, the student senate could only recommend committee members, McClusky said.

In the aftermath of everything there were many reasons given by the school newspaper and the news media for the vast majority of the problems that the university faced. The primary one was unplanned growth; UNO went relatively quickly from a small community college to a large urban university. Some felt that the university's problems resided in incompetence and racism, while others felt it was a lack of concern or acknowledgment of the needs and desires of the students.

As the days and weeks passed, the community began calling us "The Amazing 54."

On November 10, 1969, many young men and women, especially those in BLAC, put their education and their jobs in jeopardy to support a cause that they possibly would never benefit from. On that day some were confused, afraid for us, not knowing how the police would react if anyone lost their temper and got out of hand. We really had no idea how long it would take for the school to see our side of things. I was sure that some of us would lose our right to attend the school and others would lose their federal student loans and scholarships. In my mind it was a crapshoot; we were in some ways shooting blindly, and I also feared that we could be shooting blanks. Sometimes you never see the positive results of your efforts. I had no idea whether my role in the Miss America Pageant would ever yield any benefit for our youth, but I always was taught to walk in faith without any promises. We were hopeful that future students would somehow benefit from our sacrifice on that winter day. We may never know the price that many of them later had to pay or how the actions they took changed their lives. We were among many courageous and noble leaders in the civil-rights movement.

Results came slowly but were positive. We brought about an awareness of racism in our educational institutions, called attention to inadequate black studies departments, brought about necessary changes in policy in student organizations and government, and created departments to address the educational and social needs of minority students. Our actions were also a strong contributor to bringing together most students on the campus, white and black, to improve and build upon the decision-making processes in the university so that both campuses, the University of Nebraska at Lincoln and the University of Nebraska at Omaha, could meet the needs of all of their students. We also taught those within the community that they have a responsibility to speak for those who may not be able to speak for themselves.

Over time I began to recognize that I was caught between two worlds: the demands of my responsibilities and obligations to my family and myself, and my personal desire to become Miss America. I often found myself struggling with my social and political obligations. Was it right for me to use my title of Miss Omaha to try and improve the conditions in my school and in my community? I knew that I was taking controversial stands. I spoke out against what I considered to be social and legal injustices. Although I was not well known, I was known by those within my academic circle, acting community, and modeling community. I had appeared in several national magazines and newspapers across the country. I modeled for Finder Instruments, Mary Kay Cosmetics, and national modeling agencies, and I continued to act and sing in local venues.

I found myself loved and hated by individuals in and out of my community. My family continued to receive both hate mail and letters of encouragement from people living in Omaha and as far away as California and New York. Many of the letters of encouragement I received came from family, my cousins the Hawkins, and close friends, but I also received letters and telegrams from around the country. Most of the mail was encouraging, but there were some critical phone calls and letters and distasteful opinions written in to our newspaper's open forum, the Public Pulse. It was bad enough after I won the Miss Omaha Pageant. It became worse during the Miss Nebraska Pageant, and now—well, it goes without saying: my participation in BLAC became a reason for a public outcry by some outspoken individuals who demanded my head on a platter. This type of mail was torn up and destroyed by my parents as fast as it arrived, but the mean and frightening words spoken on the telephone could not be destroyed. Those harsh words were imbedded in my mind and dug scars into my heart that will probably remain with me for the rest of my life. I knew I had school files and heard that I had an FBI file. I had an academic record of excellence and a police record of condemnation.

All over Omaha and across Nebraska, people were surprised and shocked when they heard that the first black Miss Omaha was among the

Omaha 54. Several people from across the state wrote letters to me, and others made comments to my parents and friends on my involvement. Because I was a strong, young, black woman who was raised with pride and dignity, I may have been to some extent surprised, but I wasn't shocked.

    I never imagined myself in this space or on this journey, but here I was, and I had no intention of hiding or running away.

The UNO Administration Building.

The UNO Administration Building and student center.

Modeling during my college years: out of doors . . .

... summertime ...

... and wintertime.

27

A Breath of Fresh Air

I struggled with my loss at the Miss Nebraska Pageant. At the age of twenty, I thought I should be able to handle my disappointment, but I wasn't the only one having problems accepting the loss. Like most people my age, I was focused on just me: my pain, my misfortune, and my anger.

To keep my spirits up I used to go to the Fair Deal Café to meet people, watch people, and eat. They had the best fish and chicken dinners: chitterlings with greens and yams were one of my favorite soul-food meals. Sometimes I went alone and sometimes with my friend Diane. Diane and I always found time to hang out and share our day-to-day experiences with each other. She lived in South Omaha near the South Omaha Packing Plant where my father worked. When he finished work on Friday evenings, he would go by Diane's house and bring her to our house.

"I'm here!" I heard Diane's voice coming from the bottom of the stairs.

"You should come on up. I'm just getting ready."

"Are you dressed?" I could hear her feet move quickly up the stairs. She called me girl and gave me a big hug and a kiss on the cheek. Our plans that night were somewhat vague, but we intended to have a good time.

Diane spread out on her belly across the worn cotton bedspread and propped herself on her arms, surrounded by several stray pillows. "I like that picture of you, Cathy," she said, pointing to a small picture of me cut out from the *World-Herald* and framed. "What? I think the newspaper took a good picture of you," she said as I abruptly turned it face down to change the subject. I plopped down on the end of the bed.

My room was messy. I had hurried home from school that day and spent hours destroying the closet trying to find something appropriate to wear. Finding shoes was the easiest: I only had a few pairs, and even fewer pairs of boots. It was especially important for me to dress as well as I would on a first date. We planned to attend a BLAC meeting.

The meeting wasn't going to last long, so from there we planned to go over to the Live Wire Cafe and get some shrimp and crackers. Waiting in line at the cafe gave us an opportunity to boy watch. The Live Wire didn't open until 6 p.m., and the small, white building didn't have much room inside to sit down and eat. Nevertheless, Diane and I loved going there, even in the freezing cold. After we ate we'd drive over to Twenty-Second Street and go to an "after-hours joint," an old house that was turned into a club on Friday and Saturday nights, where you could dance and, for hungry folks, eat. A lot of "bootstrappers," students from Omaha and all across the country who had served in the military and were now taking advantage of the UNO Bootstrapper Program, would show up at the after-hours clubs to dance and talk with the local girls while they listened to the music. We both planned to meet a guy over there. Before we left the house we meticulously applied makeup to each other's face. Because it was evening, we put more of everything on each other without regard to the opinions of my parents, who always looked us over before we left.

"Last time I heard, boys weren't the only ones that were allowed to ask a date out." Diane was always so sure of herself. She usually knew what she wanted, Now she knew who she wanted, so she wanted me to be sure of myself, too. But I wasn't. I wasn't ready for a serious relationship. I needed space, and I was trying to get over a loss. This time it was the pageant. Not long before that it was a boyfriend who always drifted in and out of my life.

My mom called to us from the kitchen. "Do you want to eat before you leave?"

"We don't, but thank you," we answered in unison.

"Hey, Cathy." The tone of our conversation changed abruptly. "Did you read the article on the 'plan'? I mean really read it? It's kind of scary to think that anyone in our government would enact that plan."

A man by the name of Ferguson was speaking about Nixon's

"contingency plan" to anyone who was willing to listen to him. Black student unions around the country gave him formal invitations to speak. Most of the time, Ferguson would speak to a standing-room-only crowd. One of the things that Ferguson talked about was how the president would control any and all civil disobedience, to the extent of sending out troops. I don't know if I really believed all of that stuff or not, but again anything is possible, and Nixon wasn't going out of his way to earn our trust. As a matter a fact, he was a divisive individual, especially when it came to Vietnam.

As we left through the living room, we grabbed our coats off the coat tree. I put on my favorite wool-knotted hat. We put our gloves on, made sure we had our purses, keys, and IDs, and drove off in my dad's car.

At the meeting, Honore was going to talk about an unusual military plan, so Diane and I had no intention of skipping the meeting. Some of my friends weren't interested in attending the meeting, because the information had already come out in articles Honore had written for the school newspaper, *The Gateway*. As a result of all the conflict that erupted in Omaha over the summer, organizations all over the state were meeting and coming up with ideas about how they would handle any future disorders, especially disobedience in major cities.

At the meeting, Honore described several tactics the government would use to quell civil disobedience. He spoke of the contingency plan called "King Alfred." He had our total attention. He told how any widespread disturbance would be curtailed by our government putting this plan into action. Armed military and the National Guard would be put into our neighborhoods fully armed and ready to use force if necessary. They were authorized to place individuals in custody and block off any streets, neighborhoods, or passageways in and out of the city.

When it was all over, everyone had their own take on the information that was presented. During and following the meeting there were those times when I felt that I had a greater interest in the speaker than in the information that he was sharing, but I wasn't the only one. A lot of girls in UNO were attracted to him. It was probably his uniform. A man in a uniform always looked good to us.

Both my friend and I were also sizing up the other two men that were seated at the head table. "What do you think of him?" I murmured to Diane.

"Will you two be quiet?" Someone behind us was becoming annoyed with our sly remarks and jests. Both of us felt a little embarrassed at being singled out. Ever since I was a kid in elementary school I was known for talking too much and at the wrong time. I guess there are always some things that we have a hard time growing out of. Anyway, it was difficult for me to stop admiring the fine young men in the room. I thought that most of the fine-looking men hung out in clubs, but intelligent fine men could also be found in black organizations and political rallies. Although I was attending a serious political meeting I was still distracted by the young men in attendance. It wasn't my plan to meet young men at the rally, but I did. I met them at school, dances, rallies, meetings, or church. But in the sixties, no doubt the vast majority of the men that I met were in meetings, especially political meetings. That's where I spent a great deal of my time when I wasn't working or at home. Despite how it may have looked from time to time, I never lost focus of my true intentions, to fight injustice and to improve the plight of blacks in Omaha. Even so, I couldn't help but admire the intelligence of young, black, committed men, in and out of uniform.

When the meeting was over I asked several of my friends what they thought about the speech. Some of them compared the contingency plan with the internment of the Japanese during World War II. Doug, a politically astute student at Creighton University, said that there had always been plans in place to quell any uprisings in major inner cities across the United States, especially in black, urban areas. Several days before, I'd heard Ferguson speak at our university on this very subject. So I wasn't surprised at anything I heard that night.

In one article published in *The Gateway,* Honore had written, "On a deeper level, however, the threat is real. The disorders express black rage against white power. In the post disorder period, the rage still lives and so does its threat against white security, in the status quo. Is the white community willing to sacrifice its own freedom in order to suppress black protest and to prevent basic change?"

While attending UNO, Honore ran for the president of the Student Senate against the incumbent president S. Ken Wild, but he lost by a landslide. He was always creating controversy through his articles in *The Gateway.* He was driven to put himself front and center to unify black students and create a university that supported, educated, and represented all of its students. His detractors labeled him a radical and a troublemaker. He was gathering like-minded people that refused to sit patiently by and let history happen to them without contributing to needed change. We were trying to have a say in our destinies.

I clung feebly to my purse as I clumsily slid on the icy spots in the parking lot, searching my pockets for my wooly gloves. Diane stood by the car, beckoning me to hurry up and open the car door. "You need to hurry up, my hands and feet are freezing," she kept repeating.

I stomped my feet on the outside of the door to clear away the excess snow, unlocked the car doors, and we quickly got inside. I rubbed and blew into my covered hands and with two tries started the engine.

"Look at the trees. The wind's picking up," I observed. "I think it's going to snow again. Don't you think we'd better hurry and get back to the house?" Diane was more interested in our original plan to stop off at the Live Wire and pick up some shrimp and saltines before dancing the night away with our boyfriends. But as it began to snow harder we changed our minds. We were both disappointed, but we knew the reasonable thing to do was not to take any chances. It wasn't worth it to get stuck or have an accident, so we headed for home.

When we arrived home and got settled in my room, I read some of the *Gateway* article to Diane. "The plan under the Nixon administration is that in the event of widespread and continuing and coordinated racial disturbances in the United States, 'King Alfred,' at the discretion of the President, is to be put into action immediately. People and their leaders will be detained, some indefinitely. Roads will be blocked and those in the armed forces will immediately be relieved of their positions and posts."

Even though I didn't want to believe that the city would ever use such a plan, I felt like this wasn't the America that I knew. This so-called plan was frightening, to say the least, and made me feel that if it ever did happen we would be considered a police state. What was the most frightening was we could move in that direction and never become a free country where every man has a voice.

It was still early and we weren't tired enough to just put on our pajamas and go to bed, so we decided to stay up longer listening to music and watching TV. "Have you learned any new dances?" she asked, as she moved to the music of The Supremes. It was my favorite group. I began singing along with the music as we played the songs: "Come See about Me," "Reflections," "Baby Love," "Where Did our Love Go."

When Diane got tired of listening to me sing she put on "Stop in the Name of Love." We both hurried to the center of the floor in front of the bedroom mirror, and in our raggedy house shoes we fought for space and began to shake our hips, doing the "Supreme stance" and dance. We both sang, mimicking our favorite girls. We always argued over who could sing the best, why this singer or that one was loved by Motown, and who was the prettiest or the best looking.

"Hey you girls! What's that noise up there? You'd better go to sleep before you wake your father," my mom scolded.

We turned off the record player and carefully placed the seventy-eights back in their individual jackets, after looking over the covers one last time. We rolled each other's hair on large, pink, foam rollers, covered it all with black hairnets, and then tied scarves around each other's heads. Then we took turns in the bathroom. I turned the radio on low before we got into bed. We continued to laugh and talk about school and boys, keeping our voices low and the topic away from the serious discussions a few hours earlier.

This was the quiet time when we stared at the ceiling and shared our secrets. "You know the bootstrapper who always sits at the table when everyone leaves?" Diane started. "We've been seeing each other for several months, and I think he's the one."

"The one for what" I quickly responded. I was very serious now and somewhat confused.

"The one I could spend the rest of my life with," she answered.

I couldn't understand her. She was so sure, so adamant. I was dating someone. I just couldn't imagine feeling ready to settle down.

Guys would date me and later not call, or they would see me in the halls at school and act like they didn't know me. I was so ashamed because several of them I liked very much. I cared for several of them, but for some reason it was a pre-act, not good-enough material for the final stage production. Some of my friends said that the guys thought I was too smart, too ambitious, that I just wanted too much out of life, and they just didn't have a whole lot to give. I thought my friends were just making up excuses for them. I think that what they left off was the fact that I just wasn't ready to become serious with anyone.

Right before we closed our eyes I again thought about the special times that we shared. Then one of us remembered that we'd forgotten to say our prayers. I don't know what her prayers were about, but I prayed that the things we heard in the meeting would never have a reason to become fact. I also prayed that someday I would make a difference in this world. We fell asleep listening to the sounds of Smokey Robinson and the Miracles. His voice made the best background for my dreams.

Time for a swim.

Play time.

350

28

Going Forward

❦

Looking back can be difficult for some of us, and looking ahead is frightening for others. As for me, I prefer to look ahead at the possibilities, and I can only do that based on faith. I can't do anything to change what has already happened in my life, but if I stop and stand still in my truth, I can learn a lot from it. I call that gaining wisdom.

On January 11, 1970, as I looked over my dad's shoulder while he was reading the headlines in the newspaper, I noticed the lead story, "Racial Violence and Unrest Occurring in Omaha and across the United States." As I read the story, I wasn't at all surprised to see that in 1969 racial turmoil again had been among the top headlines. Remembering the headlines of 1968, I realized that things hadn't changed very much.

My dad was becoming annoyed, and he offered me a seat so that we could peruse the other stories. The paper had chosen the following other major 1969 headlines: the defeat of Cunningham for mayor, the wanted and unwanted changes in the downtown skyline, the adoption of a one-half-percent tax, ongoing and rising problems with drugs, the city placing the decision to have urban renewal on the ballot, altercations between the police and attorneys, the debate over Lincoln State Hospital's open-door policy, proposed parking changes at UNO, major fires, the packing industry closings and expansions, and of course my participation in the November 1969 sit-in at UNO in President Naylor's office.

In my small piece of the world I continued to work hard. When I wasn't at home or at work then you would probably find me at school.

"Cathy, we're going to be late to the meeting." I looked up from the notes I was studying in the student center. My friends were encouraging me to put my books away so we could arrive early to a meeting of the Young Democrats. I quickly put my notes away, stacked and grabbed my books, and headed for our meeting place off-campus. In 1968, some of us had an opportunity to be delegates to the Democratic National Convention in Chicago, and now, even with all of the many things that I was already committed to, I still felt that I had to serve on the McGovern Reform Commission. This twenty-eight-member committee was made up of people in the Democratic Party: blacks, whites, Mexican Americans, Indians, dissidents, young militants, people representing both sides of the Vietnam War, and student leaders. Because the party was open to new and different ideas, I took every opportunity to share my opinions.

Specifically, we were studying the rules and procedures of the Nebraska Democratic Party. Chairman Richard Fellman said the party had historically opened itself to new ideas and had never been afraid of different points of view and that the commission's goal was to open the party and allow it to respond to necessary change. The commission was composed of regular party elements, dissidents, whites, blacks, Indians, Mexican Americans, student militants, elected student leaders, and those on both sides of the Vietnam question. The commission had scheduled a public hearing that day, February 20, at 1 p.m. at the Fontenelle Hotel. During the hearing we asked questions.

Two informal commission sessions were held: February 8 at Kearney, for central- and western-Nebraska residents, and the other on February 14 in Omaha at the Fellman home. I was excited to learn that I had been chosen to participate. I told the commission that I was committed to taking an active role and becoming a strong contributor in meeting the needs of my community.

As a participant in the McGovern Reform Commission, I presented a plan to the state Democratic Party. I felt that the African American community wasn't being fairly represented in Omaha, so along with the others on the commission I fought to reestablish a stronger democracy. Part of our platform was to integrate neighborhood government service centers. These centers would regulate schools and would even serve as neighborhood courts. The plan would further solve inequities of the legal system in Omaha by appointing an African American judge, having cops live where they worked, and requiring jury duty based on census information rather than voter-registration rosters. I felt that these changes would best provide the equality that the system was lacking, but I wasn't fooling myself. I also knew that we would be climbing uphill and the changes would not happen overnight. We would have to remain vigilant. I was committed to improving the health and welfare of the families and individuals living in my community and throughout Omaha.

Although the winter months paralyzed some, I continued to thrive and have fun outdoors as well as in. On Valentine's Day I forged out against the elements and had dinner with several of my close friends. After our dinner we spent time looking through all of the letters and telegrams that I received around the time of the Miss Omaha pageant. Some of the letters I hadn't even read yet because I needed the support of my friends to withstand the mean and unjust remarks. Thankfully there were fewer of those types of letters this time around, and they were in an unopened bag. I had already separated the letters into two groups: those that had been read previously and the ones still needing to be opened. I placed the pleasant, encouraging ones in one large envelope and the sad, degrading ones in another. All of the envelopes were clearly marked and placed securely in a box that resembled a small trunk. I usually kept the box locked and placed in my closet on the shelf above my clothes rack. It wasn't unusual for girls to keep private keepsakes in undisclosed locations in their rooms. They kept their hiding places a secret because they wanted something for themselves: something safe and secure. My dad always said, "If you have a secret and you don't want anybody to know about it, you'd better look in a mirror while alone and tell it to yourself, preferably in silence. Then, never speak of it again, not even to yourself," and this advice I took to heart.

Whenever I would receive a letter or something small and special I would move my step stool from the other side of the room and push it carefully across the discolored and cracked red-and-gray linoleum floor.

With the help of several of my friends I carefully climbed up and reached for the box. I pulled on the chain attached to the light switch and turned on the exposed bulb. I found the box that I was looking for and handed it down, then retrieved the key to the box from my dressing table. I spent several hours with my friends looking over the contents.

The end of February was quickly approaching, and the nights were getting shorter. Political figures were traveling around the country speaking about the plight of African Americans across the country. Democratic New York Congressman Adam Clayton Powell Jr. made a brief stop in Omaha. While listening to him at the airport, my mother and I decided that if at all possible we would attend his speaking engagement at the University of Nebraska on the Lincoln campus. During his brief stop at Eppley Airfield he said that most blacks were disappointed and disillusioned with the idea of integration. As he spoke passionately to the crowd, I couldn't help but notice how handsome he was. Then I remembered hearing my mother's friends speaking about his looks as well as his smarts. He commented on the Nixon Administration not being responsive to black people, and finally he said that the administration was not concerned about Indians, Mexican Americans, or poor whites. He felt that it was insensitive to the education or health of Americans and was wasting billions on an unjust, insane Vietnam War.

Later that evening when the newspaper arrived I learned that my involvement in the H-LCC had been time well spent. We received a $303,202 federal grant to finance local Head Start programs for six months, something for which my family and community had worked hard. The money came to Omaha from the Department of Health, Education, and Welfare. The original request was for $630,000 to cover the program's expenses for the entire year. Several of us told our group that we should take these funds graciously and commit to obtaining the other funds later because of budget cuts.

I was still involved in BLAC on and off campus and knew all too well that our trial was coming up. *The Gateway* called it the trial of the Omaha 54. The trial was scheduled for Monday, February 16, at 9:00 a.m. at the Municipal Court on Eleventh and Dodge Streets. Students and the public were encouraged to attend in support of us. After the date had been announced in every publication across the city, including most church bulletins, it was postponed by the court. At first I couldn't believe that the Omaha 54 had to go back to court. I thought our attorneys must have resolved the problems and therefore the city had dropped the charges. Now I was missing school again, fighting the early-morning, downtown business traffic and fighting for scarce parking. There were a lot of people milling around and talking nervously outside and in the long, narrow hall. Some of them were seated on benches. There were people with signs both for and against us. If I had known that so many parents were going to be there I would have asked my mom and dad to come.

Soon the doors opened, and everyone moved into the courtroom. I spied a seat next to another student and quickly sat down. I had never liked scary movies, and this courtroom drama epitomized a frightening scene from a B-movie. I needed a distraction. I pulled a small paperback out of my purse and began reading. Hearing muffled voices coming from the front of the courtroom, I glanced up from the ruffled pages resting in my hands. Our trial was being reset for March 26. Our defense attorney, Martin A. Cannon, wanted a different judge to hear the case and requested a change of venue. Still free on a $25 bond, I had no idea what was going to happen to me. All of us had been charged with a misdemeanor, and I was haunted by the possible outcome. I hurried back to my car so I wouldn't have to put another dime in the parking meter.

On Thursday, March 26, the trial was again postponed. Judge Cropper spoke from the bench to a small group of policemen, attorneys, and court personnel. He told them that during the court proceedings we were the most orderly, attentive group that he'd had so far this year. The judge set April 15 as the deadline for defense attorneys Martin Cannon, Charles Scudder, Wilbur Phillips and William Staley to submit a list of legal authorities in support of a motion to dismiss the charges. The city attorneys, Gary Bucchino and Richard Dunning, were given until May 1 to reply to the material submitted by the defense attorneys. Most bonds remained set at $25, although a few were higher. Our attorneys argued that "the state failed to prove an offense." They said that the arrests were "unlawful," and that the charges were "vague and indefinite" and sought to "forbid actions protected by the Bill of Rights of the U.S. Constitution and by the Nebraska Constitution."

The judge also said, "The defendants led a peaceful demonstration and did not resort to throwing bricks and bottles, foul language and preventing the activities of others to be carried out." Cannon then eloquently recapped the events that led to our arrest. He made clear to the court that the "demands were presented three days earlier, the meeting was set by joint consent, Naylor arrived with a response already written before they were heard, and there was no discussion only a, 'get out of here in fifteen minutes or I'll call the law.' " Because the meeting was jointly called, Cannon said, "It was not subject to adjournment by one side without the agreement of the other." Finally, he noted that Naylor had indicated to one of us that he was willing to work toward a solution.

Bucchino, representing the state, alleged, "The crucial point from the legal standpoint came when Robert Honore stated that they intended to remain until their demands were met." He said that "the defendants had a right to air their grievances, attend meetings with Naylor, and present their demands." However, the students had acted illegally when "they took it upon themselves to cut off debate." It was stated that we didn't stay "for further discussions," but rather until our "demands were met." Bucchino said this violated provisions of the state law. He further went on to say, "The law says, in part, that a school's chief administrative officer can order a person off school property if the person, 'is committing or threatens to commit . . . any act which unreasonably interferes with or obstructs the lawful missions, processes, procedures, functions, or disciplines' of the school." His final remark was to note the penalty of "punishment, upon conviction, or a fine of $500, six months in jail, or both." You could have heard a feather hit the floor. My mouth remained opened for most of the proceedings. I hoped I'd never see a picture of myself with my sash and crown on behind bars.

Some time later, I was hanging out in the student union, reflecting on the past three years instead of studying, and thinking I should slip inside the school library to study. School wasn't over yet, and as much as I wanted to believe that I would pass my exams without a hitch I knew that wasn't realistically the case. I always studied for long hours and worked very hard to achieve an A in most classes, and for the more difficult classes a B with the help of tutors when I could afford it. There was one thing that I hardly ever did, and that was to fool myself. I could daydream, but when it came to school I always took my education seriously.

I was caught completely off-guard when I was approached by several reporters from the school newspaper.

"Cathy, now that you've ended your reign as Miss Omaha, what are your plans?" the reporter loudly asked me as he put a microphone and blinding lights directly in my face. "Well, Miss Pope, can you give our readers ideas of what your future plans are?"

"I really don't know," I responded anxiously. I assumed they wanted some well-thought-out answer, which I honestly couldn't give them. I wish I could have said that I was preparing to go on tour with Motown, or that I was going to New York to be discovered by a Broadway director. But at the moment none of that appeared to be in the cards for me.

"Well, if you really want to know," I said as the reporter was turning away, "I do plan to continue working with handicapped kids. I am now interning at Dr. J. P. Lord School, and I'm also working at Uta Halle Home for Girls, and I'm very proud about that."

"Oh, that's great," he politely said, somewhat bored, as his assistant began turning off the lights and taking down the light stands.

I had become used to the news media, and I always tried to look and be my best, but on several occasions I was thrown a curve. A number of times they showed up unannounced right in front of my house. When we didn't come out they interviewed our neighbors.

"Thanks, Cathy," the reporter respectfully said. "By the way," he added, "your birthday's just around the corner. How will you celebrate?" I hadn't thought about that. And how did he know it was my birthday?

My birthday was April 23, and I hadn't expect to receive a surprise gift, but I did. The members of the Omaha 54 received a special award from the UNO Student Achievement Awards Program. This award is the highest student nonacademic award given, according to UNO's Student Senate guidelines. Honore accepted the award for our group.

But sometimes things like happiness can be taken away as quickly as they are given. According to *The Gateway,* the university's Office of Information omitted including us on the list of special awards for the Achievement Awards Banquet a few days later. I was pleased to read, though, that the school's newspaper felt that we deserved the award. I was also pleased Omaha's media—Lee Terry, the *World-Herald,* the *Sun,* and others desired to know students' opinions. After reading that statement in *The Gateway* I was not only pleased, but some of my confidence was restored in my school.

Thanks to Brown Baggin' It, a column by Richard D. Brown devoted to campus entertainment and feature news, my name was mentioned in *The Gateway* more than two dozen times. In his final column on May 15, 1970, Brown said that as the winner of the Miss Omaha Contest, I made good copy in his column and captured a heavy readership. He also said that I was to be congratulated for my reign as Miss Omaha. He said that I was not only "terrifically talented," but also "a proven leader and dedicated worker for which I stand." I was mentioned in his final column, which looked back at some of the highlights of the previous thirty columns and offered a look into the future of many of the subjects that had been discussed in his column.

On June 3 Omaha 54 were found guilty of obstructing an educational facility. In July many of us were placed on probation. Part of the terms of our probation was that we "not participate in any unlawful activities."

Because of student unrest on campuses across the country, a President's Commission on Campus Unrest was developed. Richard E. Spelts Jr. of Grand Island, who had separately investigated disturbances on the University of Nebraska Lincoln campus, felt the commission's report was political rather than an unbiased inquiry. Nevertheless, as a result of the commission's findings the University of Nebraska at Omaha was directed by the White House to take a long, hard look at schoolwide policies and procedures. The outgrowth of our sit-in was more participation of all stakeholders and the creation of a more diverse faculty and student campus. It was vindication for many of us.

By the beginning of the new school year it was rumored that the hard-liner approach to the sit-in and the university's unresponsiveness to demands presented convinced members of BLAC that they could not be effective at UNO. There were many reasons some felt that the organization was not effective, but I beg to differ. We were very effective.

Speaking out.

29

I Did It My Way

❧

There was a knock at the door, and I opened it. A black attendant was there with a large bouquet of flowers in his hand.

"Where would you like for me to put these, ma'am? I think there's a vase under the sink."

"Oh, that will be just fine. Thanks." I was standing in my robe.

"Ma'am, may I ask you something? Not giving me a chance to respond, he continued, "Aren't you Catherine Pope, last year's Miss Omaha? I'm just asking because one of the guys at the front desk said you were." I could tell he was nervous and really didn't know what to say.

"Why, yes," I answered, trying to show interest. He continued to stand in the same spot, looking at me as if he had more to say, but saying nothing.

"Is there anything else?" I said as I handed him a tip of several dollars.

"You can keep the vase," he said politely. "It's plastic." Should I put the flowers in water for you?" He was somewhat shy, but his slim frame stood straight, and by his diction I could tell that he had gone to school, maybe even college.

"That would be great, but quickly. I need to get ready."

"Can I have your autograph?" The attendant was nervous, as he put water in the vase and my flowers in the water. "It's not for me; it's for my little girl. She wants it."

I asked her name, and it was the same as mine: Cathy. "The short version of your name," he said as I was writing on the program he'd handed me. "What is it like?"

"I beg your pardon?"

"What's it like to be a beauty queen, a black beauty queen?"

"Sir, will you please excuse me, I don't have time now, I need to get ready."

"Oh, I apologize. ma'am. I get off soon and I was wondering, if I bring my daughter back and you're still here, I mean if the pageant is just getting out, can I bring my daughter here to meet you?"

"Why, yes," I answered. I was impressed with the fact that he would take time to bring his daughter back to his workplace to meet me. He told me that his daughter was nine, and he thought it would be good for her to meet me. I was humbled by that. He quickly left the room with the signed program tucked tightly under his left arm.

The next time I saw him it was after the pageant. He approached me with a hundred other people out front. The pageant was over, and there was a new Miss Omaha. I stepped through the crowd, even passing by my family to get a closer look at his little girl. He'd done just as he said he would: he returned with his daughter. She was polite and listened while her dad spoke.

"See, honey, this is her, the lady I was telling you about, Miss Omaha."

"No, she isn't," she said defiantly.

Even I was puzzled because she was holding my autographed program with my picture inside of it. "Honey, but I am—at least I was 1969's Miss Omaha."

She showed concern on her face and wanted to know where my crown was. I looked around for it. But my family had all of my things, and were probably loading them into our car. I understood the confusion and quickly responded. "The crown is on my head. It's always there, you just can't see it. You even have one on your head."

At that point she reached up and touched her head, seriously, anxiously reaching, searching for her crown.

"It's there, honey, but you can't see it or feel it. It has a permanent place there, and no one can take it away." I turned to her dad. "Sir, as she grows, help her understand that if she walks in faith, with pride and inner strength as she embarks on her journey in search of her own crown, she too will discover that it has been there all the time." He just looked at me with a curious smile.

As I walked away to join my family waiting patiently by our car, I looked back at her and thought, *Wearing the crown is sometimes heavy; it often weighs you down more than you expect. At times it will lose its shine, get cracks, or you may even discover that several of the jewels are missing. Of course there will be those who will deny its existence. You may even lose your crown at times, but don't worry. If you embrace who you are and always do your best, always be truthful and honest with yourself, you'll find it again. People continuously search for so many things in their lives. For me it was a crown that I was searching for on my journey. I thought I lost it, but I soon discovered that it wasn't lost. I had it all the time.*

I will never say that I walk my journey alone. I know that I stand on the backs of so many people that came before me. I drank from the cup of pain filled with their blood and life sacrifices. I can hear their stories when I walk the streets of Omaha where I grew up. That is why I struggle to remember so much and why those things that were not remembered or told to me became a reason to study, to research, and to never forget the past. To forget would mean to be forgotten.

I took the stage for the last time as Miss Omaha. For my final act, I sang the song, "My Way."

Duchesne College and Academy.

Graduation Day: University of Nebraska at Omaha.

Epilogue

"When you came home, everyone was very concerned about you. You were in terrible pain; your legs seemed to hurt you a lot. Not a day or hour went by that you weren't tormented or that you didn't cry out. And as you got older, I can remember you trying, desperately at times, to move your legs, actually trying to walk. You were still trying to walk at three, when other kids your age were running. No one tried or wanted to stop you, even though you constantly fell. Even as a baby, there was something in you, something that pushed you ahead even if ahead meant a steep, uphill climb."

—Joyce Pope Goodwin

I decided that I had a lot of living to do in this world. Of course I would get hurt, but those are the lessons that you learn along the way. They are the rare and precious stones in the crown. Life is one long practice, a challenge. You will knowingly and unknowingly practice on unsuspecting individuals, and they will practice and act out their lives on you. Hopefully you won't hurt them too much, and they won't inflict too much pain on you. You'll fight, kick, and scream through life, sometimes leaving a bloody path. But what is the alternative? What else is there? We all look for our crowns in so many ways. We wear it when it's cracked or broken as we struggle to put the pieces back together again. We must wear it through the pain and the tears. There will also be times when we will wear it outright, in the light of day, proudly and without regret, laughing through our tears.

We need to openly display sometimes those things that are deep inside of us, the part of us that we want to leave to others. These are our legacies. No matter how quiet or small we think we are, we are all important. It is through our stories that we become examples for others as they go forward. Our life will speak to others, whether we know it or now. Though we may fall, we will rise again and again, and we will stand wearing our crowns.

Some people say that my decision to participate in the Civil Rights Movement was a poor one, because otherwise I might have been chosen as Miss Nebraska or later Miss America. They wonder if the controversy surrounding me changed the course of my life. I am very proud of my choices. I found my crown my way, and I wear it proudly without regrets. All races and generations need to find their own crowns and wear them proudly.

I thank God for my journey in this life. My journey has made me who I am. Of course I continually face challenges and struggles. Life is a struggle and a test. Sometimes it seems as if there is no way out of dire situations. You will fall down—it's not the fall but the recovery that matters. There are times when I feel like no one is listening, no one understands, and no one even cares, but I know that someone is listening, someone does understand, and there are people in my life all around me that do care. They are the women in my life, both past and present, who taught me how to love myself. They are the men who through love and even disrespect taught me how to stand up for myself and recognize that loneliness does not mean that you have to accept or even live with abusive treatment.

On my journey I am discovering that my humanity is not based on what others say about me or even think of me. It is based on my stewardship, my compassion for others, my need to contribute and give freely to others, and above all my genuine love for all people, including myself. I am no longer searching for my crown; I wear it proudly and securely. After I won the Miss Omaha title I discovered that it was only the beginning. This would be but one season of many in my long life.

I discovered that I was always special, worthy of love, respect, compassion, kindness, and forgiveness. I found it through the acknowledgment of my personal journey and all of my struggles along the way. The paths that I chose I was willing to fearlessly walk down, alone and even in darkness. Through self-study and intentional effort I came to the conclusion that I was wearing my crown all the time in truth and grace. It made me proud of the person that I am today, and for that I am very grateful.

Travels: Leaning Tower of Pisa, Arles Amphitheatre, Trevi Fountain . . .

... Manhattan Theater District, Eiffel Tower, the Paris Art District.

Resources

In writing this account I have drawn on personal notes and diaries as well as a number of other texts. For those who are interested in further exploration of any of the events described in the book, the following resources may be helpful.

Online

American Antiquarian Society
http://www.americanantiquarian.org

Child Saving Institute
http://www.childsaving.org

Encyclopedia of Children and Childhood in History and Society
http://www.faqs.org/childhood/Me-Pa/Orphanages.html

GenealogyBank.com
http://www.genealogybank.com/static/exp/hp/v2/a.php

Jet Magazine Archives
https: //books.google.com/books?id=uMADAAAAMBAJ&dq= jet&source =gbs_all_issues_r&cad=1&atm_aiy=1950#all_issues_anchor

Jewish Women's Archive
http://jwa.org/encyclopedia/article/civil-rights-movement-in-united-states

Miss America Pageant Omaha Affiliate
http: //omahadouglascounty.tripod.com/

Miss America Pageant Nebraska Affiliate
http: //missnebraska.org/

Nebraska State Historical Society
http: //www.nebraskahistory.org/index.shtml

Newsbank
http://www.newsbank.com

Newspapers.com
http://www.newspapers.com

Omaha World-Herald Archives
http://nl.newsbank.com/nl-search/we/Archives?p_product= HA-OWHB &p_theme=histpaper&p_action=keyword

The Gateway UNO Student Newspaper Archives
http://digital.olivesoftware.com/Default/Skins/Nebraska/ Client.asp?Skin= Nebraska&AW=1432838908459&AppName=2

The Omaha Star
http: //theomahastar.com/

University of Nebraska Omaha Alumni Association Archives
http://unoalumni.org/unoalum

University of Nebraska Omaha Alumni Association Facebook Page
https://www.facebook.com/UNOAlumni/posts/this-day-in-uno-history-2-28-82uno-sophomore-lori-lynn-novicki-is-named-miss-neb/10150633215134383/

University of Nebraska Omaha Women's Archive Project
http: //wap.lib.unomaha.edu/

York News-Times
http: //www.yorknewstimes.com/

Articles

"She 'dared to challenge ... an unjust system,' " Janice Gilmore, *Omaha World-Herald,* July 28, 2015, https://www.omaha.com/eedition/sunrise/articles/she-dared-to-challenge-an-unjust-system/article_df84b62f-eb5c-5b81-af71-d516154105bc.html

"Omahans Return to Nebraska for Native Omaha Days," DaVonté McKenith, KETV.com, July 31, 2015, https://www.ketv.com/article/omahans-return-to-nebraska-for-native-omaha-days-1/7654227

"Catherine Pope: A Worker for Others," The Women's Archive Project, University of Nebraska at Omaha, 2015, http://wap.lib.unomaha.edu/index.php/women/catherine-pope/

"Catherine Grace Pope," UNO Magazine, Class Notes, p. 49, Summer 2018, https://issuu.com/aflott/docs/uno_magazine_summer_2018

Conference Presentations

"Break the Silence: Retrieving That Which Was Historically Stolen Through Literary Engagement," Strategizing for Success, University of San Diego, April 12, 2016

"Author's Discussion of *In Search of the Crown*," Authenticity: Striving to Live Your Best Authentic Life, Miami, Florida, June 21–24, 2018

Video

"Dr. Catherine Pope 7-29-15," KMTV 3 News Now, https://www.youtube.com/watch?v=hV68WvNh068

Recognitions & Awards

Dr. Catherine Pope Week–—Miss Omaha 1969, declared in July 2015 by Omaha Mayor Jean Stothert, citing her courage during the Civil Rights Movement

Nova Southeastern University Phi Gamma Sigma Award for contributions to the community at large, 2009

Educational Leadership Award, Association of African-American Educators, San Diego, March 9, 2018

Educational Leadership Award, San Diego City Council, for addressing multicultural education; staff development; classroom instruction; and the intersection of culture, race, ethnicity, teaching, and learning, March 9, 2018

Other Outstanding Educator Leadership Awards: State of California; California Senate; California Legislature Assembly; United States Congress, March 9, 2018

Community Engagement Spotlight: Storytelling Exhibit at KANEKO, July 27, 2017

Contributors

Terese Danner

Joyce Goodwin

Melissa Hawkins

Reagan Jackson

Samantha Miller

Dr. Melody Moore

Rose Mary Moore

Ryan Ravelomanantsoa